## Do You Know . . .

- Which country singer has a child named **Shelby Stephen**? (Reba McEntire)

- What Dave Thomas' daughter is really named? It's NOT **Wendy**. (**Melinda Lou**)

- What Larry Holmes, Dr. Joyce Brothers, and John Laroquette have in common? (a daughter named **Lisa**)

- The most popular baby name for celebrity boys and girls? (**John** and **Elizabeth**)

- What heartthrob Mel Gibson named his *six* kids? (**Christopher, Edward, Hannah, Louis, Lucian, Will**)

- What actress named her baby **Dakota Paul Mayi**? (Melissa Gilbert)

NO BABY NAME BOOK IS MORE FUN . . .
OR INFORMATIVE!

# THE CELEBRITY BABY NAME BOOK

# THE CELEBRITY BABY NAME BOOK

*Thousands of distinctive names
inspired by the children of
your favorite personalities,
past and present*

## Stephen J. Spignesi

A SIGNET BOOK

SIGNET
Published by the Penguin Group
Penguin Books USA Inc., 375 Hudson Street,
New York, New York 10014, U.S.A.
Penguin Books Ltd, 27 Wrights Lane,
London W8 5TZ, England
Penguin Books Australia Ltd, Ringwood,
Victoria, Australia
Penguin Books Canada Ltd, 10 Alcorn Avenue,
Toronto, Ontario, Canada M4V 3B2
Penguin Books (N.Z.) Ltd, 182–190 Wairau Road,
Auckland 10, New Zealand

Penguin Books Ltd, Registered Offices:
Harmondsworth, Middlesex, England

First published by Signet, an imprint of Dutton Signet,
a division of Penguin Books USA Inc.

First Printing, June, 1996
10 9 8 7 6 5 4 3 2 1

 REGISTERED TRADEMARK—MARCA REGISTRADA

Printed in the United States of America

BOOKS ARE AVAILABLE AT QUANTITY DISCOUNTS WHEN USED TO PROMOTE
PRODUCTS OR SERVICES. FOR INFORMATION PLEASE WRITE TO PREMIUM
MARKETING DIVISION, PENGUIN BOOKS USA INC., 375 HUDSON STREET, NEW YORK,
NY 10014.

For my grandmothers,
TERESA VALANZANO RAPUANO
and
ANGELINA MAZZARELLA SPIGNESI,
*two loving women who always made*
*their children and grandchildren*
*feel like celebrities*

# Contents

## THE MOST POPULAR BOYS & GIRLS NAMES OVER THE LAST 160 YEARS

| YEAR | BOY | GIRL |
|------|-----|------|
| 1830 | JOHN | MARY |
| 1900 | JOHN | MARY |
| 1925 | ROBERT | MARY |
| 1950 | ROBERT | LINDA |
| 1970 | MICHAEL | JENNIFER |
| 1975 | MICHAEL | JENNIFER |
| 1980 | MICHAEL | JENNIFER |
| 1982 | MICHAEL | JENNIFER |
| 1990 | MICHAEL | ASHLEY |

# Read Me First

This book is in two sections: "The Names" and "The Celebrities."

The first part, "The Names," provides more than 5,200 boy and girl names, organized into entertaining and informative sections that span the popular culture landscape, including children of celebrities, names from movie titles, names of TV characters, names from song titles, and names of presidential children.

Here is what you should know about the organization of the name lists:

1. In the celebrity children section, the first name is provided (in ALL CAPS), and then following that name is the celebrity or celebrities who have used that name for their child.

   This will allow you to scan the list of names for something that appeals to you and then see if a favorite celebrity has used the same name.

2. If a celebrity baby name is suitable for either gender (Tyler, Shannon, etc.), then the name is included in *both* lists.

   Thus, these lists are *not* meant to be a biographical guide to the children of celebrities, but rather a compilation of celebrity children's names to assist you in finding a name for your own child.

[**A Note about Spelling:** Often, a child's name was spelled differently in varied sources. When this occurred, I elected to provide both spellings (sometimes as separate listings, sometimes as alternate endings). Roseanne's daughter Brandy has also been referred to as "Brandi." Since both names are pretty, I listed both. I also included nicknames as separate choices. Jack Lemmon's son Chris, whose full name is Christopher, is known widely in the movie industry as Chris Lemmon, thus both names are listed.]

3. The best way to start is probably by reviewing the "Names" lists for something appealing.

However, you might find it interesting to browse through the massive listing of celebrities in Part II (close to 2,500 celebs in almost 50 professions, including over 1,500 actors, actresses, singers, directors, writers, and professional athletes) for famous people you admire and check out what they named their kids. This could lead you back to the celebrity baby name sections to see who else has chosen a particular name.

Also, since the celebrity children's middle names are also provided in the **Celebrity Master Index,** you might find some ideas for names by checking them out as well. (And by the way, when the child is the off-spring of a celebrity *couple,* I listed the mom first, no matter how much more famous the father might be. This is just my way of acknowledging the incalculable importance of mothers.)

The **Celebrity Master Index** also offers fascinating details on a multitude of celeb vocations, from the arts, to politics, to science, and more.

As to what makes a celebrity a celebrity: Essentially, that weird aura we call "celebrity" is conferred upon people when they are repeatedly examined by the media. It seems that something intangible yet real happens when a person is on TV or the radio, or he or she appears in newspapers, magazines, or perhaps writes an intriguing book. Our perception of them is changed. A gravity (sometimes justified, sometimes not) is attached to the thoughts, habits, and beliefs of a person when these are communicated or covered via mass media.

Thus, my criteria for including a person depended on the amount of media exposure he or she has received in their lifetime. This allowed me to include people who were not only in entertainment, sports, or other high-profile popular culture endeavors, but also people who are well known in their fields and who have been extensively covered by the media (or, in the case of important historical figures, written about for centuries).

Therefore, in this book, you will find a wide-ranging spectrum of "professions," including:

| | | |
|---|---|---|
| Actors | Directors | Political Activists |
| Actresses | Doctors | Politicians |
| Architects | Economists | Professional |
| Artists | Editors | Athletes |
| Astronauts | Educators | Professional |
| Beauty Pageant | Environmentalists | Athletic |
| Winners | Explorers | Coaches |
| Bureaucrats | Fashion Designers | Psychiatrists |
| Choreographers | Financiers | Psychologists |
| Civil Rights | Inventors | Royalty |
| Leaders | Journalists | Scientists |
| Clergy | Judges | Sculptors |
| Comedians | Lawyers | Singers |
| Composers | Military People | Songwriters |
| Conductors | Models | Televangelists |
| Corporate | Movie Producers | Theatrical |
| Executives | Musicians | Promoters |
| Dancers | Poets | Writers |

And there are also a few quirky "job" titles, such as "Oil Well Fire Fighter" (Red Adair) and "Sexual Assault Victim & Actor" (John Wayne Bobbitt).

Some of the celebs included in this list may not be immediately recognizable by name, but all are well known in their respective fields.

If you come across a baby name you like while browsing through the Boys and Girls list but can't recognize the celebrity's name, flip to the Celebrity Index and check out what he or she is famous for.

[**NOTE:** Scattered throughout *The Celebrity Baby Name Book,* for your entertainment and enlightenment, are dozens of delectable bits of trivia related to names and celebrities. These tidbits are low in sodium and cholesterol and rich in fiber, so feel free to indulge in them at will!]

## ACKNOWLEDGMENTS

Special thanks to Roger Ebert; Ed Stackler; Elaine Koster and Penguin USA; Trish at the Blackstone Memorial Library in Branford, CT; Marcia at the Hagaman Library in East Haven, CT; and John White.

# THE NAMES

# Celebrity Baby Names

## THE BEST-LOVED NAMES
## OF THE ALPHABET

### Boys

| | | |
|---|---|---|
| ANDREW | JASON | STEVEN |
| BRIAN | KEVIN | THOMAS |
| CHRISTOPHER | LAWRENCE | URIAH |
| DAVID | MICHAEL | VINCENT |
| ERIC | NICHOLAS | WILLIAM |
| FREDERICK | OWEN | XAVIER |
| GREGORY | PETER | YALE |
| HOWARD | QUINTON | ZEBEDIAH |
| ISAAC | ROBERT | |

## CELEBRITY BABY NAMES FOR BOYS

AAGE (Neils Bohr)
AARON (Ken Kercheval; Paul O'Neill)
ABDEL (King Fahd)
ABRAHAM (Estelle Parsons; Herman Wouk)
ADAM (Alan Arkin; Saul Bellow; Herschel Bernardi; Barry Bremen; Jim Dale; Larry Gelbart; Maurice Gibb; Jack

Klugman; Peter Max; Leonard Nimoy; Albert Shanker;
Dick Shawn; Anna Strasberg; Leroy Van Dyke; Bill
Walton)

ADLAI (Adlai Stevenson)

ADRIAN (Edie Brickell & Paul Simon)

AHMET (Frank Zappa)

AKBAR (The Honorable Elijah Muhammad)

AL (Al "Scarface" Capone)

ALAA (Hosni Mubarak)

ALAN (Robert Alda; David Brinkley; John Kenneth
Galbraith; Samuel Hayakawa; Olive & George Osmond;
Warren Rudman)

ALBERT (Harry "Parkyakarkus" Einstein; Tipper & Al
Gore)

ALEC (Mary Hart & Bert Sugarman)

ALEX (Chris Evert; Bill Graham; Richard Heckert; Bob
Hoskins; Lindsay Wagner)

ALEXANDER (Jane Asher; Leonard Bernstein; Brenda
Boozer & Robert Klein; James Boswell; Ingrid & James
Caan; Liz Claiborne; William Sloane Coffin; Cleopatra &
Antony; Colleen Dewhurst; Chris Evert & Andy Mill;
Melanie Griffith & Steven Bauer; Alexander Haig; Wil-
liam Hurt; Olivia Hussey & Dean Paul Martin; Roy Innis;
Aristotle Onassis; King Peter; Ken Russell; George
Shultz; Yakov Smirnoff; Aung San Suu Kyi)

---

### A BUSINESS MAJOR, EH? BET HE MADE THE DEAN'S LIST.

Gangster Al Capone's son Al, Jr., used the alias "Al
Brown" when he attended the University of Miami,
majoring in Business Administration. In 1966, Al
had his name legally changed to "Albert Francis"
(perhaps in honor of Frank "Francis Albert"
Sinatra?)

ALEXIS (Charles Diggs, Jr.; Czar Nicholas II)

ALFIE (Lesley Manville & Gary Oldman)

ALFRED (Charles Dickens; Martin Luther King, Sr.; Al Unser)

ALFREDO (Enzo Ferrari)

ALJOSHA (Nastassja Kinski)

ALLEN (Russell Baker; Patty Duke & John Austin; C. Everett Koop; Doc Severinsen)

ALPHONSE (Morgan Freeman)

ALVARO (Placido Domingo; Lorenzo Lamas)

ALY (Aga Khan)

AMADEO (John Turturro)

AMIRI (Imamu Amiri Baraka [LeRoi Jones])

ANAUKAP (Admiral Robert Peáry)

ANDERS (Michael Eisner)

ANDERSON (Gloria Vanderbilt)

ANDRE (Henry Heinz)

ANDREA (Princess Caroline)

ANDREI (Leo Tolstoy)

ANDRÉS (Andrés Segovia)

ANDREW (Erma Bombeck; John Wayne Bobbitt; Mario Cuomo; Faith Daniels; William DeVries; Queen Elizabeth; Rudy Giuliani; Ira Glasser; Abbie Hoffman; Ann Jillian; Alan King; Ted Koppel; Ralph Lauren; Albert Nipon; Paul O'Neill; Phyllis Schlafly; Arthur Schlesinger; Dickie Smothers; David Stern; Stella Stevens; David Susskind; Laurence Tisch; Marvin Traub; Corinna Tsupei & Freddie Fields; Andrew Young)

ANDY (Andy Griffith)

ANGEL (Angel Cordero)

ANGUS (Amanda Pays & Corbin Bernsen; Donald Sutherland)

ANTHONY (Alan Arkin; John Avildsen; Albert Broccoli; Erik Estrada; A.J. Foyt; Tony Hillerman; Bob Hope: Judith Krantz; Angela Lansbury; Jerry Lewis; Archie Moore; Jerry Orbach; Geraldine Page & Rip Torn; Joe Papp; Gregory Peck; Osgood Perkins; Mario Puzo; Lee

Radziwill; Donna Reed; David Rogers; Rebecca West &
H.G. Wells; Julann Wright & Merv Griffin)

ANTONIO (Alberto Salazar)

ANTONY (Robert Alda)

ART (Charlie Walker)

ARTHUR (Arthur Sulzberger; Queen Victoria)

ARVO (Gus Hall)

ASHU (James Stevens)

AUBREY (Mary Robinson)

AUGUST (Lena Olin; Garth Brooks; Johann Von Goethe)

AUSTIN (Danny Ainge; Tracey Bregman; Clyde Drexler;
Tommy Lee Jones; Huey Lewis; J. Eddie Peck; Craig
Rivera; Boz Scaggs; Sela Ward)

BAILEY (Anthony Edwards)

BAIRD (John Hershey)

BARNABE (Isabelle Adjani & Bruno Nuytten)

BARNABY (John Chancellor)

BARRY (Bobby Bonds; Michael De Bakey; Barry Goldwater; Larry Speakes; Dick Van Dyke)

BASHAR (Hafez al-Assad)

BASIL (Hafez al-Assad)

BART (Bobby Hull)

BAY (Paul Rigby)

BEAU (Joseph Biden; Lloyd Bridges; Louis L'Amour;
Tanya Tucker & Ben Reed; Tommy Smothers)

BEAUREGARD (Ted Turner)

BELA (Bela Lugosi)

BEN (Jeff Daniels; Richard Dreyfuss; Jane Hamilton; Mary
Kay; Anne Meara & Jerry Stiller; Budd Schulberg; Ted
Stevens; Tanya Tucker; Hicks Waldron; Neil Young)

BENEDICK (Alan Bates)

BENEDICT (Brian Mulroney)

BENIGNO (Corazon Aquino)

BENJAMIN (Ben Bradlee; Benjamin Chavez; Olivia De
Havilland; Richard Dreyfuss; Pierre Du Pont; Harrison
Ford; Dexter Gordon; Russell Hoban; Perri Klass; Nor-
man Lear; Bob Kerrey; Anne Meara & Jerry Stiller; Lisa

Marie Presley; Marilyn & Dan Quayle; Lynn Redgrave; Carly Simon & James Taylor; Ben Vereen; Judy Woodruff)

BENJIE (Benny Goodman)

BERNARD (Stanley Elkin)

BERRY (Berry Gordy; Smokey Robinson)

BERTIE (Queen Victoria)

BEXLEY (Cordell Jackson)

BILL (Terry Jones; Ring Lardner; Red Sovine)

BILLY (Milton Berle; Bill Carlisle; Bill Caspar; Billy "Crash" Craddock; Billy Grammer; Billy James Hargis; Mickey Mantle; Billy Martin; Archie Moore; Willie Nelson; Wayne Rogers)

BION (Madeline L'Engle)

BJORN (Thor Heyerdahl)

BLAIR (Michael Deaver; Warren Moon; Charles Scribner, Jr.)

BLAKE (Bobby Hull; Brent Musburger)

BOB (Robert North Bradbury; Bob Guccione; Bob Jones)

BOBBY (Bill Caspar; Bobby Helms; Bobby Hull; Stan Jaffe; Brian Keith; Alan King; Bobby Unser; Robert Weiss; Kitty Wells; Johnny Wright)

BOGDAN (Lech Walesa)

BONGI (Miriam Makeba)

BORYS (Joseph Conrad)

BOSTON (Kurt Russell)

BRAD (Brad Bell; John Bradshaw; Jackie Kallen)

BRADFORD (George Peppard)

BRADLEY (Bryant Gumbel; Claude King; F. Story Musgrave)

BRAISON (Leticia & Billy Ray Cyrus)

BRANDEN (Erik Estrada)

BRANDON (Bruce Jenner; Bruce Lee; Richard Marx; Ron Guidry; Karyn White & Terry Lewis)

BRANFORD (Ellis Marsalis)

BRAWLEY (Nick Nolte)

BRENDAN (John Irving; Bruce Jenner)

BRENNAN (Gloria Loring and Alan Thicke)
BRENT (Lou Ferrigno; Orrin Hatch; Jimmy Johnson; Sumner Redstone; Robert Shapiro)
BRETT (Wade Boggs; Jimmy Connors; Bobby Hull)
BRIAN (Marv Albert; Steve Allen; Art Carney; Roger Corman; Rodney Dangerfield; Tennessee Ernie Ford; Alexander Haig; David Hartman; Jim Henson; Robert Keith; Sam Nunn; Sandra Day O'Connor; Andy Rooney; Lowell Weicker)

---

**THIS IS MY FATHER.
YOU CAN JUST CALL HIM "MAN."**

You'd think that if a parent went through the trouble of selecting a unique spelling for their child's name, they'd *use* it once in a while. Well, Joseph Conrad, author of *Heart of Darkness,* named his son "Borys" (deliberately replacing the "i" in "Boris" with a "y") and yet consistently addressed his heir as "Boy."

---

BRIGHAM (Brigham Young)
BRODIE (Edward James Olmos)
BRODY (Bruce Jenner)
BROM (Russell Hoban)
BROOKLYN (Jonathan Demme)
BRUCE (John Carradine; Gordon MacRae; Roberta Peters; Phyllis Schlafly; Suzanne Somers)
BRYAN (Jack Anderson; Jackie Kallen; Bryan Trottier)
BUCKY (Beverly Sills)
BUD (Bud Abbott)
BUDDY (Buck Owens)
BURT (Bruce Jenner)
BYRON (Tony Brown; Bill Caspar; Mel Harris)
CAESAR (Melvin Belli)

CAL (Glen Campbell)
CALEB (Susan Anspach & Jack Nicholson)
CAMERON (Michael Douglas; Marjorie Vincent)
CAMPBELL (Colleen Dewhurst & George C. Scott)
CAREY (Gregory Peck)
CARL (Johann Sebastian Bach; Goldie Hill; Don King; Carl Laemmle; Carl Rowan; Carl Smith; Carl Stokes)
CARL-GUSTAF (Sven Nykvist)
CARLO (Sophia Loren & Carlo Ponti; Vanessa Redgrave & Franco Nero)
CARLOS (Andrés Segovia; Martin Sheen)
CARMEN (Claudio Arrau)
CARTER (Gloria Vanderbilt)
CASEY (Beau Bridges; Rita Coolidge & Kris Kristofferson; Carlton Fisk)
CASPAR (Caspar Weinberger)
CASSIDY (Robert Vaughn)
CEDRIC (Roy Innis)
CESARE (Pope Alexander VI)
CHAD (Jimmy Johnson; Steve McQueen; Dale Murphy; Johnny Unitas)
CHANGA (Harry Edwards)
CHANNING (Carol Channing; Jeff Smith)
CHARLES (Ed Asner; Shirley Temple Black; Bill Caspar; Charles Dickens; Charles Diggs, Jr.; Robert Duncan; Thomas Edison; Queen Elizabeth; Lita Grey & Charlie Chaplin; Mark Hatfield; Jesse Helms; Jimmy Hoffa; John Houseman; Rex Humbard; Edmund Kean; Charles Lindbergh, Jr.; Henry Wadsworth Longfellow; J.E. Mainer; Walter Matthau; Henry Morgan; Harold Prince; Charlie Rich; John D. Rockefeller; Susan St. James & Dick Ebersol; James Schlesinger; Charles Schulz; Charles Scribner, Jr.; Percy Bysshe Shelley; Robert Stack; Mary Steenburgen & Malcolm McDowell; Danny Thomas; Charles Walgreen III; Byron White)
CHARLEY (John Boorman; Robert Irwin Chartoff)
CHARLIE (Susan St. James & Dick Ebersol; Charlie Mc-

Coy; Walter Matthau; Mary Steenburgen & Malcolm McDowell)

CHELSEA (Hillary Rodham & Bill Clinton)

CHESARE (Sonny Bono)

CHESTER (Rita Wilson & Tom Hanks)

CHRIS (Johnny Carson; Joan Crawford; Mario Cuomo; Bob Elliott; Rusty Kanokogi; Elia Kazan; Pat Kennedy Lawford; Jack Lemmon; Jerry Lewis; Craig T. Nelson; Robert Mitchum; Henry Morgan; Leo Penn; Kenny Rankin; Paul Rogers; Mickey Rooney; Leo Ryan; Bobby Sherman; Leslie Anne Warren & Jon Peters)

---

### A NOD TO THE HOMELAND

Educator Harry Edwards's son's name "Changa" means "strong as iron" in the African language spoken in the central region of the continent.

---

CHRIST (Charles Walgreen III)

CHRISTIAAN (Catherine Deneuve & Roger Vadim)

CHRISTIAN (Elizabeth Ashley & George Peppard; Bruce Babbitt; Neils Bohr; Eric Braeden; Klaus Maria Brandauer; Marlon Brando; Catherine Deneuve & Roger Vadim; Dick Gregory; Roger Moore; Telly Savalas; Norman Schwarzkopf; Dick Van Dyke; Andy Williams)

CHRISTOPH (Heinrich Böll)

CHRISTOPHER (Claudio Arrau; Hoyt Axton; Clive Barnes; Peter Benchley; Bill Bixby; Jimmy Breslin; Dave Brubeck; William F. Buckley; John Candy; Harry Caray; Leslie Caron; John Carradine; Alexander Cohen; Broderick Crawford; Mario Cuomo; Billy Ray Cyrus; Alphonse D'Amato; James Dickey; Tony Dow; Malcolm Forbes; Tony Franciosa; David Gergen; Mel Gibson; Nicholas Graham; Gene Hackman; Cassandra Harris & Pierce Brosnan; Henry Heinz; Keith Jackson; Peter

Jennings; Walter Kerr; James Kilpatrick; Harvey Korman; Michael Landon; Carol Lawrence & Robert Goulet; Jack Lemmon; Henry Mancini; A.A. Milne; Robert Mitchum; F. Story Musgrave; Bill O'Donnell; Tip O'Neill; Jerry Orbach; Claiborne Pell; Leo Penn; Anna Quindlen; Robert Rauschenberg; Tim Reid; Nelson Riddle; Kenny Rogers; Carole Bayer Sager & Burt Bacharach; Antonin Scalia; John Sununu; Jessica Tandy & Hume Cronyn; Elizabeth Taylor; Johnny Unitas; Gloria Vanderbilt; Sander Vanocur; Bob Vila; Mike Wallace; Orson Welles; Morris West)

CIPI (Sophia Loren & Carlo Ponti)

CLARENCE (Aretha Franklin)

---

### FAMILY INSPIRATION

A.A. Milne's son Christopher Robin was the inspiration for the author's *Winnie the Pooh* character of the same name.

---

CLARK (Judy Collins; Ann Richards)

CLAS (Max Von Sydow)

CLAUDE (W.C. Fields; Pierre-Auguste Renoir)

CLAY (Alan L. Bean; Peter Benchley; Annie Potts)

CLAYTON (Peter Benchley)

CLIFFORD (Patricia Wettig & Ken Olin)

CLIFTON (Ray Price)

CLINT (Rance Howard)

CLOVIS (Paul Gauguin)

CODY (Kathie Lee & Frank Gifford; Marsha & Robin Williams)

COLE (David Brenner)

COLIN (Bob Denver; John Irving; Walter Kerr; Michael McKean; Alan K. Simpson; Rita Wilson & Tom Hanks)

COLLIN (Jeanne Cooper)

COLM (Caitlin & Dylan Thomas)
COLUMBUS (The Duke and Duchess of Kent)
CONNOR (Ruth Pointer; Jean Smart & Richard Gilliland)
CONOR (Eric Clapton; David Hartman; Robert Kennedy, Jr.)
CONRAD (Bertrand Russell)
CONWAY (Conway Twitty)
COOPER (Tim Matheson; Kimberley Conrad & Hugh Hefner)
CORBIN (Jeanne Cooper)
CORDELL (Carl Stokes)
COREY (Bob Eubanks; Billy Dee Williams)
CORIN (Michael Redgrave)
CORNELIUS (Cornelius Vanderbilt)
CORY (Johnny Carson)
CRAIG (Hal David; Richard R. Green; Dean Martin; Charles Schulz; Del Shannon; Tina Turner; Steve Walsh)
CURTIS (Rex Allen; Curt Gowdy)
CUTTER (Lenny Dykstra)
CYRIL (Christo; Oscar Wilde)
D'AMATO (Mike Tyson)
D'ANGELO (Archie Moore)
DAEGAL (Tony Bennett)
DAKOTA (Melissa Gilbert & Bo Brinkman; Melanie Griffith & Don Johnson)
DALE (Yogi Berra; Dale Bumpers; Rose Lee & Joe Maphis; Ray Pillow; Hank Stram; Dottie West)
DALL (John Forsythe)
DALTON (Linda Hamilton; J. Eddie Peck)
DAMIEN (Richard Harris)
DAMION (Dionne Warwick; Faron Young)
DAMON (Mitch Williams; Raquel Welch)
DAN (Ann Richards)
DANA (Cordell Jackson)
DANE (Karen Velez & Lee Majors)
DANIEL (Adrienne Allen & Raymond Massey; Bob Allen; John Barth; Saul Bellow; Jimmy Breslin; Dave Brubeck;

Robert Campeau; Robert Coles; Alphonse D'Amato; Phil Donahue; Julia Duffy; Betty Friedan; Tony Hillerman; Celeste Holm; Daniel Inouye; Glenda Jackson; Anselm Kiefer; Ray Milland; Harry Morgan; Henry Morgan; Roger Mudd; Brian Mulroney; Allen Neuharth; Harold Pinter; Dan Rather; Judith Rossner; Pete Seeger; Anna Nicole Smith; Maureen Stapleton; Laurence Tisch)

DANNY (Danny Aiello; Pancho Gonzales; Mickey Mantle; Regis Philbin; Anthony Quinn; Jerry Tarkanian)

DAREK (Howard Baker)

DARIUS (Dave Brubeck)

DARRELL (Medgar Evers; Eva Marie Saint; Jonas Salk)

DARRYL (George Clinton)

DARYL (James Brown; Ray Pillow)

DASHIELL (Harry Anderson)

DAVE (Harry "Parkyakarkus" Einstein)

DAVID (Steve Allen; Isaac Asimov; Harry Belafonte; Daniel J. Boorstin; Dave Brubeck; Daniel Callahan; John Carradine; Bill Caspar; Ray Charles; William Sloane Coffin; Dom De Luise; Ray Milton Dolby; Pete Domenici; David Dinkins; Patty Duke & John Astin; Deidre Hall; William Randolph Hearst; Richard Kiley; Stan Getz; Ira Glasser; William Golding; Eydie Gormé & Steve Lawrence; Bill Graham; Bill Hanna; Hugh Hefner; Hal Holbrook; Shirley Jones & Jack Cassidy; Henry Kissinger; Jack Klugman; C. Everett Koop; Alan Ladd; Angela Lansbury; Ring Lardner; Ralph Lauren; Michele Lee & James Farentino; Alfred Lennon; Dorothy Letterman; Joseph Levine; Roy Lichtenstein; Gavin MacLeod; Mickey Mantle; Walter Matthau; Robert Merrill; Arnold Newman; Robert Redford; David Reuben; Jason Robards; David Robinson; David Rockefeller; Mike Royko; Dean Rusk; Vidal Sassoon; Budd Schulberg; Willard Scott; Don Shula; Isaac Stern; Potter Stewart; Curtis Strange; Dick Thornburgh; Texas T. Tyler; John Updike; Irving Wallace; Joseph Wapner; Dionne Warwick; Theodore White; Frank Lloyd Wright)

DEAN (Dean Martin)
DEGEN (E.G. Marshall)
DEION (Deion Sanders)
DENIS (Michael De Bakey)
DENNIS (Bing Crosby; Merle Travis)
DESIDERIO (Lucille Ball & Desi Arnaz)
DEVADAS (Mahatma Gandhi)
DEVIN (Vanessa Williams; Roger Zelazny)
DEX (Dana Carvey)
DEXTER (Coretta Scott & Martin Luther King, Jr.)
DHANI (George Harrison)
DICKIE (Eddy Arnold; Stan Musial)
DILLON (Glen Campbell)
DINO (Enzo Ferrari; Dean Martin)
DION (Charley Pride)
DIRK (Dan Blocker)
DMITRI (Ursula Andress & Harry Hamlin; Vladimir Ashkenazy)
DODD (Sandra Dee)
DOMINIC/CK (Kelly LeBrock & Steven Seagal; Ben Bradlee; Dan Fouts)
DOMINIK (Andy Garcia)
DON (Hawkshaw Hawkins; Rex Humbard)
DONALD (James Boggs; Stepin Fetchit; Katharine Graham; Don Nickles; Donny Osmond; Ivana & Donald Trump)
DONN (Jean & George Ariyoshi)

---

### BUT HIS MIDDLE NAME MEANS "ROYALTIES," RIGHT?

Contrary to rumors widely spread by the press, George Harrison's son Dhani's name does *not* mean "wealthy" in Hindu. George derived the name from two ascending notes of the Indian musical scale, "dha" and "ni."

DONNEL (Rosalynn & Jimmy Carter)
DONNIE (Jimmy Swaggart)
DONNY (Olive & George Osmond; Ivana & Donald Trump)
DONOVAN (Donovan Leitch)
DONTE (Phil Spector)
DORIAN (Lindsay Wagner)
DORION (Carl Sagan)
DORNIN (Oliver Stone)
DOUGLAS (Gary Carter; Charles Durning; Douglas Fairbanks, Sr.; Robert Hofstadter; Doug Kershaw; Jean Kirkpatrick; Arthur Liman; Douglas Wilder)
DREW (Brett Saberhagen; Roger Smith; Paul Tagliabue)
DREXEL (O.B. McClinton)
DUANE (Dick Clark; Claude King)
DUNCAN (Anthony Quinn; James Watson)
DWEEZIL (Frank Zappa)
DYLAN (Jim Bartling; Beau Bridges; Mia Farrow & Woody Allen; Ralph Lauren; Alex North; Stephanie Seymour & Peter Brant; Bob Welch; Robin Wright & Sean Penn)
EARL (J.E. Mainer; Earl Wilson)
EARVIN (Earletha Kelley & Earvin "Magic" Johnson)
ED (Ed Begley, Sr.)
EDDIE (Anita Baker)
EDEN (Don Everly; Vidal Sassoon)
EDMOND (Keenan Wynn)
EDMUND (Ben Kingsley)
EDOARDO (Sophia Loren & Carlo Ponti)
EDSEL (Henry Ford II)
EDSON (Pelé)
EDUARD (Albert Einstein)
EDWARD (Eddie Albert; Mel Brooks; Lawton Chiles; Charles Dickens; Queen Elizabeth; Aretha Franklin; Ray Flynn; Mel Gibson; Henry VIII; Edward Kennedy; Rose & Joseph Kennedy; Linus Pauling; Edward G. Robinson; Susan St. James & Dick Ebersol; Abigail Van Buren; Fay Vincent; Frank Yablans)
EDWIN (Frank Borman; George Hamilton IV)

EFREM (Efrem Zimbalist, Sr.)
ELAN (Vidal Sassoon)
ELI (Sally Fields; Sophia Loren & Carlo Ponti)
ELIAU (Shlomo Mintz)
ELIJAH (Cher & Gregg Allmann; Janet Hubert-Whitten; The Honourable Elijah Muhammad; Tiffany)
ELIOT (Sting)
ELLIOT (Fyvush Finkel)
ELLIOTT (Laura D'Andrea Tyson)
ELON (Alan Dershowitz)
ELVIS (Anthony Perkins)
EMANUEL (Debra Winger & Timothy Hutton)
EMIL (Paul Gauguin)
EMILE (Paul Gauguin)
EMILIANO (Carlos Salinas)
EMILIO (Martin Sheen)
EMMANUEL (The Honorable Elijah Muhammad)
ENNIS (Bill Cosby)
ENZO (Patricia Arquette)
ERIC (Bruno Bettelheim; Marva Collins; Kirk Douglas; Michael Eisner; John R. Galvin; Bruce Greyson; Walter Heller; Robert Hooks; Don King; Ted Knight; Sherrill Milnes; Arnold Newman; Mike Norris; Adele Smith Simmons; David Stern; Ivana & Donald Trump; Willie C. Williams)
ERIK (Neils Bohr; Gaby Landhage & Thierry Reussel; Gypsy Rose Lee & Otto Preminger)
ERNEST (Neils Bohr; Michael De Bakey; Ernest Hollings; Henry Wadsworth Longfellow; Loretta Lynn)
ERROL (Russell Train)
ERWIN (Max Planck)
ETHAN (Jackson Browne; Stephen Jay Gould)
EUGENE/EUGÈNE (Josephine, Napoleon's Empress; Eugene O'Neill; Mario Puzo; Gene Roddenberry; Antonin Scalia)
EUSTACE (Eustace Gay)

EVAN (Diana Ross; Patti Scialfa & Bruce Springsteen; Paul Stanley)
EVANDER (Evander Holyfield)
EVIN (Bill Cosby)
EWIN (Evander Holyfield)
EZEKIEL (Beau Bridges)
EZRA (Marion Wright Edelman)
FAISEL (King Fahd)
FEDERICO (Dino De Laurentiis)
FELIPE (Juan Carlos I)
FELIX (Felix Grucci)
FEODOR (Ivan the Terrible)
FERNANDO (Fernando Valenzuela)
FIDEL (Fidel Castro)
FINN (Terrence McKenna)
FLEETWOOD (Tom Robbins)
FLETCHER (Mia Farrow & André Previn; Michael McKean)
FLYNN (Cecila Hart & James Earl Jones)
FOREST (Jack Greene)
FORREST (Forrest Tucker)
FOSTER (Mary Baker Eddy)
FRANCESCO (Caitlin Thomas & Giuseppe Fazio; Anthony Quinn)
FRANCIS (Charles Dickens; Johnny Unitas)
FRANK (Jay Gould; Pee Wee King; Jennings Randolph; Frank Robinson; Frank Sinatra; Jackie Stallone)
FRANZ (Wolfgang Amadeus Mozart)
FRASER (Charlton Heston)
FRED (Fred Astaire; Gordon Lightfoot)
FREDDY (Karl Marx)
FREDERIC (Barry Commoner; Maurice Strong)
FREDERICK (Frank Borman; Joseph Wapner)
FREDRIC (Gene Barry)
FREE (Barbara Hershey & David Carradine)
FRIEDRICH (Kaiser Wilhelm)
FUDDY (Daman Wayans)

FYODOR (Fyodor Dostoyevsky)

GABRIEL (Joan Baez; Paul Butterfield; Rosemary Clooney & José Ferrer; Amy Irving & Bruno Barreto; Geraldo Rivera; S. Brian Willson)

GAELAN (Gina & Michael Biehn)

GALE (Gale Sayers)

GAMAL (Hosni Mubarak)

GARRETT (Bo Jackson)

GARRY (Jimmy Dean; Goldie Hawn & Bill Hudson; Jane Pauley & Gary Trudeau; Gary Wills)

GARTH (Colleen Carroll; Vincent Persichetti)

GARY (Hank Aaron; Bing Crosby; Larry Gelbart; Jerry Lewis; Jimmy "C" Newman; Jack Nicklaus; Earl Scruggs; Phil Spector; Hank Stram; Henny Youngman)

GASTON (Jaclyn Smith)

GAVIN (Lenny Dykstra)

GENE (Pee Wee King; Les Paul)

GENEROSO (Generoso Pope)

GENTRY (Marvelous Marvin Hagler)

GEOFFREY (Philip Caputo; Greg Le Mond; Ashley Montagu; Roger Moore; Carl Rowan; George Will)

GEORGE (Tina Brown; Barbara & George Bush; Mary Baker Eddy; George Foreman; George Gallup III; Jay Gould; William Randolph Hearst; James Joyce; Meadowlark Lemon; George S. Patton; Babe Ruth; Jerry Tarkanian; Cornelius Vanderbilt; George Wallace)

GEORGIE (George Clinton)

GERALD (Alexander Cohen)

GERARD (Yehudi Menuhin)

GIAN-CARLO (Francis Ford Coppola)

GIB (Connie Sellecca & Gil Gerard)

GIDEON (Kathryn Grody & Mandy Patinkin)

GILBERT (Walter Kerr)

GILLIAN (Patty Hearst; Jeff Sagansky)

GLEN (Barbara Cartland; J.E. Mainer)

GLENN (Hank Greenberg; Kenneth H. Olsen; Bo Schembechler)

GORDON (Pat Robertson)

GRADY (Lynn Herring; Harry Smith)

GRANT (Kenneth Auchincloss; David Guyer)

GRAY (Lowell Weicker)

GREG (Carl Perkins)

GREGG (Marjorie Lord)

GREGORY (Saul Bellow; Elmer Bernstein; Mickey Gilley; Don King; Ernest Hemingway; Maurice Hines; Wanda Jackson; Walter Kerr; Greg Norman; William Smith)

GRIFFIN (Dominick Dunne; Ryan O'Neal)

GROVER (Grover Washington, Jr.)

GUILLAUME (Gerard Depardieu)

GUION (Guion Bluford)

GUNNAR (Rick Nelson)

GUY (Maya Angelou; Ruby Dee & Ossie Davis)

GYROMAS (Joseph Newman)

HADRIAN (Antoine Predock)

HAL (Hal Wallis)

HALLAM (Alfred Lord Tennyson)

HAMNET (William Shakespeare)

HAMZAH (King Hussein)

HANK (Hank Aaron)

HANS (Neils Bohr; Albert Einstein; Martin Luther)

HARDY (Archie Moore)

HARILAL (Mahatma Ghandhi)

HAROLD (Hawkshaw Hawkins; George Steinbrenner)

HARPER (Paul Simon)

HARRIS (Eric Bogosian)

HARRISON (Leslie Wexner)

HARRY (Richard Dreyfuss; Harry Caray; Harry Carey)

HARTLEY (Samuel Coleridge)

HASHIM (King Hussein)

HEDWIG (Maria Von Trapp)

HEINRICH (Karl Marx)

HENRY (Hank Aaron; Corbin Bernsen; Gwendolyn Brooks; Princess Diana & Prince Charles; Charles Dickens; Henry Heinz; Henry VIII; Dennis Hopper; Julia Louis-Dreyfus

& Brad Hall; Amanda Pays & Daniel Stern; Martin Short;
George Steinbrenner; Hank Stram; Meryl Streep)
HERBERT (The Honorable Elijah Muhammad; Claiborne
Pell; Joseph Pulitzer)
HIRO (Akihito; Kiichi Miyazawa)
HISAO (Akira Kurosawa)
HOLDEN (Dennis Miller)
HOMER (Matt Groenig; Bill Murray)
HOOPER (Robin Wright & Sean Penn)
HORACE (Julian Bond)
HORASHI (Arata Isozaki)

---

## YEAH, BUT HE'LL PROBABLY CHANGE IT LATER

John Mellencamp (formerly John Cougar, and then
John Cougar Mellencamp) named his son Hud for
the main character in Paul Newman's memorable
1963 Martin Ritt-directed drama, *Hud.* Mellencamp
and his wife, Elaine Irwin, are very good friends
with Larry McMurty, author of the novel *Horseman
Pass By,* which was made into the 1963 flick.

---

HORATIO (Horatio Nelson)
HOWELL (Howell Heflin)
HUD (John Mellencamp)
HUGER (Shelby Foote)
HUGH (William Joseph Brennan; Hugh Downs; Carroll
O'Connor)
HUGO (Jane Goodall)
HUNT (Joseph Biden)
HUNTER (Karen Black)
IAN (Zbigniew Brzezinski; Barbara Cartland; Roz Chast;
Nicolas Coster; Fyvush Finkel; Hal Linden; John
Lithgow; Robert MacNeil; Robert Maxwell; Adele Smith
Simmons)

IB (Lauritz Melchior)
ICILIO (Giuseppe Verdi)
IGNAT (Aleksandr Solzhenitsyn)
IGOR (Peter Ustinov)
IKE (Tina Turner)
ILANN (Lorin Mazel)
ISAAC (Kathryn Grody & Mandy Patinkin)
ISAIAH (Mia Farrow)
ISRAEL (Isaac Bashevis Singer)
IVAN (Ivan the Terrible)
JACHIN (Russell Hoban)
JACK (Ellen Barkin & Gabriel Byrne; Annette Bening &
    Warren Beatty; Christie Brinkley; Willem Dafoe; Jack
    Haley; Ernest Hemingway; Irene Hervey & Allan Jones;
    Bob Hoskins; Caroline Kennedy; Joanne Whalley-Kilmer
    and Val Kilmer; Denis Leary; Timothy Leary; Barry
    Levinson; Virginia Madsen & Antonio Zapato; Ozzie
    Osbourne; Art Linkletter; Loretta Lynn; Jack Nicklaus;
    Donna Pescow; Nathan Pritikin; Jeanne Pruett; Charlie
    Rich; Meg Ryan & Dennis Quaid; Susan Sarandon & Tim
    Robbins)

---

### HEEEERE'S JACK!

Annette Bening and Warren Beatty's second child,
Jack, was named for Warren's best friend, Jack
Nicholson.

---

JACKIE (Jack Greene; Katherine & Joe Jackson)
JACKSON (Morgan Englund; Patti Smith)
JACOB (Jason Epstein; Nora Ephron & Carl Bernstein;
    Dustin Hoffman; Lawrence Kasdan; Willie Nelson;
    Roseanne)
JACQUES (Robert Campeau)
JADEN (Frank Dicopoulos)

JAKE (Gary Busey; Shaun Cassidy; Blythe Danner & Bruce
Paltrow; William Devane; Dustin Hoffman; Lawrence
Kasdan; Sinead O'Connor; Rhea Perlman & Danny
DeVito; Jason Robards; Roseanne; Kim Zimmer)

JAMAL (Clarence Thomas)

JAMES (Jacques Barzun; Guion Bluford; James Boggs;
James Boswell; Sarah & Jim Brady; Jimmy Breslin; Jim
Ed Brown; Abe Burrows; James Cagney; Lynda Carter;
Rosalynn & Jimmy Carter; James Coburn; Medgar Evers;
John Kenneth Galbraith; Art Garfunkel; Ruth Bader
Ginsburg; Felix Grucci; Marvelous Marvin Hagler; Jerry
Hall & Mick Jagger; Oscar Hammerstein II; Helen Hayes;
Clifton Keith Hillegas; James Hoge; John Hughes; Stacy
Keach, Sr.; Jack Kemp; Gladys Knight; Burt Lancaster;
Ring Lardner; John Major; Mary, Queen of Scots; Paul
McCartney; J. Michael McCloskey; Gates McFadden &
John Talbot; Larry McMurtry; Charles Merrill; Robert
Mitchum; Art Monk; Bill Monroe, Rupert Murdoch;
Kenneth H. Olsen; Carrie Saxon Perry; Annie Potts; Wil-
liam Rehnquist; Ken Russell; James Schlesinger; John
Sununu; Laurence Tisch; Marvin Traub; Gwen Verdon;
Jon Voight; Paul Volcker; Kurt Vonnegut, Jr.; Molly Yard)

JAMIE (Jim Abrahams; Jim Bakker; Leonard Bernstein;
Lynda Carter; Ron Guidry; Richard Harris; James Lehrer;
Janet Leigh & Tony Curtis; Joan Lunden & Michael
Krause; Mike Krzyzewski; Jim Palmer; Robert Redford;
John D. Rockefeller, Jim Valvano)

JAMIN (Alan Dershowitz)

JARED (Richard Harris; Andy Van Slyke; Paula Zahn)

JAROSLAW (Lech Walesa)

JARREL (Sugar Ray Leonard)

JARRETT (Walter Payton)

JASON (Jane & Robert Alexander; Kent Bateman; John
Bonham; Diane Cilento & Sean Connery; Jill Ireland;
Ellis Marsalis; Jason Miller; Michael Nesmith; Barbra
Streisand & Elliott Gould; Antoine Predock; Jason
Robards, Sr.; Talia Shire; Marqueritte & O.J. Simpson;

Jeff Smith; Ringo Starr; Leslie Uggams; Johnny Ray Youngblood)

JAY (Bob Allen; Leona Helmsley; Sandra Day O'Connor; Olive & George Osmond; Mark Sandrich)

JAYSON (Jay Kordich)

JEAN (Paul Gauguin; Henri Matisse; Pierre-Auguste Renoir)

JEAN PAUL (Robert Campeau)

JEAN-CLAUDE (Josephine Baker)

JEAN-JACQUES (Jean-Pierre Rampal)

JEAN-MICHEL (Jacques Cousteau)

JED (Ken Kesey; Henry Winkler)

JEDD (Peter Nero)

JEFF (Lloyd Bridges; Sammy Davis, Jr.; Linda Gray; Jack Kemp)

JEFFERSON (Ellen Burstyn)

---

### THIS IS OUR SON. WE NAMED HIM IN HONOR OF ONE OF OUR FAVORITE VEHICLES.

John Travolta, a licensed pilot, named his son Jett after his beloved plane.

---

JEFFERY (Frank Gifford)

JEFFREY (Mario Andretti; Anne Archer; Julian Bond; Alan Cranston; Sandy Duncan; Tennessee Ernie Ford; Leon Gorman; Michael Jordan; Jack Kemp; Ed McMahon; Warren Moon; F. Story Musgrave; George Segal; Bernie Siegel; Judy Woodruff; William Zander Zalm)

JELANI (Wesley Snipes)

JEMAJO (Stepin Fetchit)

JENNINGS (Jennings Randolph)

JEREMY (Yehudi Menuhin; Carl Sagan; Larry Speakes; Reggie White)

JERMAINE (Katherine & Joe Jackson)

JERONE (Claude King)

JERRY (Ernie Banks; Pat Corley; Jerry Falwell; A.J. Foyt)

JERRY LEE (Jerry Lee Lewis)

JESS (James Brolin)

JESSE (Steven Bochco; Patti D'Arbanville & Don Johnson; Neil Diamond; Stephen Jay Gould; Orrin Hatch; Jesse Jackson; Leon Max Lederman; Sam Shepard; Dee Snider; Twyla Tharp)

JESSIE (Lorrie Morgan & Keith Whitley)

JETT (Kelly Preston & John Travolta)

JEVON (Bobby McFerrin)

JIM (Jim Brown; Jerry Buss; Hal David; Phil Donahue; Robert Mitchum)

JIMMIE (Jimmie Davis; Al Dexter; Hank Snow)

JIMMY (Red Adair; Joel Grey; Oscar Hammerstein II; Jack Kemp; Olive & George Osmond; Conway Twitty)

JO JO (Joe Louis)

JOAQUIN (Jimmy Smits)

JÖCHI (Genghis Khan)

JODY (Rose Lee & Joe Maphis)

JOE (Kevin Costner; David Hare; Istvan Eszterhas; Ethel & Robert Kennedy; Christine Lahti; Joe Louis; John Madden; Sting)

JOEL (David Brinkley; Mac Davis; Kirk Douglas; Mickey Katz; Dr. Ruth Westheimer; Johnny Ray Youngblood)

JOEY (Naomi Baka & Joe Eszterhas; Ernie Banks; Florence Henderson; Joe Piscopo; Mario Puzo)

JOHANN (Johann Sebastian Bach)

JOHANNAS (Maria Von Trapp)

JOHN (Caroline Astor; John Jacob Astor; Richard Avedon; Adrienne Barbeau & John Carpenter; John Barrymore, Sr.; John Barth; John Bradshaw; David Brinkley; Jensen Buchanan; Barbara & George Bush; Jerry Buss; Daniel Callahan; John Carradine; Rosalynn & Jimmy Carter; June & Johnny Cash; Henry Cisneros; John Connally; Alistair Cooke; Morris Dees; Johnny Dollar; Georgiana Drew & Maurice Barrymore; Michael Dukakis; John

Elway; Dale Evans & Roy Rogers; Geraldine Ferraro; Betty & Gerald Ford; Clark Gable; John Glenn; Arthur Hailey; Kay Hammond; Gary Hart; William Randolph Hearst; Jim Henson; John Hershey; John Houseman; Walter Huston; Candido Jacuzzi; Nancy Kassebaum; Caroline Kennedy & Ed Schlossberg; Jacqueline & John F. Kennedy; Rose & Joseph Kennedy; Walter Kerr; Jay Kordich; Jeane Kirkpatrick; Kris Kristofferson; Bert Lahr; Burt Lancaster; Ring Lardner; Paul Laxalt; Timothy Leary; Julia Lennon; Doris Lessing; Robert Loggia; John D. Loudermilk; Norman Mailer; Thurgood Marshall; Stewart McKinney; John Miller; Bill Moyers; Daniel Moynihan; Norman Vincent Peale; Michelle Pfeiffer & David Kelley; Bucky Pizzarelli; Norman Podhoretz; Paul Revere; Tex Ritter; John D. Rockefeller; Bertrand Russell; Johnny Rutherford; Antonin Scalia; Phyllis Schlafly; Charles Scribner, Jr.; Rudolph Serkin; Dinah Shore; Benjamin Spock; John Sununu; John Thompson; Dick Thornburgh; Spencer Tracy; Tracy Ullman & Allan McKeown; Johnny Unitas; John Warner; Denzel Washington; Jack Welch; Gary Wills; Frank Lloyd Wright; Molly Yard; Brigham Young; John Young)

---

### A NAME GAME

Aretha Franklin's son's name, "Kecalf," is an acronym of his parents' names, Ken E. Cunningham and Aretha L. Franklin.

---

JOHNNY (Chris Schenkel; Tracy Ullman; Jimmy Wakely; Johnny Ray Youngblood)

JOHNSE (William Hatfield)

JOHNSON (William Hatfield)

JON (William DeVries; Bob Edwards; Charles Lindbergh, Jr.; Madelyn Murray O'Hair; Gregory Peck)

JONA (Bert Convy)

JONAH (Marion Wright Edelman)

JONAS (Jamie Farr)

JONATHAN (Daniel J. Boorstin; Dave Dravecky; Jerry Falwell; José Feliciano; Betty Friedan; Mark Goodson; Jesse Jackson; Lawrence Kasdan; Oliver Koppell; John Larroquette; Meadowlark Lemon; Robert Ludlum; Burgess Meredith; Roger Mudd; Geraldine Page & Rip Torn; Gregory Peck; Paulina Porizkova & Ric Ocasek; Harry Reasoner; Shanna Reed; Tex Ritter; Jonas Salk; Mike Schmidt; Daniel Schorr; Artie Shaw; Bernie Siegel; Jon Vickers; George Will; Jonathan Winters)

JONATHAN-RUFUS (John Avildsen)

JORDAN (Bono; Beau Bridges; John Elway; Leeza Gibbons & Steve Meadows; Orel Heshiser; Cheryl Ladd; Jason Miller)

JOSÉ (Placido Domingo)

JOSEPH (Naomi Baka & Joe Eszterhas; Joseph Biden; Joe Garagiola; Jack Gilford; Jascha Heifetz; Ethel & Robert Kennedy; Rose & Joseph Kennedy; Ring Lardner; Jerry Lewis; Joe Louis; Joe Piscopo; Joseph Pulitzer; Paul Revere; Rudolph Schildkraut; Sting; Joe Theismann; Herman Wouk)

JOSH (James Brolin; William Devane; Mike Farrell; Michael Landon; Ali MacGraw; Zero Mostel)

JOSHUA (Bert Convy; Marion Wright Edelman; Linda Ellerbee; Larry Gatlin; Jacob Javits; Patti LuPone; Ali MacGraw; Mike McCartney; Warren Moon; Roger Schank; Isiah Thomas; Zero Mostel)

JUAN (Alicia De Larrocha; Carlos Salinas; Hunter Thompson)

JULIAN (Anselm Kiefer; John Lennon)

JUNIOR (Carl Laemmle)

JUSTIN (Adolph Caesar; Chris Cross; Bill Kreutzman; Andie MacDowell & Paul Qualley; John D. Rockefeller; Nicole & O.J. Simpson; Ernie Tubbs)

JUSTIS (Pam & Dave Mustaine)

KADEEM (Bethann Hardison)
KAGLE (Betty Carter)
KALI (Admiral Robert Peary)
KAN (Arata Isozaki)
KANE (Glen Campbell)
KARL (Wolfgang Amadeus Mozart; Max Planck)
KAWAI (Walter Becker)
KECALF (Aretha Franklin & Kenneth Cunningham)
KEENAN (Ed Wynn)
KEITH (John Carradine; Bob Costas; Bruce Hornsby; Gavin
    MacLeod; Jesse McReynolds; Bernie Siegel)

---

### "THIS IS MY BROTHER DARYL; THIS IS MY OTHER BROTHER DARYL" DEPARTMENT

Boxer Joe Louis had two sons named Joe: One, Joe
Louis, was a legitimate son born when he was
married; the other, Joseph, was his illegitimate son
by a prostitute.

---

KEN (Ken Griffey)
KENDALL (Ramsey Lewis)
KENNEDY (Berry Gordy)
KENNETH (Candido Jacuzzi; Elisabeth Kübler-Ross; Bar-
    bara Mandrell; Nathan Pritikin; Kenny Rogers; Irving
    Stone; Maurice Strong; Dave Thomas; Johnny Unitas; Jon
    Vickers)
KENNY (Marv Albert)
KENT (Conrad Bain)
KERRY (Berry Gordy; Gene Kelly; Kathleen Kennedy &
    David Townsend; Dottie West)
KEVIN (Rocky Aoki; Pat Corley; Patty Duke; Jack
    Anderson; Jimmy Breslin; Jim Brown; James Dickey; Phil
    Donahue; Joycelyn Elders; Paula Hawkins; Lou Holtz;
    Robert Hooks; Norman Jewison; James Kilpatrick; Paul

Laxalt; Robert Maxwell; Tatum O'Neal & John McEnroe;
Leo Ryan; Vince Scully; Tom Selleck; Adele Smith Simmons; Charles Walgreen III; Faron Young)

KIEFER (Donald Sutherland)

KIERNAN (Kit Culkin)

KIMBERLY (Merle Kilgore)

KIM (Kim Il Sung)

KIN (Herb Shriner)

KINGSLEY (George Gallup III)

KIP (Malcolm Forbes)

KLAUS (Thomas Mann)

KOBY (Roger Clemens)

KORY (Roger Clemens)

KRAIG (Charley Pride)

KRIS (Kris Kristofferson)

KRISTIAN (Paul Roebling)

KRISTOFFER (Viveca Lindfors)

KROV (Yehudi Menuhin)

KURT (Alfred Adler; Kurt Vonnegut, Jr.)

KWAMAE (The Reverend Ralph David Abernathy)

KYLE (Natalie Cole; Clint Eastwood; Frank Gifford; Margaret Trudeau Kemper; Richard Petty)

LACHLAN (Rupert Murdoch)

LAFFIT (Laffit Pincay, Jr.)

LAMAR (Buster Douglas)

LAN (Lloyd Bentsen)

LANCE (Jack Anderson; Barbara Hutton)

LAND (Charles Lindbergh, Jr.)

LARRY (Hank Aaron; Larry Flynt; Goldie Hill; Pee Wee
King; Mary Martin; Carl Smith)

LARY (Hank Aaron)

LAWRENCE (Yogi Berra; Judy Blume; Albert Nipon; Don
Rickles; Lawrence Taylor; L. Douglas Wilder)

LAWTON (Lawton Chiles)

LEAR (Frances Lear)

LEE (Jane Brody; Paul Butterfield; Lee Mazzilli; Roger

Tory Peterson; Cokie Roberts; Ringo Starr; Leroy Van Dyke)

LEIGH (David Guyer)

LEO (Geoffrey Holder; Elia Kazan; Leo Tolstoy)

LEON (Albert Nipon; Leon Payne)

LEONARD (Estee Lauder)

LEONARDO (Andrés Segovia)

LEOPOLD (Queen Victoria)

LESLIE (Charles Walgreen III)

LESTER (Geraldine McCullough; Les Paul)

LEVI (Carole King)

LEWIS (David Hare; Arthur Liman; Lewis Powell; Charlie Weaver)

LIAM (Faye Dunaway; Rachel Hunter & Rod Stewart)

LINCOLN (Gutzon Borglum; Phyllis George & John Brown)

LINDSEY (Keith Jackson)

LINLEY (Lord Snowden)

LINUS (Linus Pauling)

LIONEL (Georgiana Drew & Maurice Barrymore; Edward III)

LLEWELYN (Caitlin & Dylan Thomas)

LLOYD (Dan Aykroyd; Lloyd Bentsen; Cynthia Gregory; Robert Louis Stevenson; Frank Lloyd Wright)

LON (Lon Chaney, Jr.)

LORENZO (Arlene Dahl & Fernando Lamas; Anthony Quinn)

LORET (Loret Miller Ruppe)

LORIN (Jane Brody)

LOUIE (Lou Ferrigno)

LOUIS (Charlemagne; Mel Gibson; Rosanna Scotto; Phil Spector; Princess Stephanie; Louis Stokes; Friedrich Wilhelm)

LOWELL (Lowell Weicker)

LUC (Dave Coulier)

LUCA (Audrey Hepburn)

LUCAS (Mort Janklow; Willie Nelson; Carl Reiner)

LUCIAN (Jo Andres & Steve Buscemi; Mel Gibson)
LUDWIG (Cicciolona & Jeff Koons)
LUKAS (Willie Nelson)
LUKASZ (Krzysztof Penderecki)
LUKE (Howard Jensen; Bill Murray; Tim Russert; Bill Walton)
LYNDON (Mildred Evelyn & Clive Brook)
LYON (Mark Messier)
MAC (Roxanne Pulitzer)
MACAULAY (Kit Culkin)
MACKENZIE (John Astin & Patty Duke)
MAHIR (Hafez al-Assad)
MAJD (Hafez al-Assad)
MALCOLM (Kenneth Auchincloss; Malcolm Forbes; Harrison Ford; Herman Melville; Pauletta & Denzel Washington)
MALIK (Bobby Seale)
MANLIO (Giuseppe Garibaldi)
MANNY (Sammy Davis, Jr.)
MARC (Philip Caputo; Tony Danza; Neil Sedaka)
MARCO (Tony Franciosa)
MARCUS (Robert Gallo; A. Bartlett Giamatti; Michael Jordan; Ramsey Lewis)
MARIO (Claudio Arrau; Mario Montessori; Mario Van Peebles)
MARION (Marion Barry)
MARK (Rex Allen; Ernie Ashworth; Dan Aykroyd; Conrad Bain; Marilyn Beck; Zbigniew Brzezinski; Daniel Callahan; Tommy Cash; John Connally; Sammy Davis, Jr.; Mike Ditka; Jack Greene; Arthur Hailey; Tom Harmon; Mark Hatfield; Samuel Hayakawa; Gordie Howe; Evan Hunter; Grandpa Jones; Tom Jones; Charles M. Jordan; Michael Landon; Ed McBain; Ricardo Montalban; Otto Preminger; Mickey Rooney; Margaret Thatcher; Leon Uris; Kurt Vonnegut, Jr.; Jack Welch; Donald Wildmon)
MARLAN (Lefty Frizell)

MARLON (Katherine & Joe Jackson; Anita Pallenberg & Keith Richards)

MARSHALL (Paul MacCready)

MARSTON (Hugh Hefner)

MARTIN (John Hershey; Martin Luther King, Sr.; Coretta Scott & Martin Luther King, Jr.; Paul Simon)

MARTY (Merle Haggard; Gordie Howe)

MARVIN (Barbara & George Bush; Marvelous Marvin Hagler)

MARVIS (Joe Frazier)

MATHEW (Mike Singletary)

MATT (Barbara Mandrell)

MATTHEW (Robert Altman; Alan Arkin; Ed Asner; Erma Bombeck; Carol Moseley Braun; James Broderick; Dave Brubeck; Genevieve Bujold; Dick Butkus; Mike Ditka; Mia Farrow & André Previn; Richard Gephardt; Alec Guinness; Penelope Leach; Rob Lowe; George Morgan; Michael Moriarty; Roger Mudd; Rick Nelson; Sam Peckinpah; Arthur Penn; Christopher Reeve; Lee Remick; Antonin Scalia; Talia Shire; Wayne Thiebaud; Alex Trebek)

MAURICE (Sarah Bernhardt; Hank Locklin)

MAX (Nora Ephron & Carl Bernstein; Dustin Hoffman; Amy Irving & Steven Spielberg; Mike McCartney; Henry Winkler; Kim Zimmer)

MAXIMILIAN (Sinead Cusack & Jeremy Irons)

MAXIMILLIAN (Anne Bancroft & Mel Brooks; Don King)

MAXWELL (Robert Burns; Andrew Dice Clay)

McCANNA (Moira Harris & Gary Sinise)

MELVIN (Melvin Belli; Mel Tillis)

MERCER (Duke Ellington)

MERLE (Chet Atkins; Doc Watson)

MERLIN (Vyvyan Holland)

MERRILL (Olive & George Osmond)

MERWAN (Zubin Mehta)

MESSENGER (Sidney Poitier)

MICAH (Robert Bly)

MICHAEL (Robert Altman; Mario Andretti; Earl Anthony; Hoyt Axton; Catherine Bach; Russell Baker; Gene Barry; Herschel Bernardi; William Peter Blatty; Julian Bond; Charles Boyer; Albert Broccoli; Ron Brown; Dave Brubeck; Stephen Breyer; Robert Coles; Bette Davis; Michael De Bakey; Dom De Luise; Ronald Dellums; Mike Ditka; Phil Donahue; Kirk Douglas; Sandy Duncan; Michael Eisner; Geraldine Fitzgerald; Betty & Gerald Ford; Barry Goldwater; Pancho Gonzales; Eydie Gormé & Steve Lawrence; Ernest Hollings; Katherine & Joe Jackson; Eliot Janeway; Norman Jewison; Casey Kasem; Alfred Kazin; Brian Keith; Richard Kiley; James Kilpatrick; Michael Landon; Carol Lawrence & Robert Goulet; Sinclair Lewis; John D. Loudermilk; Robert Ludlum; Eugene McCarthy; Ed McMahon; Jesse McReynolds; Norman Mailer; Thomas Mann; Willie Mays; Don Meredith; Michael Moorer; Jack Nicklaus; Tip O'Neill; Joe Papp; Colin Powell; Ethel & Julius Rosenberg; Vince Scully; Albert Shanker; Don Shula; Benjamin Spock; Isaac Stern; Jimmy Stewart; John Sununu; Elizabeth Taylor; Tina Turner; John Updike; Leon Uris; Tom Watson; Earl Weaver; Jerry Weintraub; Morris West; Jane Wyman & Ronald Reagan)

MICKEY (George Dolenz; Mickey Mantle; Mickey Rooney)

MICO (Edward James Olmos)

MIGUEL (Rosemary Clooney & José Ferrer)

MIKE (Ernie Ashworth; Zbigniew Brzezinski; Big Jim Hogg; Casey Kasem; John Madden; Chuck Norris; Buck Owens; Ted Schwinden; Red Sovine; Mickey Spillane; Conway Twitty)

MIKLOS (Jayne Mansfield)

MILES (Ron Carter; Nicole Mitchell & Eddie Murphy; Lionel Richie; Susan Sarandon & Tim Robbins)

MITCHELL (Roy Lichtenstein)

MONTEL (Montel Williams)

MORGAN (Rae Dawn Chong; Marvin Mitchelson; Lorrie Morgan & Ron Gaddis)

MORRIS (Morris Dees; Dottie West)
MORTON (Morton Downey)
MOSES (Mia Farrow & Woody Allen)
MUMTAZ (Stevie Wonder)
MURPHY (Howard Jensen)
MURRAY (Jim Dale; Gordie Howe)
MYLES (Betty Carter)
NANHOI (Klaus Kinski)
NARVEL (Narvel Felts)
NATHAN (Daniel Boone; Mark Hamill; John Lithgow; Merlin Olsen; Bill Walton)
NATHANIEL (Bill Baker; Barbara Mandrell; The Honorable Elijah Muhammad; Herman Wouk)
NAVARONE (Priscilla Presley & Marco Garibaldi)
NAYIB (Gloria & Emilio Estefan)
NEAL (Joseph Barbera)
NEIL (Barbara & George Bush)
NELSON (Billy Graham; Nelson Riddle)
NICHOLAS (Tony Curtis; Chris Evert; Stan Getz; Marilu Henner; Nat Hentoff; S.E. Hinton; Judith Krantz; Sylvia Plath & Ted Hughes; Gena Rowlands & John Cassavetes; Carl Sagan; Telly Savalas; Sander Vanocur; Andrew Lloyd Webber; Vanna White)
NICK (Elia Kazan)
NICKLAUS (Glen Campbell)
NICKOLAS (Pamela Sue Martin)
NICKY (Mel Brooks)
NICOLAS (Alain Prost)
NIGER (Roy Innis)
NIKI (Deborah Norville)
NILAS (Peter Martins)
NILE (Jim Bartling)
NOAH (Kim Alexis & Ron Duguay; Boris Becker; Noah Berry, Sr.; Robert Bly; Barry Bremen; Debra Winger & Timothy Hutton)
NORM (Debbie Allen)
NORMAN (C. Everett Koop)

NUALA (Claiborne Pell)

OBALAJI (Imamu Amiri Baraka [LeRoi Jones])

ÖGÖDEI (Genghis Khan)

OLIVER (Amanda Pays & Corbin Bernsen; Martin Short; Goldie Hawn & Bill Hudson)

OREL (Orel Hershiser)

OREN (Evelyn Rosenberg)

OSCAR (Oscar Arias Sanchez; Dan Aykroyd; Barry Humphries; Boz Scaggs)

OSGOOD (Anthony Perkins)

OWEN (Phoebe Cates & Kevin Kline; Otto Gray; Tabitha & Stephen King; Christopher Reeve)

PALMER (Lowell Weicker)

PARKER (Paul MacCready)

PAT (Pat Harrington; Peter O'Toole)

PATON (Daphne Ashbrook & Lorenzo Lamas)

PATRICK (Tom Berenger; Eileen Brennan; Jimmy Breslin; Marva Collins; Dennis De Concini; Isadora Duncan; Edward Kennedy; Jacqueline & John F. Kennedy; Bobby Knight; Maria Shriver & Arnold Schwarzenegger; Leigh Taylor-Young & Ryan O'Neal; Joe Theismann; John Wayne; Tuesday Weld & Dudley Moore)

PAUL (Daniel J. Boorstin; Art Carney; Martha Lou Carson; Catherine the Great; Larry Gelbart; A. Bartlett Giamatti; Paul Harvey; Martin Luther; Bernard Malamud; Herbie Mann; Henry Morgan; Roberta Peters; Generoso Pope; Paul Revere; Antonin Scalia; Mitzi & Sammy Shore; Studs Terkel; Wayne Thiebaud; Strom Thurmond; Morris West; Gahan Wilson)

PAULY (Mitzi & Sammy Shore)

PEN (Robert Browning)

PER (Max Von Sydow)

PERCY (Percy Bysshe Shelley)

PERRIN (Edward Ziegler)

PERRY (Phyllis Diller)

PETER (Princess Anne; Fred Astaire; Mikhail Baryshnikov; Meredith Baxter & David Birney; Polly Bergen & Freddie

Fields; Elmer Bernstein; Tony Bill; Daniel Callahan; Dom De Luise; Phyllis Diller; Pete Domenici; Kirk Douglas; Olympia Dukakis; Sally Field; Henry Fonda; John Kenneth Galbraith; Ira Glasser; Julie Harris; Lou Harris; Henry Heimlich; Doris Lessing; Martin Luther; Hans Namuth; Maureen O'Sullivan & John Farrow; Linus Pauling; Pete Rose; Jonas Salk; Rudolph Serkin; Stephanie Seymour & Peter Brant; Peter Shultz; Beverly Sills; John Sununu; Dick Thornburgh; Mike Wallace; Eli Wallach; Edward Woodward)

PETEY (Pete Rose; Kristina & Jack Wagner)

PHILIP (Archie Campbell; Joe Cates; Bing Crosby; Stanley Elkin; Henry Heimlich; Robert Maxwell)

PHILIPPE (Arman; Jacques Cousteau)

PHILIPPE-LOUIS (Henry-Louis Vuitton)

PHILLIP (Joan Crawford; Phil Spector)

PIERO (Enzo Ferrari)

PIERRE (Valerie Campbell; Princess Caroline; Pierre Du Pont; Henry Matisse; Pierre-Auguste Renoir)

PLACIDO (Placido Domingo)

PLORN (Charles Dickens)

PO-YU (Confucius)

POLA (Paul Gauguin)

POTTER (Potter Stewart)

PRESTON (Larry Hagman)

PRINCE (Cecil Fielder)

PRZEMYSLAW (Lech Walesa)

---

### NAMESAKE DEPARTMENT

Ryan O'Neal and Farrah Fawcett's son Redmond was named for the character Ryan played in the 1975 Stanley Kubrick epic, *Barry Lyndon*. Redmond's complete name is Redmond James Fawcett O'Neal.

PTOLEMY (Cleopatra & Antony)
QUIN (Anna Quindlen)
QUINCY (Quincy Jones)
QUINDLEN (Anna Quindlen)
QUINN (Ben Bradlee)
QUINTON (Loni Anderson & Burt Reynolds)
RAFAEL (Rosemary Clooney & José Ferrer)
RAIMUND (Heinrich Böll)
RAINEY (Andi MacDowell & Paul Qualley)
RAISHUN (Kei Takei)
RALPH (The Reverend Ralph David Abernathy; Mary
   Forbes; Nathan Pritikin; Joseph Pulitzer)
RAMON (Martin Sheen)
RAMSEY (Ramsey Emanuel)
RANDALL (Aaron Spelling)
RANDOLPH (Winston Churchill; Dabney Coleman; Wil-
   liam Randolph Hearst)
RANDY (Jack Anderson; Judy Blume; Bobby Helms; Kath-
   erine & Joe Jackson; Jesse McReynolds; Boots Randolph;
   Earl Scruggs; Gahan Wilson)
RAPHAEL (Juliette Binoche & André Hallé; Gloria &
   Emilio Estefan; Diahnne Abbott & Robert DeNiro)
RASJUA (Imamu Amiri Baraka [LeRoi Jones])
RAY (Ray Charles; Ella Fitzgerald; Sugar Ray Leonard)
RAYMOND (Rebecca Broussard & Jack Nicholson; Ray
   Flynn; Ray Floyd; Raymond St. Jacques)
REBOP (Todd Rundgren)
REDMOND (Farrah Fawcett & Ryan O'Neal)
REED (Ron Howard; Thomas Kean)
REID (Nolan Ryan)
REESE (Branford Marsalis; Nolan Ryan)
REIS (Jennifer O'Neill)
REMICK (Dickie Smothers)
RENE (Martha Lou Carson)
RENÉ (Heinrich Böll)
REX (Rex Allen; Rex Humbard)
RHETT (Ted Turner)

RICCARDO (Rosanna Della Corte)

RICCI (Dean Martin)

RICH (Charlie Rich)

RICHARD (Melvin Belli; Dick Butkus; Admiral Richard Byrd; Sid Caesar; Dick Clark; Charlie Correll; Oliver Cromwell; E.L. Doctorow; Pancho Gonzales; Lou Harris; Tommy Hilfiger; Evan Hunter; Nancy Kassebaum; Mary Kay; Dick & Ruth Marx; Ed McBain; Mary Tyler Moore; Eugene O'Neill; Joan Plowright & Laurence Olivier; Jane Pauley & Gary Trudeau; Richard Pryor; David Rockefeller; Dean Rusk; Richard Thomas; Lee Trevino; Porter Wagoner; Darryl Zanuck)

RICK (Danny Aiello; Lefty Frizell; Dennis Weaver)

RICKY (Johnny Carson; John D. Loudermilk)

RIDDICK (Riddick Bowe)

RILEY (Bob Welch)

RING (Ring Lardner)

RITCHIE (Mary Tyler Moore)

ROB (Carl Reiner)

ROBBIE (Evel Knievel)

ROBBY (Dave Barry; Ann Benson & Jerry Segal; Bob Osborne; Sally Jessy Raphaël; Bobby Unser; Dennis Weaver)

ROBERT (Robert Altman; Bob Atcher; Bobby Bare; Carl Belew; Jim Belushi; Joseph Biden; Henry Bloch; Robert Burns; Robert Campeau; John Carradine; Ray Charles; Natalie Cole; Robert Coles; Malcolm Cowley; Jimmy Dean; Robert DeNiro, Sr.; Ray Floyd; Malcolm Forbes; Robert Gallo; Geronimo; Stephen Hawking; Jascha Heifetz; Florence Henderson; James Hoge; Bruce Jenner; Jennifer Jones & Robert Walker; Robert Kenney, Jr.; Rose & Joseph Kennedy; Art Linkletter; Bobby Lord; Rollo May; Arthur Miller; Robert Mondavi; Brian Mulroney; Robert Overmyer; Les Paul; Admiral Robert Peary; Nathan Pritikin; Carl Reiner; Admiral Hyman Rickover; Ethel & Julius Rosenberg; Mike Royko; Arthur Schlesinger; Robert Schuller; Willard Scott; Talia Shire;

Eunice & Sargent Shriver; Barbara Sinatra; Ted Turner; Johnny Unitas; Andy Williams; Frank Lloyd Wright; Frank Yablans)

ROBERTO (Isabella Rosselini)

ROBIN (Herschel Bernardi; Bjorn Borg; Madeline Hunter; Gloria Loring & Alan Thicke; Bob Mackie; Faron Young)

ROCK (Yul Brynner)

RODERICK (Carla Hills)

RODGER (Texas T. Tyler)

RODNEY (Jack Anderson)

ROEG (Donald Sutherland)

ROGER (Jacques Barzun; Roger Corman; Arthur Hailey; Roger Miller; Phyllis Schlafly; Roger Smith; Red Sovine; Suzy)

ROHAN (Bob Marley)

ROMAN (Francis Ford Coppola)

RON (Lon Chaney; Rance Howard)

RONALD (Gracie Allen & George Burns; Victor Borge; Ron Carter; Leslie Howard; Estée Lauder; Ronnie Milsap; Nancy & Ronald Reagan; Jimmy Stewart; John Thompson; Tina Turner)

RONNIE (Gracie Allen & George Burns; Rance Howard; Jerry Lewis; Marty Robbins; Charlie Walker)

ROONE (Roone Arledge)

ROSS (Jane Pauley & Gary Trudeau; H. Ross Perot; Diana Ross)

ROSSIF (Donald Sutherland)

ROY (Roy Disney; Mildred Douglas & Roy Acuff; Dale Evans & Roy Rogers; Roy Drusky)

RUBY (Rudy Perpich)

RUDOLPH (Werner Herzog)

RUDY (Johnny Wright)

RUFUS (James Watson)

RUPERT (Barry Humphries; Maria Von Trapp)

RUSS (Paula Prentis & Richard Benjamin)

RUSSELL (Lucille Gleason; Bruce Hornsby; William Janklow)

RUSTY (Dennis Weaver)

RYAN (Cal Ripkin, Jr.; Robert Urich)

SAGE (Sylvester Stallone)

SAM (Lauren Bacall & Jason Robards; Timothy Daly & Amy Von Nostrand; Sally Field; Jack Gilford; Elliott Gould; William Hurt; Barry Levinson; Rick Nelson; Tracy Pollan & Michael J. Fox; Patti Scialfa & Bruce Springsteen)

SAMUEL (Harold Arlen; Eileen Brennan; Sinead Cusack & Jeremy Irons; Sally Field; Jessica Lange & Sam Shepard; Sam Snead; Anne Truitt)

SASCHA (Mia Farrow & André Previn)

SATCHEL (Mia Farrow & Woody Allen)

SATIE (Louis Gossett, Jr.)

SAWYER (Kate Capshaw & Steven Spielberg)

SCOT (Lowell Weicker)

SCOTT (Francis Lee Bailey; James Caan; James Garner; Orrin Hatch; Brenda Marshall & William Holden; Garry Marshall; Virginia Johnson-Masters; Charles Lindbergh, Jr.; Brent Musburger; Paul Newman; Sandry Day O'Connor; Robert Redford; Gale Sayers; William Smith; Andy Van Slyke)

SCOTTIE (F. Scott Fitzgerald)

SCOTTY (Mac Davis; Jerry Lewis)

SEAN (John Astin & Patty Duke; Pierce Brosnan; Pam Dawber & Mark Harmon; Errol Flynn; Cassandra Harris; Mariette Hartley; Audrey Hepburn & Mel Ferrer; David Hartman; Michael Keaton; Jim McKay; Michael Landon; Tatum O'Neal & John McEnroe; Yoko Ono & John Lennon; Leo Penn; Elizabeth Clare Prophet; Jane Seymour; Alana & Rod Stewart)

SEBASTIAN (James Spader)

SELASSIE (Solomon Burke)

SERGIO (Sylvester Stallone)

SETH (Juliet Prowse & John McCook; Sylvester Stallone)

---

### GOOD THING WOODY WASN'T A FAN OF MOOKIE WILSON, EH?

Woody Allen and Mia Farrow's son, Satchel, was named in honor of black baseball legend, Satchel Paige.

---

SHANE (Nicole Mitchell & Eddie Murphy; Eugene O'Neill)
SHANNON (Richard Dawson; Glen Campbell; Emmylou Harris; Ken Kesey; Jason Robards; Del Shannon; Roger Zelazny)
SHARRON (Louis Gossett Jr.)
SHAWN (Sherrill Milnes; Dale Murphy)
SHELBY (Reba McEntire)
SHELLEY (Howard Metzenbaum)
SHELLY (Dottie West)
SHLOMO (Elie Wiesel)
SIDNEY (Lita Grey & Charlie Chaplin)
SIEGFRIED (Richard Wagner)
SIMON (Marlon Brando; Phil Collins; Albert Finney; Laurence Luckinbill; Laurence Olivier)
SKIP (Lou Holtz)
SLAVA (Oleg Vidov)
SLAWOMIR (Lech Walesa)
SLY (Jackie Stallone)
SONNY (Arlene Dahl; Lowell Weicker)
SOULIMA (Igor Stravinsky)
SPECK (Elaine Irwin & John Mellencamp)
SPENCER (Robin Gibb; David Groh)
SPIKE (Bill Lee)
STACY (Stacy Keach, Sr.)
STAN (Carl Perkins)
STANISLAUS (Gloria Vanderbilt)
STANWIX (Herman Melville)

## HART TO HEART

Grateful Dead drummer Mickey Hart recorded his son Taro's heartbeat when the lad was still in the womb and then overdubbed the beat with drums, bass harmonics, and wooden flute. He later released this biological "piece" as *Music To Be Born By*. ("Taro" is the name of a tropical plant with broad leaves and a large, starchy edible plant. Why Hart chose to name his child after a plant or vegetable isn't clear.)

STEFAN (Olympia Dukakis; Berry Gordy)

STEPAN (Aleksandr Solzhenitsyn)

STEPHEN (Steve Allen; Robert Altman; Lauren Bacall & Humphrey Bogart; Daniel Callahan; Archie Campbell; Joe Garagiola; Barry Gibb; Katharine Graham; Hank Greenberg; Merle Kilgore; Joseph Levine; Marie Osmond; Arthur Schleslinger; Budd Schulberg; Bernie Siegel)

STERLING (Raymond St. Jacques)

STEVE (Billy "Crash" Craddock; Malcolm Forbes; Alan Hamel; Glenn Miller; Alex North; Sonny Osborne; Gregory Peck; Carl Perkins; Earl Scruggs; Bill Walsh)

STEVEN (Judith Crist; Joe Eszterhas; Betty & Gerald Ford; Stan Getz; Arthur Hailey; Tony Hillerman; Norman Mailer; George McGovern; Jack Nicklaus; Sydney Pollack; Charles Rangel; Earl Scruggs; Artie Shaw; Corinna Tsupei & Freddie Fields; Kurt Vonnegut, Jr.)

STEWART (Stewart McKinney)

STONEWALL (Stonewall Jackson)

STUART (Jeane Kirkpatrick; Harry Reasoner; Barry Slotnick; Oliver Stone; Hank Stram)

SULTAN (King Fahd)

SUMNER (Sylvia Porter)

SVIATOSLAV (Igor Stravinsky)

SYDNEY (Charles Dickens; Pat Kennedy; Sidney Poitier; Nicole & O.J. Simpson)

SYLVESTER (Jackie Stallone)

TAD (Charles Walgreen III)

TAIT (Oliver Stone)

TAJ (Steven Tyler)

TAMON (Teddy Pendergrass)

TANDY (Lawton Chiles; Jessica Tandy & Hume Cronyn)

TANNER (Danny Ainge)

TARO (Mickey Hart)

TAYLOR (Garth Brooks; Rob E; Emilio Estevez; Don Mattingly; Bobby McFerrin; George Plimpton)

TED (Meredith Baxter; Evan Hunter; Ed McBain; Ted Knight; Chris Schenkel)

TEDDY (James Brown; Aretha Franklin; Lena Horne; Rusty Kanokogi; Teddy Pendergrass)

TEIHOTU (Marlon Brando)

TERENCE (Thomas Eagleton)

TERRANCE (Sam Snead)

TERRY (James Brown; Doris Day; Berry Gordy)

TEX (Vivian Ayers)

THADDEUS (Chick Corea)

THEO (Kate Capshaw & Steven Spielberg; Patricia Neal & Roald Dahl)

THEODOR (Celeste Holm)

THEODORE (Thomas Edison; Joseph Heller; Ursula K. Le Guin; Joan & Walter Mondale; Ted Stevens; Igor Stravinsky)

THERAN (Mike McCartney)

THOMAS (Anne Archer; Bruce Babbitt; Henry Bloch; Clifford Carlisle; Dana Carvey; Ramsey Clark; Ray Milton Dolby; Patty Duke & John Astin; Thomas Edison; Nikki Giovanni; Bill Graham; Nat Hentoff; Bobby Ray Inman; Thomas Kean; Don Knotts; Tom Landry; Thomas Mattingly; Tip O'Neill; Tommy Overstreet; Pocahantas;

Tex Ritter; James Schlesinger; Curtis Strange; William Styron; Kiri Te Kanawa; Laurence Tisch)
THOR (Thor Heyerdahl)
THURGOOD (Thurgood Marshall)

---

### I'LL BET HE'S GLAD SHE WASN'T AN "ALLEY OOP" FAN!

Doris Day named her son Terry Melcher for her favorite comic strip, "Terry and the Pirates." Terry later went on to cowrite the Beach Boys's 1988 hit single, "Kokomo."

---

TIM (Jack Holt; Hope Newell & James Daly; Tim Reid)
TIMOTHY (Bruce Babbitt; Yogi Berra; Roy Disney; Malcolm Forbes; Stephen Hawking; Jim Hutton; Gene Kelly; Bobby Knight; Robert Mondavi; Daniel Moynihan; Hope Newell & James Daly; Donna Reed; Pat Robertson; Gale Sayers; Leo Tolstoy; Edward Woodward)
TITO (Katherine & Joe Jackson)
TITUS (Rembrandt)
TOBY (Jim Dale; Ken Russell)
TOD (Eleanor Smeal)
TODD (Jean & George Ariyoshi; Ronnie Milsap; Debbie Reynolds; Vince Scully)
TOLUY (Genghis Khan)
TOM (Barbara Hershey & David Carradine; Big Jim Hogg; Tommy Lasorda; Irving Penn)
TOMMY (Bill Caspar; Gary Trudeau)
TONIO (Giacomo Puccini)
TONY (Pearl Bailey; John Baldessari; Merv Griffin; Jayne Mansfield & Matt Cimber; Gregory Peck; Tyrone Power; Soupy Sales; Lee Trevino)
TOPO (Dorothy McGuire)

TORY (Roger Tory Peterson)
TRACY (Roy Drusky)
TRAVIS (Glen Campbell; Dale Murphy; Kyra Sedgwick & Kevin Bacon)
TREMAYNE (Karyn White & Terry Lewis)
TRENT (Roger Zelazny)
TREVOR (Curt Gowdy; Janet Jones & Wayne Gretzky)
TREY (Karen Valez & Lee Majors)
TRISTAN (Alan Bates)
TROY (Pat Corley; Leeza Gibbons & Steve Meadows; Tom Hayden & Jane Fonda; Lee Trevino)
TUCKER (Marilyn & Dan Quayle)
TY (Pam Dawber & Mark Harmon; John Grisham; Janet Jones & Wayne Gretzky)
TYRON (Sandy Denton)
TYRONE (Jerry Greenfield; Tyrone Power)
TYLER (Molly & Roger Clinton; Barbara Gallagher & Perry Ellis; Robert Jarvik; Paul MacCready; Dana Plato; Pete Rose; Bobby Sherman)
UDO (Werner Breitschwerdt)
VICTOR (Victor Borge; Doug Kershaw; Ricardo Montalban)
VINCENT (John Jacob Astor; Heinrich Böll; Alex Katz; Vincent Price; Dick Van Patten)
VINCENZIO (Galileo Galilei)
VITTORIO (King Umberto)
VLADIMIR (Vladimir Ashkenazy)
VYVYAN (Oscar Wilde)
WALKER (Julie Brown)
WALLACE (The Honorable Elijah Muhammad)
WALTER (Anita Baker; Walter Cronkite; Charles Dickens; Rodney Grant; Walter Heller; Leo Slezak; Ted Stevens; Arturo Toscanini)
WARD (Mickey Spillane)
WARWICK (Adlai Stevenson)
WASHINGTON (John Roebling)
WAYMAN (James Boggs)

WAYNE (Al Dexter; Olive & George Osmond)

WEBB (Webb Pierce)

WENZEL (Joseph Beuys)

WERNER (Maria Von Trapp)

WESTON (Christina Fulton & Nicholas Cage)

WIELAND (Russell Hoban)

WILHELM (Johann Sebastian Bach)

WILL (Mel Gibson; Big Jim Hogg; Laurie Metcalf; Peggy Noonan; Christopher Reeve; Will Rogers; Herb Shriner)

WILLARD (Ralph Bellamy; Harrison Ford; Brigham Young)

WILLEM (Billy Idol)

WILLIAM (Kirstie Alley & Parker Stevenson; William Joseph Brennan; Dale Bumpers; William Burroughs; Glen Campbell; Princess Diana & Prince Charles; Robert Irwin Chartoff; William DeVries; Thomas Edison; Eng; Benjamin Franklin; Billy Graham; Katharine Graham; William Grayson; Barbara Hale & Bill Williams; Alex Haley; Hedda & DeWolf Hopper; Bobby Ray Inman; Eliot Janeway; Nancy Kassebaum; Burt Lancaster; Robert MacNeil; Joan & Walter Mondale; Bill Moyers; Anne Murray; Madelyn Murray O'Hair; Bill Phillips; William Randolph; Phylicia Rashad; Mary Robinson; William Ruckleshaus; Susan St. James & Dick Ebersol; James Schlesinger; Percy Bysshe Shelley; Fred Silverman; Alan K. Simpson; William Smith; Dick Thornburgh; Cornelius Vanderbilt; Jon Vickers; Fay Vincent)

WILLIE (Willie C. Williams; Mary Wilson)

WILSON (Christine Lahti)

WIM (William Zander Zalm)

WINSTON (Betty Bao & Winston Lord)

WOLFGANG (Valerie Bertinelli & Eddie Van Halen; Wolfgang Amadeus Mozart)

WOODY (Dexter Gordon)

WYATT (Goldie Hawn & Kurt Russell)

WYNN (Bob Osborne)

WYNTON (Ellis Marsalis)

XAVIER (Ken Russell)
YELLOW BIRD (George Armstrong Custer)
YUSEF (Jesse Jackson)
YUVAL (Yitzhak Rabin)
YVES (Arman)
ZACH (Roxanne Pulitzer; Jane Wallace)
ZACHARIAH (Cybill Shepherd; Jane Wallace)
ZACHARY (Philip Glass; Gregory Hines; Murray Schisgal;
   Cheryl Tiegs & Tony Peck; Robin Williams)
ZACK (Darren Daulton)
ZAFAR (Salman Rushdie)
ZAK (Ringo Starr)
ZANE (Ken Kesey)
ZEKE (Carrie Snodgrass & Neil Young)
ZEPHYR (Karla DeVito & Robby Benson)
ZIGGY (Bob Marley)
ZOLTAN (Jayne Mansfield)
ZOWIE (Angela & David Bowie)

# THE BEST-LOVED NAMES
# OF THE ALPHABET

## *Girls*

| | | |
|---|---|---|
| AMANDA | JENNIFER | SARAH |
| BARBARA | KRISTIN | TIFFANY |
| CHRISTINA | LAURA | URSULA |
| DAWN | MICHELLE | VALERIE |
| ELIZABETH | NICOLE | WENDY |
| FRAN | OLIVIA | XENA |
| GLORIA | PATRICIA | YVONNE |
| HEATHER | QUINTINA | ZELDA |
| ILENE | REBECCA | |

## CELEBRITY BABY NAMES FOR GIRLS

AAREN (Margueritte & O.J. Simpson)
ABBI (Mike McCartney)
ABBIE (Estelle Parsons)
ABBY (David Rockefeller)
ABIGAIL (Roy Disney; Anthony Hopkins; Calvin Trillin)
ADA (Lord Byron)
ADELE (Loret Miller Ruppe)
ADÈLE (Victor Hugo)
ADREANA (Harold Robbins)
ADRIE (William DeVries)
ADRIENNE (Harry Belafonte)
AERONWYN (Cailtin & Dylan Thomas)
AFRIKA (Roland Hayes)

AGATHE (Maria Von Trapp)
AIMEE (Rex Humbard; Marc Von Arx)
AINSLIE (Leon Gorman)
AISHA (Stevie Wonder)
AKEIBA (M.C. Hammer)
AKIVA (Chaim Potok)
ALANA (Kenneth Feld; Alana & Rod Stewart; Faron Young)
ALBA (Candido Jacuzzi)
ALEKSANDRA (Mikhail Baryshnikov)
ALESSANDRA (Armand Assante; Andy Garcia)
ALEXA (Christie Brinkley & Billy Joel; Brent Jasmer)

---

### NAMESAKE DEPARTMENT

The "Ray" in Billy Joel and Christie Brinkley's daughter Alexa Ray's name is an homage to Ray Charles, one of Billy's all-time favorite musicians.

---

ALEXANDRA (Alfred Adler; Paul Anka; Vladimir Ashkenazy; Peter Bogdonovich; Ray Bradbury; Joe Cates; Tony Curtis; Edvard Grieg; Patti Hansen & Keith Richards; Dustin Hoffman; Thomas Kean; Jessica Lange & Mikhail Baryshnikov; Robert Lutz; Joe Montana; Christopher Reeve; Gene Rowlands & John Cassavettes; Carl Sagan; Leo Tolstoy; Anne Truitt; Tom Wolfe)
ALEXANDRE (Konstantin Costa-Gavras; Diane Von Furstenberg)
ALEXANDREA (Whoopi Goldberg)
ALEXANDRIA (Adolph Caesar; Tommy Hilfiger)
ALEXANDRINE (Madame de Pompadour)
ALEXES (Kimberlin Brown)
ALEXIA (Ted Danson)
ALEXIS (Charles Diggs, Jr.; Martha Stewart)
ALI (Alan Jackson; Ruth Pointer)

ALICE (Henry Wadsworth Longfellow; Bill Moyers; Christopher Patten; Queen Victoria)

ALICIA (Paul Anka; Alicia De Larrocha; James Hoge; Margaret Trudeau Kemper; Charles Rangel; Johnny Unitas)

ALINE (Paul Gaugin)

ALISON (Clint Eastwood; George Gallup III; Carla Hills; Robert MacNeil)

ALISSA (David Guyer)

ALLEGRA (Christine Kaufman & Tony Curtis; Henry Wadsworth Longfellow; Rollo May)

ALLISON (Tom Berenger; Sally Jessy Raphaël; Jon Vickers)

ALLY (Charlotte Sheedy)

ALLYN (Elizabeth Roberts & Robert Morse)

ALMA (Barbara Tuchman)

ALTA (John D. Rockefeller)

ALVA (Hank Greenberg)

ALY (Pat Morita)

ALYSA (Orrin Hatch)

ALYX (Faith Daniels)

ALYXANDRA (Georg Stanford Brown & Tyne Daly)

AMANDA (Paul Anka; Michael Deaver; Leonard Goldberg; Cynthia Gregory; Tammy Grimes & Christopher Plummer; Evan Hunter; Jean Kennedy; Gordon MacRae; Ed McBain; James Lehrer; Willie Shoemaker)

AMARAH (Alexandrea Martin)

AMBER (Neil Young)

AMELIA (Paul Anka; Hal Linden)

AMY (Bob Allen; James L. Brooks; Rosalynn & Jimmy Carter; William Sloane Coffin; Norman Cousins; Mick Fleetwood; Terry Gilliam; Thomas Harkin; Sidney Lumet; Anne Meara & Jerry Stiller; Howard Metzenbaum; Willie Nelson; Noel Perrin; Regis Philbin; Priscilla Pointer; Maury Povich; Robert Redford; David Reuben; Charles Schulz; Dick Shawn; Joe Theismann; Irving Wallace; Robin Yount)

AMY SUE (Alan L. Bean)

ANABEL (Morgan Englund)

ANANSA (Beverly Johnson)

ANASTASIA (Czar Nicholas II)

ANDRA (Richard Heckert)

ANDREA (Marilyn Beck; Tom Brokaw; Norman Cousins; Michael Dukakis; Pancho Gonzales; Gary Hart; Ted Koppel; George Mitchell; Sally Jessy Raphaël; Peter Ustinov; Andrew Young)

ANETTE (Thor Heyerdahl)

ANGELA (Mort Janklow; Anita Pallenberg & Keith Richards; Charley Pride; William Raspberry; Johnny Rutherford; Louis Stokes; Donald Wildmon)

ANGELICA (John Huston; Geraldine Page & Rip Torn; Thurman Thomas)

ANGELINA (John Voight)

ANGELIQUE (Louis L'Amour)

ANIKA (Sidney Poitier)

ANITA (Ricardo Montalban; Jimmie Rodgers)

ANJE (Johnny Duncan)

ANN (Bob Allen; John Hershey; George McGovern; Lewis Powell; Harry Reasoner; Del Reeves; Pat Robertson; Antonin Scalia; James Schlesinger; William Wordsworth)

ANN MARIE (Pete Rozelle)

ANNA (Claire Bloom & Rod Steiger; Sigmund Freud; Tony Goldwyn; Kelly LeBrock & Steven Seagal; Lisa Rinhart & Mikhail Baryshnikov; Richard Leakey; Lee Radziwill; Penelope Spheeris; Lech Walesa)

ANNABEL (Lynn Redgrave)

ANNABELLE (Jerry Garcia; Davey Jones)

ANNAMARIE (John Baldessari)

ANNE (Arman; Queen Elizabeth; Henry Ford II; Billy Graham; Tony Hillerman; George S. Kaufman; Charles Lindbergh, Jr.; June Lockhart; Marjorie Lord & John Archer; Robert Maxwell; John Milton; Phyllis Schlafly; Willard Scott; Tom Seaver; Don Shula; William Makepeace Thackeray; Fay Vincent; Jack Welch; Richard Widmark)

ANNE-MARIE-THERESE (Eugene Ionesco)
ANNELEISE (Kelly LeBrock & Steven Seagal)
ANNEMARIE (Colin Powell)
ANNETTE (Bob Gibson)
ANNIE (Glenn Close; Kevin Costner; Jamie Lee Curtis & Christopher Guest; David Dukes)
ANTHEA (Paul Anka)
ANTOINETTE (Loret Miller Ruppe)
ANTONIA (Tony Bennett; Peter Bogdanovich; Kiri Te Kanawa)
ANYA (Armand Assante)
APRIL (Hoyt Axton; David Baker; Billy "Crash" Craddock)
AQUINNAH (Tracy Pollan & Michael J. Fox)
ARABEL (Herbert Von Karan)
ARETHA (Bennett Cohen)
ARIANA (Telly Savalas; Theodore White)
ARIANNA (Pinchas Zukerman)
ARIEL (Daniel Goldin; Cybill Shepherd)
ARIELLE (Christina & Anthony Randalls)
ARISSA (Kelly LeBrock & Steven Seagal)
ARLIN (Caspar Weinberger)
ARNELLA (Errol Flynn)
ARNELLE (Margueritte & O.J. Simpson)
ASHLEE (Danny Ainge)
ASHLEY (Lee Atwater; Joseph Biden; Glen Campbell; Alana Collins & George Hamilton; Barry Gibb; Evander Holyfield; Naomi Judd; Nancy Lopez; Howard Stern; Paul Tsongas; Karyn White & Terry Lewis; Doug Williams)
ASIA (Imamu Amiri Baraka [LeRoi Jones])
ASSISSI (Jade Jagger)
ASTRIDUR (Vigdís Finnbogadóttir)
ATHINA (Christina Onassis & Thierry Reussel)
ATTALLAH (Betty Shabazz)
AUDREY (Ashley Montagu)
AUGUST (Sandy & Garth Brooks)
AURORA (Corazon Aquino)

AUTUMN (Don Gibson)
AVA (Fred Astaire)
AVA-LISA (Kenneth H. Olsen)
AYA (Akihito)
AYANNA (Dick Gregory)
BARBARA (Albert Broccoli; Alexander Cohen; Bette Davis; Wilson Follett; John Ford; Jack Greene; Alexander Haig; Gus Hall; Florence Henderson; Elisabeth Kübler-Ross; Marcello Mastroianni; Howard Metzenbaum; Ashley Montagu; Albert Nipon; Joe Papp; Carl Rowan; George Shultz; Richard Thomas; Robert Young)
BARBRA (Mario Andretti)
BARTLETT (Bernadine Healy)
BEA (Princess Fergie & Prince Andrew)
BEATRICE (Arlene & Alan Alda; Princess Sarah Ferguson & Prince Andrew; George S. Patton; Andrés Segovia; Queen Victoria; Orson Welles)
BECKY (Larry Gelbart; Billy James Hargis)
BEIGE (Don Adams)
BEKKA (Bonnie Bramlett)
BELINDA (Jim Dale)
BELLE (Donna Dixon & Dan Aykroyd; Robert Louis Stevenson)
BENNA (Mike McCartney)
BERNADETTE (William Casey)

## IN HONOR OF BABS, I WOULD LIKE TO . . . NEVER MIND

Early prepartum news reports revealed that Garth Brooks had planned to name his unborn daughter August Barbra in honor of Barbra Streisand, but the baby was ultimately named August Anna. Think Barbra's feelings were hurt?

BERNICE (Coretta Scott & Martin Luther King, Jr.)

BERTHA (Charlemagne)

BERYL (Herschel Bernardi)

BETH (Hank Locklin)

BETHANY (George Morgan; Del Reeves)

BETSY (Barbara Bel Geddes; Erma Bombeck; Stan Jaffe)

BETTINA (Ray Bradbury; Thor Heyerdahl; Nelson Riddle)

BETTY (Red Foley; Jerome Kern; Loretta Lynn)

BEVERLY (Joan Davis; Stan Getz; Meadowlark Lemon; Peter Nero; Jesse Owens; Sidney Poitier)

BIANCA (Gerardo)

BILLIE (Carrie Fisher & Bryan Lourd)

BLAKE (Robin Morgan; Opal Stone & Ron Perelman)

BLANCHE (Carroll Baker)

BOBBI (Whitney Houston & Bobby Brown)

BOBBIE JO (George Wallace)

BONITA (Rex Allen)

BONNIE (Buddy Ebsen; Bill Hanna; Billy James Hargis; John Raitt)

BRANDI (Roseanne)

BRANDY (Wilson Pickett; Roseanne)

BREA (Nicole Mitchell & Eddie Murphy)

BREAN (Bob Edwards)

BRENDA (Riddick Bowe; John Bradshaw; Lester Flatt; Billy James Hargis)

BRIA (Rich Little)

BRIDGET (Robert Bly; Peter Fonda; David Hartman; Gene Kelly)

BRITTNEY (Walter Payton)

BRONWEN (James Dickey)

BROOK (John Hershey; Donna Summer)

BROOKE (John Forsythe; Teri Shields)

BRYCE (Ron Howard)

BRYGIDA (Lech Walesa)

BUBBA (Edye Tarbox-Weill)

BUSHRA (Hafez al-Assad)

### MY DAUGHTER, THE PUNCH LINE

When Russian emigré comedian Yakov Smirnoff and his wife Linda were expecting their daughter Natasha, Linda suggested thay give her an American name, like "Brandy," Yakov replied, "Brandy Smirnoff? Why don't we just send her to the Betty Ford Day-Care Center?"

CABELLA (Cab Calloway)
CAIRO (Beverly Peele)
CAITLIN (Christopher Buckley; Shaun Cassidy; Robert Vaughn)
CALEIGH (Jon Peters)
CALEY (Chevy Chase)
CALLIE (Gene Siskel)
CAMERA (Arthur Ashe)
CAMILLA (John Cleese)
CAMILLE (Louis Pasteur)
CANDACE (Nicolas Coster; Telly Savalas)
CANDICE (Edgar Bergen)
CANDIS (Norman Cousins)
CANDY (George Morgan)
CARA (Pete Rose; Kerry Kennedy Cuomo & Andrew Cuomo)
CAREW (Sir Walter Raleigh)
CARLA (Bobby Bare; Pearl Lee & Carl Butler; Jacob Javits; Oliver Koppell; Karl Malden; Leroy Van Dyke)
CARLIE (Don King)
CARLYN (Carlton Fisk)
CARNIE (Brian Wilson)
CAROL (Wilma Lee & Stoney Cooper; Kenny Rogers; Robert Schuller; Montana Slim; Margaret Thatcher; Jimmy Wakely; Kitty Wells; Johnny Wright; Robert Young)
CAROLE (Arlene Dahl)

CAROLINE (P.T. Barnum; E.L. Doctorow; Rudy Guiliani; Ursula K. Le Guin; Jacqueline & John F. Kennedy; Brian Mulroney)

CAROLYN (John Glenn; Robert Lutz; J.E. Mainer; Rollo May; Robert Overmyer; H. Ross Perot; Bernie Siegel; Mickey Spillane)

CARRIE (Carol Burnett; Debbie Reynolds & Eddie Fisher; Mel Tillis; Dick Van Dyke; Charlie Walker)

CARTER (Diana D. Brooks)

CARYN (Harold Robbins)

CASEY (Beau Bridges; Rita Coolidge & Kris Kristofferson; Carlton Fisk)

CASSANDRA (Bruce Jenner)

CASSIDY (Kathie Lee & Frank Gifford; Robert Vaughn; Jackie Zeman)

CATHERINE (Dave Brubeck; Albert Camus; Roger Corman; Peter Falk; Ray Flynn; Crystal Gayle; Lynda Bird Johnson & Charles Robb; Robert Lutz; Robert MacNeil; Marcel Ophuls; David Reuben; William Ruckleshaus; Antonin Scalia; Martin Scorsese; Vince Scully; Charles Spaak; John Sununu; Frank Lloyd Wright)

CATHLEEN (James Cagney; Gordie Howe)

CATHRAEL (Alfred Kazin)

CATHY (Joan Crawford; Larry Gelbart; Arthur Sulzberger; Conway Twitty)

CATYA (Beverly & Vidal Sassoon)

CECI (Hank Aaron)

CECILE (Ann Richards)

CÉCILE (Louis Pasteur)

CECILIA (Robert Hooks; Gregory Peck; Carlos Salinas)

CECILY (Peter Drucker; Nelson Riddle)

CECILYNN (Cecil Fielder)

CELESTE (Marvelous Marvin Hagler)

CELINE (Karen Black)

CHAIA (Larry King)

CHARELLE (Marvelous Marvin Hagler)

CHARLENE (Slim Whitman)

CHARLIEN (Carry Nation)

CHARLOTTE (Caroline Astor; Princess Caroline; Cassandra Harris & Pierce Brosnan; Rickie Lee Jones; Henry Ford II; Sigourney Weaver)

CHASTITY (Sonny Bono & Cher)

CHELSEA (Tom Berenger; Hillary & Bill Clinton; Kelly McGillis; Warren Moon; Steven Tyler)

CHELSY (Scott Bakula)

CHERI (Jack Anderson; Jim Henson)

CHERISH (Charlene Tilton & Johnny Lee)

CHERRY (Pat Boone)

CHERYL (Pat Boone; Dale Evans & Roy Rogers; Curt Gowdy; Madeline Hunter; Michael Landon; Lana Turner)

CHEYENNE (Marlon Brando)

CHIANNA (Sonny Bono)

CHIARA (Catherine Deneuve)

CHIEN (I.M. Pei)

CHINA (Grace Slick)

CHLOE (Tom Berenger; Candice Bergen & Louis Malle; Stephen Breyer; Olivia Newton-John & Matt Lattanzi; Karyn White & Terry Lewis)

CHOU-CHOU (Claude Debussy)

CHRIS (Lou Costello)

CHRISTIANA (Chris Schenkel)

CHRISTIE (Hugh Hefner)

CHRISTIN (Thomas Eagleton)

CHRISTINA (Albert Broccoli; Oleg Cassini; Pat Corley; Joan Crawford; Dennis De Concini; Olympia Dukakis; Pancho Gonzales; Juan Carlos I; Naomi Judd; Reginald Lewis; Aristotle Onassis; Nancy Priddy; Anthony Quinn; Telly Savalas; Arthur Schlesinger; Maria Shriver & Arnold Schwarzenegger; John Sununu)

CHRISTINE (Robert Altman; John Barth; Sonny Bono; William Peter Blatty; Richard Gephardt; Robert Maxwell; Frank Sinatra)

CHRISTY (Sonny Bono; Gary Carter; Spinderella)

CHRYS (Ted Schwinden)

CHUDNEY (Diana Ross)

CHYNNA (Michelle & John Phillips)

CILO (Richard Moll)

CINDY (Alex Haley; Johnny Cash; Dick Clark; Doc Severinsen; Mel Tillis; Merle Travis)

CLAIRE (J. Michael McCloskey; William Styron)

CLARA (Loretta Lynn; James Schlesinger; Mark Twain)

CLARE (Peter Domenici)

CLARISSA (Brigham Young)

CLAUDE-EMMA (Claude Debussy)

CLAUDETTE (Claude Debussy)

CLAUDIA (Werner Breitschwerdt; Herbie Mann; Dean Martin; Ed McMahon; Michelle Pfeiffer; Sir George Solti)

CLEA (Joanne Woodward & Paul Newman)

CLEMENTINE (Cybill Shepherd)

CLEO (Katharine Ross & Sam Elliott)

CLEOPATRA (Cleopatra & Antony)

COCO (Kim Gordon & Thurston Moore; Sting)

COLETTE (Henry-Louis Vuitton)

COLLEEN (Les Paul)

CONDOLA (Phylicia Rashad)

CONNIE (Jimmy Dean; Bobby G. Rice; Mel Tillis)

CONSTANCE (Richard Bennett; Paul Erdman)

CORA (James Schlesinger)

CORDI (Carl Stokes)

CORINNE (Roy Innes)

CORRIE (Larry Bird)

COSIMA (Franz Liszt)

COURTNEY (Carlton Fisk; Ethel & Robert Kennedy; Jack Lemmon; Natalie Wood & Robert Wagner)

CRIS (Sylvia Porter)

CRISTINA (Valerie Harper; Luciano Pavarotti)

CYDNEY (Chevy Chase)

CYNDI (Bobby Unser)

CYNTHIA (Howard Baker; John Cleese; Marva Collins; Joan Crawford; David Guyer; Alex Haley; Robert Loggia; Norman Schwarzkopf; Arthur Sulzberger; Forrest Tucker)

D'ANDREA (Tony Bennett)

DAISY (Markie Post; Mia Farrow & André Previn; Brian Keith; Harold Prince)

DAKOTA (Melissa Gilbert & Bo Brinkman; Melanie Griffith & Don Johnson)

DALE (Yogi Berra; Dale Bumpers; Hank Stram; Dottie West)

DALIA (Yitzhak Rabin)

DALINDLELA (Oliver Tambo)

DANA (Merle Haggard)

DANAE (Ann Wedgeworth & Rip Torn)

DANDELION (Anita Pallenberg & Keith Richards)

DANIELE (Jerry Lewis; Anthony Quinn; Henry Louis-Vuitton)

DANIELLE (Bobby Bonilla; Lisa Marie Presley; Norman Mailer; Art Monk; Marcel Ophuls; Leslie Uggams)

DAPHNA (Mathilde Krim)

DAPHNE (Douglas Fairbanks, Jr.)

DARA (Neil Sedaka)

DARCY (David Hare)

DARIA (Oleg Cassini; Gregory Hines)

DARLENE (Gene Roddenberry)

DARYA (Ekaterina Gordeeva & Sergie Grinkov)

DAWN (Ramsey Lewis; Art Linkletter; Anne Murray; Dan Rather; Gene Roddenberry)

DEANA (Billy Walker)

DEANNA (James Brown; Dean Martin; Jimmy Wakely)

DEBBIE (Vivian Ayers; Bobby Helms; Leon Huff; Mike Krzyzewski; Webb Pierce)

DEBBY (Pat Boone; Glen Campbell)

DEBORAH (Pat Boone; Dale Evans & Roy Rogers; Joan Fontaine; Don King; John Milton; Roger Moore; Paul Revere; B.F. Skinner; Barry Slotnick)

DEBRA (Charles M. Jordan; Carl Perkins; Warren Rudman; Howard Stern; Al Unser; Porter Wagoner)

DEBRACA (Redd Foxx)

DEE DEE (Pearl Bailey; Dexter Gordon)

DEENA (Morgan Freeman)

DEIDRA (Loni Anderson)

DEIDRE (Ted Koppel)

DEIONDRA (Deion Sanders)

DEIRDRE (Hugh Downs; Isadora Duncan; Angela Lansbury)

DELILAH (Gregg Allman)

DELPHINE (Robbie Robertson)

DENA (Danny Kaye)

DENISE (Marv Albert; Dennis De Concini; Charles Diggs, Jr.; Porter Wagoner)

DENNI (Woody Harrelson)

DESTINY (Leticia & Billy Ray Cyrus)

DETIRA (Leon Huff)

DEVIN (Denis Leary)

DEVON (Bruce Greyson)

DIANA (John Barrymore, Sr.; Judy Canova; William DeVries; Chuck Mangione; Beverly Sills; David Susskind)

DIANE (Billy Grammer; Arthur Hailey; Clifton Keith Hillegas; Art Linkletter)

DIERDRE (Errol Flynn; Richard Kiley)

DINAH (Lee Grant)

DINEAN (Nicolas Coster)

DION (Charley Pride)

DIVA (Frank Zappa)

DIXIE (Andy Griffith)

DOLORES (Maurice Costello)

DOMENICA (Martin Scorsese)

DOMINIQUE (Michael Caine; Krzysztof Penderecki)

DONNA (George Clinton; Scatman Crothers; David Dinkins; Geraldine Ferraro; Billy Grammer; Felix Grucci; Meadowlark Lemon; Don Shula)

DONNA LOU (Donald Wildmon)

DONZALEIGH (The Reverend Ralph David Abernathy)

DORA (Barry Gray)

DORE (Ted Schwinden)

DORINDA (Hank Aaron)
DOROTHEA (Richard Kiley)
DOROTHY/DORO (Barbara & George Bush; Mario Puzo; Babe Ruth)
DREAMA (James De Paiva)
DREE (Mariel Hemingway)
DREW (John Barrymore, Jr.; Paul Tagliabue)
DRINA (Diahnne Abbott & Robert DeNiro)
DUDALANI (Oliver Tambo)
DYLAN (Jim Bartling; Beau Bridges; Mia Farrow & Woody Allen; Ralph Lauren; Alex North; Stephanie Seymour & Peter Brant; Bob Welch; Robin Wright & Sean Penn)
EBONNÉ (Evander Holyfield)
EDEN (Vidal Sassoon)
EDITH (Henry Wadsworth Longfellow; John D. Rockefeller; Kurt Vonnegut, Jr.)

---

### NAMESAKE DEPARTMENT

Percy Bysshe Shelley named his daughter Eliza Ianthe for two people: Eliza for his wife Harriet's sister, and Ianthe after the maiden in his lengthy epic poem, *Queen Mab*.

---

EDWINA (Keenan Wynn)
EILEEN (Art Carney; David Rockefeller)
ELAN (Vidal Sassoon)
ELEANOR (Diane Lane & Christopher Lambert; Karl Marx; Joan & Walter Mondale)
ELENA (Juan Carlos I; A. Bartlett Giamatti)
ELEONORE (Maria Von Trapp)
ELETTRA (Guglielmo Marconi; Isabella Rosselini)
ELEUTHERE (Pierre Du Pont)
ELINOR (Katie Couric; Joanne Woodward & Paul Newman)
ELIOT (Sting)

ELISA (Linda Dano)

ELISABETH (Ursula K. Le Guin; Rupert Murdoch; Noel Perrin; Rudolph Serkin)

ELISE (Clyde Drexler; Pierre Du Pont; Grandpa Jones; Maria Tallchief)

ELISSA (Alex North)

ELIZA (Victoria Lockwood & Charles, Viscount Althrop; Percy Bysshe Shelley)

ELIZABETH (Arlene & Alan Alda; Roone Arledge; Irving Berlin; Elmer Bernstein; Henry Bloch; Anne Boleyn; Robert Burns; James Burrows; Harry Caray; Lynn & Dick Cheney; Natalie Cole; Tyne Daly & Georg Stanford Brown; Alan Dixon; James Fulbright; John R. Galvin; Katharine Graham; Gene Hackman; Jerry Hall & Mick Jagger; Mark Hatfield; Henry Heimlich; Florence Henderson; Henry VIII; Lou Holtz; Peter Jennings; Henry Kissinger; C. Everett Koop; Betty Bao & Winston Lord; John Major; Norman Mailer; Joe Montana; Robert Montgomery; Tommy Overstreet; Norman Vincent Peale; Richard Pryor; Harry Reasoner; Pat Robertson; George Segal; Robert Stack; Ted Stevens; John Sununu; Elizabeth Taylor; John Updike; Bill Walsh; Robert Young)

ELLA (Alan Dershowitz; Moira Harris & Gary Sinise)

ELLEN (Norman Lear; Eugene McCarthy; Harry Reasoner; Ann Richards; Andy Rooney)

ELLIE (Morris Dees)

ELLY (Tony Curtis)

ELOISE (Grandpa Jones)

ELYN (Neil Diamond)

ELYSE (Ted Knight)

EMANUELE (Ken Follett)

EMILY (Caroline Astor; Kenneth Auchincloss; Elmer Bernstein; Jimmy Breslin; Beau Bridges; Chevy Chase; Tony Danza; Richard Dreyfuss; Betty Friedan; Andrea Hall; Barry Humphries; William Kuntsler; Arthur Liman; Tatum O'Neal & John McEnroe; Andy Rooney; James Schlesinger; Howard Stern; Paul Tagliabue; Alex Trebeck;

Russell Train; Robert Urich; Dianne Wiest; Edward Woodward)

EMMA (Julie Andrews; Michael Crawford; Christine Lahti; Eric Roberts)

ENSA (Bill Cosby)

ERICA (Joseph Heller; Walter Slezak; Nick Turturro)

ERIKA (Bill Cosby; Thomas Mann)

ERIN (Barry Bremen; Carol Burnett; Don Everly; Mike Farrell; David Foster; Richard Kiley; Sherrill Milnes; Elizabeth Clare Prophet; Leo Ryan; Vince Scully)

ERINN (Bill Cosby; Nancy Lopez)

ERNESTINE (James Boggs)

ESME (Russell Hoban)

ETHEL (Georgina Drew & Maurice Barrymore; The Honorable Elijah Muhammad)

---

## LOVE LETTERS

Former Secretary of the Department of Housing and Urban Development Jack Kemp must like the letter J. He gave all of his four kids J names: Jeff, Jimmy, Jennifer, and Judith. Another "J" lover is Jerry Buss, owner of the Los Angeles Lakers. His kids are John, Jim, Jeanie, and Janie. And yet another J name fan is Debbie Fields of Mrs. Fields Cookies fame. Her daughters are Jessica, Jennessa, and Jennifer. Other famous "letter lovers" are Paul Anka, whose girls are named Alexandra, Amanda, Alicia, Anthea, and Amelia; Carlton Fisk, whose kids are Carlyn, Casey, and Courtney; and, of course, The Cos himself, Bill Cosby, whose progeny are all E names: Ennis, Ensa, Erika, Erinn, and Evin.

---

EUGENIE (Princess Sarah Ferguson & Prince Andrew)

EUNICE (Rose & Joseph Kennedy)

EUPHEMIA (James Boswell)

EVA (Harry Anderson; Meredith Baxter; Geronimo; Susan Sarandon & Franco Amurri; Richard Wagner)

EVE (Bella & Maurice Abzug; Arlene & Alan Alda; Elmer Bernstein; Bono; Marie Curie; Hal Holbrook)

FAITH (Mildred Evelyn & Clive Brook; Bill O'Donnell)

FATIMA (Harry Edwards)

FAWN (Pete Rose)

FELICE (Henry Mancini)

FELICIA (Faye Wattleton)

FERNANDA (Rita Moreno)

FIFI (Bob Geldoff)

FIONA (Lorin Maazel)

FLEETWOOD (Tom Robbins)

FLORENCE (Grantland Rice)

FOSCA (Giacomo Puccini)

FRANCES (Courtney Love & Kurt Cobain; Jackie Nespral; Paul Revere; Frank Lloyd Wright; Robin Wright & Sean Penn)

FRANCESCA (Frances Fisher & Clint Eastwood; Conrad Hilton & Zsa Zsa Gabor; Dino De Laurentiis)

FRANCOISE (Arman)

FRAZISKA (Karl Marx)

FREDERIKKE (Victor Borge)

FRIEDA (Sylvia Plath & Ted Hughes)

GABRIELLE (Larry Johnson; Dona Karan)

GAIL (Hank Aaron; Lena Horne; Paul Laxalt; Dean Martin; Dan Rostenkowski)

GAILE (Hank Aaron)

GALAXY (J.P. Getty II)

GAMILAH (Betty Shabazz)

GENEAN (Paula Hawkins)

GENEVIEVE (Jackie Gleason)

GENIE (Ivor Francis)

GENIMA (Pelé)

GEORGETTE (Tammy Wynette)

GEORGIA (Jerry Hall & Mick Jagger)

GEORGINA (Russell Chatham)

GERALDINE (Jackie Gleason; William Grayson; Oona O'Neill & Charlie Chaplin; Stan Musial)

GHISLAINE (Robert Maxwell)

GILLIAN (Patty Hearst; Jeff Sagansky)

GINA (Harry Belafonte; Tony Danza; Joe Garagiola; Wanda Jackson; Joe Mantegna; Dean Martin; Sidney Poitier; Generoso Pope)

GINGER (Charlie McCoy)

GIOVANNA (Sean Connery)

GISELE (Olivia De Havilland)

GISELLE (Robert Campeau; David Reuben)

GIULIANA (Luciano Pavarotti)

GLINORA (Martin Scorsese)

GLORIA (Enrico Caruso; William Grayson; Jesse Owens)

GLYNIS (Mervyn Jones; Robert Ludlum)

GRACE (Rocky Aoki; Meryl Streep)

GRACIE (Rhea Perlman & Danny DeVito)

GRETA (Rachel Ticotin & David Caruso)

GRETCHEN (Robert Schuller)

GRETTA (James Garner)

GWEN (Jesse McReynolds)

GWYNETH (Blythe Danner & Bruce Paltrow; Richard Thomas)

HALEY (Pat Benatar & Neil Geraldo; Paula Zahn)

HALLIE (Emmylou Harris)

HANA (Muhammad Ali; Robert Schank)

HANAKO (Billy Dee Williams)

HANNA (Gerhard Casper)

HANNAH (Jamison Elvidge & Perry King; Mel Gibson; Jane Hamilton; Jessica Lange & Sam Shepard; Jilly Mack & Tom Selleck)

HARMONY (Susan St. James)

HARRIET (Potter Stewart)

HAYLEY (Jeff Bridges; Pamela Bach & David Hasselhoff; Sir John Mills)

HAZEL (Berry Gordy)

HEATHER (Jerry Garcia; Jim Henson; Gordon MacRae; Paul McCartney; Don Meredith; Dina Merrill & Cliff Robertson)

HEIDI (Larry Hagman; Skitch Henderson; Leon Max Lederman)

HELEN (Ambrose Bierce; Al Dexter; Pete Domenici; The Duke and Duchess of Kent; Jason Epstein; Ernest Hollings; Gordon Hunt; Babe Ruth)

HELENE (Constantin Costa-Gavras)

HELLER (Mary Martin)

HILDA (Kennan Wynn)

HILLARY (Howard Cosell)

HOLLY (Michael Bolton; Richard Branson; James Clavell; Danny Gatton; Terry Gilliam; Charlton Heston; F. Story Musgrave; Dolores Robinson)

HORTENSE (Josephine)

IDA (Stanley Lupino)

ILYASAH (Betty Shabazz)

IMA (Big Jim Hogg)

IMAN (King Hussein)

IMOGEN (Andrew Lloyd Webber)

INDIA (Olivia Hussey; Catherine Oxenberg; Marianne Williamson)

INDIRA (Jawaharlal Nehru)

INGRID (Woody Herman; Gordon Lightfoot)

INNA (Vladimir Dzhanibekov)

IONE (Donovan Leitch)

IRENE (Candido Jacuzzi)

IRÉNE (Marie Curie)

ISA (Michael Bolton)

ISABEL (Jacques Barzun; Tina Brown; Robert Maxwell; Herbert Von Karajan)

ISABELLA (Ingrid Bergman & Roberto Rossellini; Nicole Kidman & Tom Cruise; Geraldo Rivera)

ISABELLE (Jean-Pierre Rampal)

ISOBEL (Bella & Maurice Abzug)

ISOLDE (Richard Wagner)

IVANKA (Ivana & Donald Trump)

JACKELYN (Howie Mandel)

JACKIE (Marv Albert; Peter Falk; Joe Louis)

JACQUELINE (James Boggs; Newt Gingrich; Jesse Jackson; Julia Lennon; Joe Louis; Robert Lutz; Barbara Walters)

JACQUELYN (Joe Frazier)

JACQUI (Julia Lennon; Jerry Rice)

JADE (Bianca & Mick Jagger)

JAEL (Jeanne Pruett)

JAIME (Danny Aiello; Barbara Mandrell)

JAMIE (Jim Abrahams; Leonard Bernstein; Lynda Carter; Ron Guidry; Richard Harris; James Lehrer; Janet Leigh & Tony Curtis; Joan Lunden & Michael Krause; Mike Krzyzewski; Jim Palmer; Robert Redford; John D. Rockefeller; Jim Valvano)

JAMIE LEE (Janet Leigh & Tony Curtis; Jerry Weintraub)

JAN (Ernie Banks; Jack Greene; Dick Howser; Stan Lee)

JANE (Julian Bond; Jim Carrey; Ruth Bader Ginsburg; Dan Jansen; Arthur Hailey; Jesse Helms; William Kuntsler; Arthur Miller; Henry Fonda; Harry Reasoner; Murray Schisgal)

JANENE (Floyd Patterson)

JANESSA (Debbie Fields)

JANET (Victor Borge; Henry Heimlich; Katherine & Joe Jackson; Tony Hillerman; Allen Neuharth; Nathan Pritikin; William Rehnquist; Red Sovine; Hicks Waldron)

JANICE (Johnny Unitas; Paul Volcker)

JANIE (Jerry Buss; George Wallace)

JANNA (William DeVries; Bernard Malamud)

JASMINE (Michael Jordan)

JAUNDALYNN (The Reverend Ralph David Abernathy)

JAYNE (Joseph Barbera; Jayne Mansfield)

JEAN (Melvin Belli; Robert Burns; Rusty Kanokogi; Rose & Joseph Kennedy; Doris Lessing; Stewart McKinney; Judith Rossner; Mark Twain)

JEANIE (Jerry Buss)

JEANINE (Charles Durning)

JEANNA (Pancho Gonzales)

JEANNE (Marcel Ophuls; Louis Pasteur; Robert Schuller; John Tower; Abigail Van Buren)

JEANNIE (Jerry Falwell; Elaine May)

JECOLIA (Reggie White)

JENIFER (Robert Irwin Chartof)

JENNA (Ann Byrne & Dustin Hoffman; Englebert Humperdinck; Susan Korn; Lee Mazzilli; Robin Yount)

JENNESSA (Debbie Fields)

JENNIE (Red Foley; Charles Loeb; Albert Shanker)

JENNIFER (John Aniston; Conrad Bain; Tom Brokaw; John Candy; Dyan Cannon & Cary Grant; Leslie Caron; Bill Caspar; Burt Convy; Billy Crystal; Paul Erdman; Debbie Fields; Vince Gill; Leon Gorman; Elliott Gould; Joel Grey; Norman Jewison; Lynda Bird Johnson & Charles Robb; Jack Kemp; Shirley Knight & Jack Nicholson; Michael Landon; Hal Linden; David Lynch; Jason Miller; Vic Morrow; Don Nickles; Floyd Patterson; Pelé; Regis Philbin; Roseanne; William Ruckleshaus; Dick Shawn; Roger Smith; George Steinbrenner)

JENNY (Leeza Gibbons & Stephen Meadows; E.L. Doctorow; Billy Crystal; William Goldman; Thomas Harkin; Sidney Lumet; Karl Marx; Walter Matthau)

JERI (Bobby Unser)

JERI ANN (Earl Anthony)

JESSE (Cassandra Delaney & John Denver)

JESSICA (Lynda Carter; John Elway; Debbie Fields; Davey Jones; Nat Hentoff; Gregory Hines; Joe Namath; Roseanne; Mike Schmidt; Budd Schulberg; Norman Schwarzkopf; Patti Scialfa & Bruce Springsteen; George Steinbrenner; Barbara Tuchman)

JESSIE (Maurice Benard; Kenny Rogers)

JESSYKA (Joseph Beuys)

JILL (Howard Cosell; Corky & Larry Elikan; William Faulkner; Dick Howser; E.G. Marshall; Paul Mazursky; Merlin Olsen; Charles Schulz; Mike Singletary)

JILLIAN (Bryant Gumbel; Vanessa Williams)

JO ANN (Eddy Arnold)

JOAN (Louise Bates Ames; Peter Drucker; Stan Lee; Jack London; Molly Yard)

JOANIE (Stan Lee; Archie Moore)

JOANNA (Clive Barnes; Tony Bennett; Regis Philbin)

JOANNE (Barry Goldwater; Burt Lancaster)

JOCELYN (Ron Howard)

JODIE (Jerry Tarkanian)

JODY (Carol Burnett; Johnny Carson; Del Shannon; Jerry Weintraub)

JOELY (Phil Collins; Vanessa Redgrave & Tony Richardson; Connie Stevens & Eddie Fisher)

JOHANNA (Maria Von Trapp)

JOIE (Bill Lee)

JOLIE (Quincy Jones; Brenda Lee)

JONETTA (Joe Frazier)

JONI (Conway Twitty)

JORDAN (Bono; Beau Bridges; John Elway; Leeza Gibbons & Steve Meadows; Orel Hershiser; Cheryl Ladd; Jason Miller)

JOSEPHA (Jascha Heifetz)

JOSEPHINE (Perri Klass; Madeline L'Engle; Linda Hamilton & James Cameron; Lewis Powell)

JOY (Jacob Javits; Bob Jones)

JOYCE (Marion Worth)

JUANITA (William Zander Zalm)

JUDITH (Bill Caspar; William Golding; Jack Kemp; Rudolph Serkin; William Shakespeare)

JUDY (Elia Kazan; Doc Severinsen; Jimmy Stewart; Billy Walker; Loretta Young & Clark Gable)

JULIA (Caesar Augustus; Julian Bond; Bill Caspar; Red Foley; David Halberstam; Russell Hoban; Julia Lennon; Clairborne Pell; Hank Stram; Richard Threlkeld)

JULIANA (Alan Shepard; Strom Thurmond)

JULIE (Robert Irwin Chartoff; Lee J. Cobb; Dennis Conner; Konstantin Costa-Gavras; Gerard Depardieu; Ray Flynn;

Casey Kasem; Brenda Lee; Gavin MacLeod; Leonard
Nimoy; Pat & Richard Nixon; Al Pacino; Joan Plowright
& Laurence Olivier; George Peppard; B.F. Skinner; Billy
Walker; Jerry Weintraub)
JULIET (Allen Funt; Philip Glass; Sir John Mills)
JULIETTE (Kenneth Feld)
JUNE (Kathleen & Gene Lockhart)
JUSTICE (John Mellencamp)

---

## REALITY BITES

Garth Brooks's real first name is Troyal. Garth is his
middle name.
Gregory Peck's real first name was Eldred. His
mother Bernice picked it out of a phone book.
Naomi Judd took her maiden name after a divorce
(she was born a Judd) and changed her first name to
Naomi, a name she got from the Bible. (Her real
first name is Diana.)
Markie Post's real first name is Marjorie. (Markie is
a childhood nickname from one of her brothers.)
Pablo Picasso's real name was Pablo Nepomuceno
Crispiniano de la Santissima Trinidad Ruiz y
Picasso. The legendary artist (who was designer
Paloma's father) signed his early paintings "P. Ruiz
Picasso."

---

JUSTINE (Kent Bateman; Peter Fonda; Mariette Hartley;
Mary McFadden; Anita Roddick)
KAAREN (Walter Heller)
KABARA (Ben Vereen)
KADY (Tim Allen)
KANDACE (Kelsey Grammer)
KARA (Michael Dukakis; Edward Kennedy)

KAREN (Carla Bley; Sid Caesar; Don Knotts; Sonny Osborne; Arthur Sulzberger; Alvin Toffler; Leon Uris)

KARENNA (Tipper & Al Gore)

KARI (Del Reeves)

KARIN (William Kuntsler)

KARINA (Ann Byrne & Dustin Hoffman)

KARIS (Marsha Hunt & Mick Jagger)

KARON (Ben Vereen)

KARYN (Irv Kupcinet)

KATE (Jane Asher; Meredith Baxter; Ted Danson; Charles Dickens; Goldie Hawn & Bill Hudson; Robert Jarvik; Frances & Norman Lear; Norman Mailer; Christopher Patten; Julia Phillips; Markie Post; Lee Remick; Bertrand Russell; Jean Simmons & Richard Brooks; Gene Siskel; Sting; John Vernon; Robert Wagner)

KATHARINA-BIANCA (Falco)

KATHARINE (Elia Kazan; Walter Kerr; Ring Lardner; Bertrand Russell; Arthur Schlesinger; Maureen Stapleton; Gene Wilder; Bill Wyman)

KATHERINE (Bob Allen; Tyne Daly & Georg Stanford Brown; James Burrows; Ted Danson; Tony Danza; Nancy Dolman & Martin Short; Dianne Feinstein; Richard Gephardt; David Gergen; Ellen Goodman; Ann Jackson & Eli Wallach; Russell Long; Ed McMahon; H. Ross Perot; Loret Miller Ruppe; Maria Shriver & Arnold Schwarzenegger; Adlai Stevenson; Sting; Robert Wagner; Jack Welch; Hank Williams, Jr.)

KATHLEEN (Russell Baker; June & Johnny Cash; Abby Dalton; Peter Drucker; John R. Galvin; William Averell Harriman; Ethel & Robert Kennedy; Robert Kennedy, Jr.; Rose & Joseph Kennedy; Richard Kiley; Paul Laxalt; Garry Marshall; Anthony Quinn; George Shultz; Robert Young)

KATHLYN (Annette Bening & Warren Beatty)

KATHRYN (Tim Allen; Ed Asner; William DeVries; Lee Iacocca)

KATHRYNE (Tyne Daly & George Stanford Brown)

KATHY (Polly Bergen & Freddie Fields; Dianne Feinstein; Buddy Rich; Mickey Spillane)

KATIA (Denzel Washington)

KATIE (Tony Danza; Jane Seymour)

KATINA (Paul Tsongas)

KATRINA (Anne Baxter; James Miller)

KATY (Joan Collins)

KATYA (Victoria Lockwood & Charles, Viscount Althrop)

KAY (Douglas Fairbanks, Jr.; Frank Faylen; Sir Guy Standing)

KAZUKO (Akira Kurosawa)

KEHLY (Linda Gray)

KEIKO (Kiichi Miyazawa)

KEITA (Stevie Wonder)

KELLEY (Broderick Crawford; Paula Hawkins)

KELLI (Glen Campbell; Morton Downey, Jr.)

KELLIE (Merle Haggard)

KELLY (Jimmy Breslin; George Carlin; Dabney Coleman; Don Drysdale; Linda Gray; Richard R. Green; Tom Harmon; Bob Hope; Janet Leigh & Tony Curtis; Huey Lewis; Billy Marshall; Merlin Olsen; Jim Palmer; Lynn Redgrave; Mickey Rooney; Richard Roundtree; Vince Scully; Jimmy Stewart)

KELSEY (Kelly McGillis; Gabrielle Carteris)

KELY (Pelé)

KENDALL (Ramsey Lewis)

KENYA (Nastassja Kinski & Quincy Jones; Gladys Knight)

KERRI (Casey Kasem)

KERRY (Berry Gordy; Gene Kelly; Ethel & Robert Kennedy; Kathleen Kennedy & David Townsend; Dottie West)

KIDADA (Peggy Lipton & Quincy Jones)

KILEY (Edward Kennedy, Jr.)

KIM (Jim Brown; Don Nickles; Jeannie C. Riley; Aung San Suu Kyi)

KIMATHIA (Roy Innis)

KIMBERLEE (Richard R. Green)

KIMBERLY (Gary Carter; James Garner; Orrin Hatch; Clifton Keith Hillegas; Rod Stewart)
KITTY (Victoria Lockwood & Charles, Viscount Althrop; Tom Landry)
KRISHA (Cindy & Steve Garvey)
KRISTEN (Ron Hextall; Sam Peckinpah; Mike Singletary)
KRISTIN (Larry Gatlin; Tipper & Al Gore)
KRISTINA (Corazon Aquino; Robert Loggia)
KRYSTA (Dennis Franz)
KRYSTEN (Robbie Knievel)

---

### BUT SHE STILL BROKE UP
### THE SCHOOL BAND, RIGHT?

When Yoko Ono's daughter (by Tony Cox) Kyoko enrolled in Walter Reed Junior High School in the U.S., she used the alias "Ruth Holman."

---

KYM (Jean Kennedy; Del Shannon)
KYOKO (Yoko Ono)
LACEY (Lee Mazzilli; Jackie Zeman)
LADONNA (Teddy Pendergrass)
LANA (Willie Nelson)
LANGLEY (Mariel Hemingway)
LARA (Bob Saget)
LARK (Mia Farrow & André Previn)
LATOYA (Katherine & Joe Jackson)
LAURA (Pat Boone; John Chancellor; Blythe Danner & Bruce Paltrow; Geraldine Ferraro; Daniel Goldin; Carla Hills; Robert Hofstadter; Diane Ladd & Bruce Dern; Tommy Lasorda; Herbie Mann; Karl Marx; J. Michael McCloskey; Ricardo Montalban; Christopher Patten; Wayne Rogers; Warren Rudman; Ted Turner)
LAURA LEE (Ted Turner)
LAUREL (Rollie Fingers)

LAUREN (Adrien Arpel; Vincent Persichetti; Judy Woodruff)

LAURETTE (Eva Marie Saint)

LAURIE (Jack Anderson; Vaughn Beals; Charlie Rich)

LAUTITIA (Uta Hagen & José Ferrer)

LAVERNE (Ruby Dee & Ossie Davis)

LAYLA (Jellybean Benitz)

LEA (Russell Chatham; Angie Dickinson & Burt Bacharach)

LEAH (Justin Tubb)

LEE (Paul Butterfield; Roger Tory Peterson; Ringo Starr)

LEE ANN (Jim Valvano)

---

## AND THEN HE CRIED
## AND RAN OFF THE STAGE, RIGHT?

Jack Parr once introduced Liza Minnelli on his show as "Dujy Landgar," an anagram of her mother Judy Garland's name.

---

LEILA (Donny Hathaway; Greta Scacchi)

LENI (Karl Marx)

LEONILDA (Giacomo Casanova)

LESLEY (Lee Trevino)

LESLIE (Lauren Bacall & Humphrey Bogart; Jackie Coogan; Johnny Duncan; Gene Hackman; Alan Hamel; Michael Landon; Reginald Lewis; William Shatner)

LEXI (Leeza Gibbons & Steve Meadows)

LI (I.M. Pei)

LIA (Lee Iacocca)

LIANA (Chick Corea; George Morgan)

LIANE (I.M. Pei)

LIBBY (Stewart McKinney)

LIBERTY (Jean & Casey Kasem)

LIBRA (Peter Max)

LILLY (Mary Steenburgen & Malcolm McDowell)

LILY (Phil Collins; Kevin Costner; Jill Krementz; Amy
 Madigan & Ed Harris; David Rabe & Jill Clayburgh; Ted
 Stevens; Meredith Viera; Dianne Wiest)
LINA (Billy Walker)
LINDA (Irving Berlin; Shirley Temple Black & John Agar;
 Pat Boone; Bill Caspar; Newt Gingrich; Jackie Gleason;
 Paul Henning; Clifton Keith Hillegas; Bob Hope; Nancy
 Kassebaum; Mervyn LeRoy; Ed McMahon; Linus Paul-
 ing; Colin Powell; Boots Randolph; Jimmy Wakely)
LINDA LOU (Dale Evans & Roy Rogers)
LINDLEY (Beverly Sills)
LINDSAY (Billy Crystal; Cheryl Ladd)
LINDSEY (Bob Kerrey)

---

### "LITTLE DID THEY KNOW" DEPARTMENT

Ulysses S. Grant's boyhood nickname was
"Useless."

---

LINDY (Mike Krzyzewski)
LINELL (Ogden Nash)
LINN (Liv Ullman & Ingmar Bergman)
LISA (Lynn Anderson; Dr. Joyce Brothers; James Coburn;
 Alphonse D'Amato; Edward J. DeBartolo, Jr.; Pete
 Domenici; Larry Flynt; Jack Gilford; Jim Henson; Larry
 Holmes; Virginia Johnson-Masters; Charles Kuralt; Tom
 Landry; John Larroquette; Richard Petty; Lafffit Pincay,
 Jr.; Daniel Schorr; Justin Tubb; Willie C. Williams; An-
 drew Young)
LISA MARIE (Priscilla & Elvis Presley)
LISABETH (William Shatner)
LISTY (Larry Holmes)
LITTLE DOE (Dale Evans & Roy Rogers)
LIV (Alicia & Steven Tyler)
LIVIA (Galileo Galilei)

LIZA (Ed Asner; Gene Barry; Judy Garland & Vincente Minnelli; W. Somerset Maugham; Elizabeth Taylor)
LIZANNE (Robert Merrill)
LOIS (Lefty Frizell)
LOLA (Annie Lennox)
LOLITA (Gale Anne Hurd & Brian DePalma)
LORELEI (F. Story Musgrave)
LOREN (L. Douglas Wilder)
LORENE (Louis Stokes)
LORENZA (Luciano Pavarotti)
LORETTA (George Morgan)

---

**ELVISISMS**

Elvis's personal Convair 880 passenger jet was named the *Lisa Marie,* in honor of his daughter, Lisa Marie Presley-Jackson.
Elvis's pet names for his and Priscilla's daughter Lisa Marie were "Yisa" and "Buttonhead."

---

LORI (Shirley Temple Black; Johnny Duncan; Goldie Hill; Eleanor Smeal; Carl Smith; Dave Thomas)
LORRAINE (Tom Bradley; Rebecca Broussard & Jack Nicholson; Alphonse D'Amato; Generoso Pope)
LORRIE (Rose Lee & Joe Maphis; George Morgan)
LOTTIE (The Honorable Elijah Muhammad; Jerry Reed)
LOUISA (Meryl Streep)
LOUISE (Carole King; Richard Leakey)
LOYAL (Nancy Reagan)
LUANNE (Lou Holtz)
LUCI (Lady Bird & Lyndon Johnson)
LUCIA (James Joyce; William Zander Zalm)
LUCIE (Lucille Ball & Desi Arnaz; Stewart McKinney)
LUCINDA (Lloyd Bridges; Lynda Bird Johnson & Charles Robb; Jonathan Winters)

LUCY (Jimmy Breslin; Barry Commoner; Michael Crawford; Stephen Hawking; James Lehrer; Patricia Neal & Roald Dahl; Rhea Perlman & Danny DeVito; Adlai Stevenson; Barbara Tuchman; Billy Ed Wheeler)

LYDIA (Alex Haley; Patty Hearst; Betty Johnson; Gary Wills)

LYNDA (Lady Bird & Lyndon Johnson)

LYNN (Liz Anderson; Jean & George Ariyoshi; Ralph Bellamy; Michael Redgrave; L. Douglas Wilder)

LYNNE (Joseph Barbera; Dick Gregory)

LYRIC (Robby Benson)

LYUBOV (Fyodor Dostoyevsky)

MABEL (Tracy Ullman; Brigham Young)

MACKENZIE (John Phillips)

MADDIE (Ken Kercheval)

MADELINE (Mario Cuomo; Thomas Edison; Lea Thompson; Mel Harris)

MADISON (Sissy Spacek & Jack Fisk)

MAGDALEN (Thea Vidale)

MAGDALENA (Lech Walesa)

MAGGIE (Judith Ivey & Tim Braine; Frances & Norman Lear; Norman Mailer)

MAISHA (Imamu Amiri Baraka [LeRoi Jones])

MAIZIE (Julie Walters)

MAKI (Nelson Mandela)

MALAAK (Betty Shabazz)

MALAIKA (Ben Vereen)

MALIKAH (Betty Shabazz)

MALLARY (Wayne Thiebaud)

MALLIKA (Carole Simpson)

MALLORY (Rick Derringer; Shari Lewis & Jeremy Tarcher)

MALU (David Byrne)

MARCI (Calvin Klein)

MARCIA (Orrin Hatch; Robert Mondavi)

MARGARET (Dale Bumpers; James Burrows; Charles V;

Mario Cuomo; Shelby Foote; Barry Goldwater; O. Henry; Hank Locklin; Eugene McCarthy; Norman Vincent Peale; David Rockefeller; Dean Rusk; Babe Ruth; Antonin Scalia; George Shultz; Danny Thomas; Tom Watson; May Whitty)

MARGAUX (Lorraine Bracco & Mark Vaughn)

MARGO (Ann Landers; Danny Thomas)

MARGOT (Bette Davis)

MARGUERITE (Henri Matisse; Rudolph Serkin)

MARIA (Corazon Aquino; Rosemary Clooney & José Ferrer; Gary Cooper; Mario Cuomo; Marlene Dietrich; John Farrow; Galileo Galilei; Harvey Korman; Madeline L'Engle; Roger Mudd; Anna Quindlen; Generoso Pope; Rasputin; Eunice Shriver; Elizabeth Taylor; Maria Von Trapp; Lech Walesa)

MARIAN (Thor Heyerdahl; John Tower)

MARIE (Marc Bohan; Bernadine Healy; Olive & George Osmond; Admiral Robert Peary)

MARIE-CHRISTINE (Katherine Dunham)

MARIE-CLAIRE (Ken Follett)

MARIETTA (Pee Wee King)

MARIAH (Kerry Kennedy Cuomo & Andrew Cuomo)

MARIKA (Samantha & Ivan Lendl)

MARILYN (Henny Youngman)

MARINA/MARYNA (Ben Bradlee; Charles Bukowski)

MARION (Thomas Edison; Dale Evans & Roy Rogers; Charles Grodin; David Guyer)

MARISKA (Jayne Mansfield)

MARJORIE (Neil Diamond)

MARKO (Bogdan Maglich)

MARLENE (Jesse Owens)

MARLO (Danny Thomas)

MARTHA (Estelle Parsons; Andy Rooney)

MARTINA (Quincy Jones; Maria Von Trapp)

MARTINA-LISA (Quincy Jones)

MARTITA (Joan Fontaine)

MARY (Bob Atcher; Malcolm Baldridge; Irving Berlin;

William Peter Blatty; Robert Bly; Catherine of Aragon; John Chancellor; Lynn & Dick Cheney; Dabney Coleman; Roger Corman; Walter Cronkite; Bing Crosby; Dale Evans & Roy Rogers; George Hamilton IV; Edward Henry Harriman; William Averell Harriman; Helen Hayes; Henry VIII; Robert Hofstadter; Eugene McCarthy; George McGovern; Jim McKay; J.E. Mainer; Don Meredith; John Milton; Mary Ann Mobley & Gary Collins; Henry Moore; Les Paul; Rudy Perpich; Lewis Powell; Vincent Price; Marilyn & Dan Quayle; Harry Reasoner; Loret Miller Ruppe; Antonin Scalia; Meryl Streep; William Ruckleshaus; Hank Stram; Anne Truitt; Al Unser; John Warner)

---

### HEAVEN FORFEND SHE MARRY AN ACCOUNTANT, EH?

In 1974, boxing fanatic Brian Brown of Wolverhampton, England, named his new daughter Maria Sullivan Corbett Fitzsimmons Jeffries Hart Burns Johnson Willard Dempsey Tunney Schmelling Sharkey Carnera Baer Braddock Louis Charles Walcott Marciano Patterson Johannson Liston Clay Frazier Foreman Brown. His fatherly dream for the lass? "I hope she marries a boxer." Maria's middle names are the names of all the World Heavyweight Boxing Champions in order from 1882 through 1974.

---

MARY ANNE (Donna Reed; Maurice Strong)
MARY ELLEN (Robert Zemeckis)
MARY JO (Henry Bloch; John R. Galvin)
MARYLYN (Mary Kay)
MARYROSE (Phil Donahue)
MATHILDA (Victor Haim)

MATTIE (Alan Jackson)

MAURA (Daniel Moynihan; Gail Sheehy)

MAUREEN (Ray Flynn; Nelson Riddle; Maurice Strong; Jane Wyman & Ronald Reagan)

MAXIMILLIA (Roy Scheider)

MAYA (Ra'uf Glasgow)

MEAGANN (Wade Boggs)

MEDEA (Thea Vidale)

MEDORA (George Plimpton)

MEG (Paul Mazursky)

MEGAN (Malcolm Baldrige; Mike Ditka; Emmylou Harris; Carla Hills; Mario Van Peebles)

MEGHAN (Wally Kurth; Gavin MacLeod)

MEGHANN (Emmylou Harris)

MELANIE (Rodney Dangerfield; Tippi Hedren; Keith Jackson; William Shatner; Morris West; Vanessa Williams)

MELIA (Melvin Belli)

MELINDA (Dave Thomas)

MELISA (Robin Yount)

MELISSA (Anne Baxter; Steven Bochco; Morton Downey, Jr.; Douglas Fairbanks, Jr.; José Feliciano; Robin Gibb; Charles M. Jordan; Penelope Leach; Bob Luman; Bill Monroe; Sam Peckinpah; Joan Rivers & Edgar Rosenberg; Dinah Shore; Fred Silverman; Barry Slotnick; Joanne Woodward & Paul Newman)

MELODY (Barry Gray)

MERCEDES (Henry Cisneros; Joanna Whalley-Kilmer & Val Kilmer)

MEREDITH (Whitney Blake; Gordon MacRae; Charles Schulz; Beverly Sills)

MERLENE (Merle Travis)

MERLY (Angel Cordero)

MIA (Joe Mantegna; Maureen O'Sullivan & John Farrow; Steven Tyler)

MICA (Evelyn Rosenberg)

MICAELA (Mirella Freni)

MICHAELA (LeVar Burton; James Clavell)

MICHELE (Sid Caesar; Benjamin Chavez; Charles Durning; Dick Gregory; Generoso Pope

MICHELLE (Harry Caray; Pat Corley; Paul Laxalt; John Mellencamp; Sam Nunn; Barry Slotnick; Keifer Sutherland)

MICHI (George Foreman)

MIKA (Pete Seeger)

MIKO (Marlon Brando)

---

### "ISN'T THERE A THIRD CHOICE, HONEY?"

When Frank Zappa's wife Gail was pregnant with their daughter Moon Unit in 1967, Frank offered her two choices for the new baby's name: Moon Unit or Motorhead. Gail went with Moon Unit. In 1994, during the 25th anniversary of the moon landing, Moon Unit was asked if her name was her father's tribute to the space program. "I don't think he chose it to directly commemorate the Apollo missions," she replied. "He just liked the name." Moon Unit is known as "Moon" to her friends.

---

MILA (Karl Malden)

MILDRED (Merle Travis)

MILENA (Ghena Dimitrova)

MILENE (Igor Stravinsky)

MILLA (Galina Jovovich)

MILLIE (Any Grant)

MIMI (Brian Keith; Donna Summer)

MINDY (Don Rickles)

MIRA (Paul Sorvino)

MIRANDA (Nat Hentoff; Joe Papp; John Updike)

MIRIAM (Dr. Ruth Westheimer)

MISS (Dick Gregory)

MISSY (Dick Gregory)

MIYAKO (Billy Dee Williams)

MOHM (Gail Sheehy)

MOIRA (Malcolm Forbes; Elizabeth Clare Prophet)

MOLLIE (Meredith Baxter & David Birney; Amy Heckerling)

MOLLY (Meredith Baxter & David Birney; Stanley Elkin; Annabeth & John Goodman; Erica Jong; Carole King; Arthur Penn; Ken Russell; Jan Smithers & James Brolin; Paul Tsongas)

MOLLY JO (Dave Thomas)

MONICA (Tony Hillerman; Henry Mancini; Art Monk; Xarolj Seles; Bob Vila)

MONSITA (Rosemary Clooney & José Ferrer)

MOON UNIT (Frank Zappa)

MORGAN (Rae Dawn Chong; Marvin Mitchelson; Lorrie Morgan & Ron Gaddis)

MORGAN-LEIGH (Greg Norman)

MORGANA (Morgan Freeman)

MORGANE (Roman Polanski)

MUFFY (Beverly Sills)

MYRTIE (Leon Payne)

NAAMA (Chaim Potok)

NADIA (Vladimir Ashkenazy)

NAJA (Ben Vereen)

NANCY (Harry Blackmun; William Joseph Brennan; Walter Cronkite; Ray Flynn; Jesse Helms; Chuck Mangione; Edwin Newman; Jack Nicklaus; H. Ross Perot; William Rehnquist; Doc Severinsen; Beverly Sills; Frank Sinatra; Strom Thurmond; Russell Train; Byron White)

NANETTE (Pete Domenici; Kurt Vonnegut, Jr.)

NAOMI (Valerie Campbell; Bruno Bettelheim; Joseph Biden; Norman Podhoretz)

NATALIA (Pinchas Zukerman)

NATALIE (Nat King Cole; Chrissie Hynde & Ray Davies; David Lander; Maureen McCormick; Michael Moore)

NATASHA (Shakira Baksh & Michael Caine; Joe Frazier;

Vanessa Redgrave & Tony Richardson; Yakov Smirnoff; Tuesday Weld; Natalie Wood & Robert Wagner)

NELL (Stephen Breyer)

NELLA (Pete Domenici)

NEVA (David Rockefeller)

NICHELLE (Frank Robinson)

NICOLE (Dick Butkus; Barbara Boxer; Edward DeBartolo, Jr.; Kenneth Feld; Lionel Richie; Richard Roundtree; Phil Spector; Jim Valvano; Gwen Verdon & Bob Fosse; Pete Weber)

NICOLETTE (Robert Goulet)

NIKKI (Angie Dickinson & Burt Bacharach)

NIKOLAI (Barry Bonds)

NINA (Leonard Bernstein; Roz Chast; Robert DeNiro; Tony Franciosa; Al Hirschfeld; John Ratzenberger)

NINNA (Marlon Brando; Christopher Reeve)

NOEL (Merle Haggard)

NOELLE (Andy Williams)

NONA (Marvin Gaye)

NORA (Gwendolyn Brooks; Ruby Dee & Ossie Davis; Bob Edwards; Bob Hope; Hal Linden)

NORI (Akihito)

NUALA (Claiborne Pell)

OLGA (Michael De Bakey; Mstislav Rostropovich; Svetlana Stalin)

OLIVIA (Patricia Neal & Roald Dahl; Thurman Thomas; Paula & Denzel Washington)

OLYA (Vladimir Dzhanibekov)

OONA (Eugene O'Neill)

OPHELIA (Patricia Neal & Roald Dahl)

PADDY (Lou Costello)

PAGE (John Forsythe)

PAIGE (Ron Howard)

PALOMA (Emilio Estevez; Pablo Picasso)

PAM (William Janklow; Mel Tillis)

PAMELA (Ronald Dellums; Little Jimmy Dickens; Phyllis George & John Brown; Stan Getz; Dick Gregory; Merle

Kilgore; Russell Long; Sidney Poitier; David Susskind; Jerry Tarkanian; Dave Thomas; Forrest Tucker)

PAOLA (William Styron)

PARIS (Corinna Tsupei & Freddie Fields; Sarah Vaughn)

PAT (Peter O'Toole; Merle Travis)

PATRICIA/PATTI/Y (Roone Arledge; Lewis Arquette; Harry Caray; Ernest Hollings; Reverend Benjamin Hooks; Roy Innis; Rose & Joseph Kennedy; Pat & Richard Nixon; Robert Overmyer; Leon Payne; Anthony Quinn; William Raspberry; Nancy & Ronald Reagan; Leo Ryan)

PATSY (Loretta Lynn)

PAULA (Tommy Cash; Benjamin Chavez; Pete Domenici; Dick Gregory; Willie Nelson; Irving Stone; Lawrence Taylor; Andrew Young)

PAULINA (Janet Jones & Wayne Gretzky)

PAULINE (P.T. Barnum; Princess Stephanie)

PAVLA (Peter Ustinov)

PEACHES (Bob Geldoff)

PEGGY (Loretta Lynn)

PEGGY ANN (Marvin Traub)

PEGGY SUE (George Wallace)

PENELOPE (Telly Savalas; John Tower)

PENNY (Donna Reed)

PETRINE (Robert Mitchum)

PHOEBE (Joe Cates; Russell Hoban; Jerry Lee Lewis; John Lithgow)

PHYLICIA (Vivian Ayers)

PHYLLIS (Julian Bond; Tom Bradley; Phyllis Schlafly)

PILAR (Richard Thomas)

PIXIE (Bob Geldoff)

POCAHANTAS (Powhatan)

POLA (Klaus Kinski)

POLLY (George Segal)

PRESLEY (Tanya Tucker & Ben Reed)

PRIMA (Connie Sellecca & John Tesh)

PRUDENCE (Rupert Murdoch; Maureen O'Sullivan & John Farrow)

QUBLIAH (Betty Shabazz)

QUINTANA (Joan Didion)

RACHEL (Robert Campeau; Benny Goodman; Marie Osmond; Cynthia Ozick; Jane Pauley & Gary Trudeau; Norman Podhoretz; Sydney Pollack; Diana Rigg; Cal Ripkin, Jr.; Donald Sutherland; Kathleen Turner; Kim Zimmer)

RAE (Tommy Chong)

RAFAELLA (Dino De Laurentiis)

RAIN (Richard Pryor)

RAINA (Evelyn Ashford)

RAINE (Barbara Cartland)

RAINEY (Andie MacDowell & Paul Qualley)

RAMONA (Ray Bradbury; Jonathan Demme)

RANDY (Earl Scruggs)

RASHEEDA (Muhammad Ali)

RASHIDA (Peggy Lipton & Quincy Jones)

REBECCA (Ernie Ashworth; Bob Atcher; Marlon Brando; Russell Chatham; Rita Hayworth & Orson Welles; Dustin Hoffman; Richard Petty; Powhatan; Cokie Roberts; Sydney Pollack; Carl Smith; Dawn Steel; David Steinberg)

REENA (Medgar Evers)

REEVE (Charles Lindbergh, Jr.)

REIS (Jennifer O'Neil)

REMINGTON (Tracy Nelson & Billy Moses)

RENA (Leon Max Lederman; Archie Moore; Chaim Potok; George Segal)

RENE (Leon Payne)

RENÉE (Bob Gibson; Rachel Hunter & Rod Stewart; Richard Pryor; Charlie Rich; Martin Sheen)

RENILDE (Mario Montessori)

REYA (Jellybean Benitz)

RHEA (Lawton Chiles)

RHONDA (Diana Ross & Berry Gordy; Earl Weaver)

RIDICIA (Riddick Bowe)

RILEY (Terry & Howie Mandel; Bob Welch)

ROBERTA (James Fulbright; Ann Jackson & Eli Wallach)

ROBIN (Herschel Bernardi; Alan Cranston; Dale Evans &

Roy Rogers; Dexter Gordon; Pat Kennedy; Meadowlark Lemon; Alfred Lennon; Robert Morse; William Ruckleshaus; Doc Severinsen)

ROBYN (Red Adair; Isaac Asimov; Don Nickles)

ROMANE (Richard Bohringer)

ROMINA (Tyrone Power)

ROMY (Ellen Barkin & Gabriel Byrne)

RONDA (Ramsey Clark)

RORY (Ethel & Robert Kennedy; Errol Flynn)

ROSA (Bob Hoskins)

ROSANNA (Lewis Arquette)

ROSANNE (June & Johnny Cash)

ROSE (Caroline Kennedy & Ed Schlossberg; Renée Russo)

ROSE ANNE (Randolph McCoy)

ROSEMARIE (Maria Von Trapp)

ROSEMARY (Jimmy Breslin; Rose & Joseph Kennedy; J. Michael McCloskey; Tip O'Neill; Nelson Riddle)

ROTRUD (Charlemagne)

ROXANNE (Patricia Wettig & Ken Olin)

ROXIE (Patricia Wettig & Ken Olin)

RUBY (Kelly Emberg & Rod Stewart; Rudy Perpich; Kitty Wells)

RUMER (Demi Moore & Bruce Willis)

RUTH (Bruno Bettelheim; Billy Graham; George S. Patton; Norman Podhoretz; Rainer Marie Rilke)

RUTH ELLEN (George S. Patton)

SABLE (James Worthy)

SABRINA (James Miller)

SACHA (Joan Collins & Anthony Newley)

SACHI (Shirley MacLaine)

SADIE (Michael Ontkean)

SALLY (Harry Blackmun; Robert Bloch; Phyllis Diller; Ira Glasser; Terry Jones)

SAMANTHA (Bibi Besch; Maurice Gibb; Ron Perelman; Anita Roddick; David Susskind; James Thompson)

SAMIRA (Richard Leakey)

SANDRA (George Burns; John Young)

SANDRINE (Gaby Landhage & Thierry Reussel)

SANNA (Victor Borge)

SANTITA (Jesse Jackson)

SARA (Samuel Coleridge; Norman Cousins; David Foster; Paul Gilbert; Boris Karloff)

SARAH (Lee Atwater; Tom Brokaw; Daniel Callahan; Bill Caspar; Winston Churchill; Susan Dey; Benjamin Franklin; Tipper & Al Gore; Bob Hoskins; Anselm Kiefer; William Kuntsler; Davey Jones; Bobby Lord; Princess Margaret; Jason Robards; Katy Sagal & Jack White; Tom Seaver; Carly Simon & James Taylor; Oliver Stone; Keifer Sutherland; Calvin Trillin; Ted Turner; Joseph Wapner; Edward Woodward)

SASHA (Kate Capshaw & Steven Spielberg; Joan Collins & Anthony Newley; Simon Rattle; David Steinberg; Leo Tolstoy)

SAVANNAH (Jimmy Buffet; Janice Dickinson)

SAYAN (Walter Becker)

SCHUYLER (Van Johnson; Tracy Pollan & Michael J. Fox; Sissy Spacek & Jack Fisk; John J. York)

SCOTTISH WARD (Dale Evans & Roy Rogers)

SCOUT (Demi Moore & Bruce Willis)

SEDINA (Jerry Reed)

SEIRA (Seiji Ozawa)

SELENA (Ray Pillows)

SEVEN (Country Joe McDonald)

SHAKARI (Willie Gault)

SHANA (Gary David Goldberg; Grover Washington, Jr.)

SHANE (Nicole Mitchell & Eddie Murphy)

SHANGA (Gladys Knight)

SHANI (Imamu Amiri Baraka [LeRoi Jones])

SHANNA (Dennis Conner; Lou Ferrigno)

SHANNIN (Arlen Specter)

SHANNON (Richard Dawson; Glen Campbell; Emmylou Harris; Ken Kesey; Jason Robards; Del Shannon; Roger Zelazny)

SHANNON JO (Leo Ryan)

SHARI (Harry Belafonte; Sumner Redstone)

SHARON (John Connally; Art Linkletter; Sam Peckinpah; Richard Petty; Bob Schieffer; Don Shula; Frank Yablans)

SHAUNA (Robert Redford)

SHAWN (Sherill Milnes; Dale Murphy)

SHAWNA (Michael Landon)

SHAYNE (Lorenzo Lamas; Nicole Mitchell & Eddie Murphy)

SHEA (John Grisham)

SHEILA (Bill Carlisle; Paul Laxalt; Robert Schuller; Paul Simon; Montana Slim)

SHELLEY (Howard Metzenbaum; Louis Stokes)

SHELLY (David Guyer; Dottie West)

SHERRI (Richard Green; Sidney Poitier; Dick Vitale)

SHERRY (Carole King)

SHIKARI (Barry Bonds)

SHIRA (Isaac Stern)

SHIRLEY (Red Foley)

SHONNA (William Janklow)

SIERRA (James Worthy)

SIGOURNEY (Pat Weaver)

SIMONE (Geraldo Rivera)

SKYE (James Aubrey)

SKYLAR (Sharise & Vince Neal)

SONDRA (Kelly McGillis; Larry Speakes)

SONIA (Vladimir Ashkenazy; Vladimir Horowitz; Nastassja Kinski)

SONORA (Kelly McGillis)

SONYA (Michael Jacobson)

SOON-YI (Mia Farrow & André Previn)

SOPHIA (Eleanor Neil & Francis Ford Coppola; Michael Richards; Ian Schrager)

SOPHIE (Moira Harris & Gary Sinise; Bette Midler; Marcel Marceau; Shannon Tweed & Gene Simmons)

SOSIE (Kyra Sedgwick & Kevin Bacon)

SPENCER (Kelsey Grammer; Jaclyn Smith)

STACEY (Don Everly; Dick Van Dyke)

STACIA (Narvel Felts)
STACY (Danny Aiello)

---

**BUT WHAT IF THEY HAD TWINS?, PARTS 1 & 2**

Before their third child was born, funnyman Eddie
Murphy and his model wife, Nicole Mitchell,
decided that regardless of the baby's sex, it would
be named "Shane." (The baby was a girl.)
Wynonna Judd (whose real name is Christina
Ciminella) decided beforehand on the names of her
unborn children: Elijah, if it was a boy, and Naomi,
if it was a girl (in honor of her mother, Naomi Judd,
whose real [maiden] name is Diana Ciminella).

---

STARLITE (Marisa Berenson)
STEFANIE (Mel Brooks)
STEFFI (Maureen O'Sullivan & John Farrow)
STELLA (Lorraine Bracco & Harvey Keitel; Charles Loeb)
STEPHANIE (Dorothea & Jon Bon Jovi; Maureen
    O'Sullivan & John Farrow; Phyllis Diller; Alan Dixon;
    Princess Grace; Dick Gregory; Shirley MacLaine; Cliff
    Robertson; William Smith; Joanne Woodward & Paul
    Newman; Efrem Zimbalist, Jr.)
SUNSHINE (Ken Kesey; Susan St. James)
SUSAN (Roone Arledge; Vaughn Beals; Barbara Bel
    Geddes; Melvin Belli; Harry Blackmun; Ray Bradbury;
    John Cheever; Alistair Cooke; Susan Dey; Roy Disney;
    Geraldine Fitzgerald; Betty & Gerald Ford; Lou Har-
    ris; Charles Kuralt; Burt Lancaster; Timothy Leary;
    Susan Lucci; Norman Mailer; Neville Marriner; George
    McGovern; Howard Metzenbaum; Paul Newman; Tip
    O'Neill; Joe Papp; Maury Povich; Bob Schieffer; Alan K.
    Simpson; Ted Stevens; Lee Strasberg; Jessica Tandy &
    Hume Cronyn; Shirley Temple; Richard Threlkeld)

SUSANNA (William Goldman; William Shakespeare; William Styron)

SUSANNAH (Bob Edwards; Bob Vila)

SUSIE (Willie Nelson; Spencer Tracy; Mark Twain)

SUSY (Mark Twain)

SUZANNE (Diahann Carroll; Phyllis Diller; Joe Eszterhas; Dan Fouts; Bill Moyers; H. Ross Perot)

SYDNEY (Charles Dickens; Pat Kennedy; Sidney Poitier; Nicole & O.J. Simpson)

SYLVIA (Oscar Arias Sanchez; Carl Reiner)

T'ING (I.M. Pei)

TAHNEE (Raquel Welch)

TAINA (Jimmy Smits)

TALA (Burgess Meredith)

TALI (Annie Lennox; Bob Woodward)

TALIA (Davey Jones)

TALLULAH (Demi Moore & Bruce Willis)

TAM (Mia Farrow)

TAMARA (Bobby G. Rice; Peter Ustinov)

TAMBI (Oliver Tambo)

TAMELA (George Jones)

TAMLA (Smokey Robinson)

TAMMI (Bill Baker)

TAMMY (Tammy & Jim Bakker)

TAMMY SUE (Tammy & Jim Bakker)

TAMON (Teddy Pendergrass)

---

### GOOD THING FOR THE KID HE DIDN'T WORSHIP FLEA!

Garth Brooks named his daughter Taylor in honor of his idol James Taylor.

---

TAMSIN (Joan Plowright & Laurence Olivier)

TANISHA (Lawrence Taylor)

TANYA (Jack Anderson)

TARA (James Caan; June & Johnny Cash; Ted Koppel; Joan Collins & Anthony Newley; J.P. Getty II)

TARITA (Marlon Brando)

TARIN (Michael Bolton)

TARYN (Michael Bolton; Tyrone Power)

TATIA (Zak Starkey)

TATIANA (Caroline Kennedy & Ed Schlossberg; Elizabeth Clare Prophet; Diane Von Furstenberg)

TATUM (Joanna Moore & Ryan O'Neal)

TAYLOR (Garth Brooks; Rob E; Emilio Estevez; Don Mattingly; Bobby McFerrin; George Plimpton)

TAZAMISHA (Harry Edwards)

TEDDI (John Mellencamp)

TEDDI JO (John Mellencamp)

TERESA (Henry Cisneros; Larry Flynt; Jerry Garcia; George McGovern)

TERRI (Dick Vitale)

TERRY (James Brown; Doris Day; A.J. Foyt)

TESSA (Barry Humphries; Hans Namuth; Patricia Neal & Roald Dahl; Mary Robinson)

THEODORA (Patti Hansen & Keith Richards)

THERESA (Bill Bradley; Mark Hatfield; Danny Thomas; Earl Weaver)

THOMASINE (James Boggs)

TIA (Pat Morita)

TIFFANIE (Edward J. DeBartolo, Jr.)

TIFFANY (Adolph Caesar; Dave Dravecky; Kato Kaelin; Marla Maples & Donald Trump; Joe Pesci; John Thompson)

TIMOLIN (Nat King Cole)

TINA (Jack Anderson; Lloyd Bentsen; Bob Osborne; Frank Sinatra)

TINYA (Pete Seeger)

TISA (Maureen O'Sullivan & John Farrow)

TISHA (Teddy Pendergrass)

TONYA (Larry Flynt; David Rogers)

TORI (Tim Reid; Aaron Spelling)

TORY (Roger Tory Peterson)

TRACEE (Diana Ross)

TRACEY (Ron Brown; Sammy Davis, Jr.; Morton Downey, Jr.; Robert Loggia)

TRACY (Earl Anthony; Peter Benchley; Kris Kristofferson; Penny Marshall; Rick Nelson; Jean Simmons & Stewart Granger; Keenan Wynn)

TRICIA (Dennis Franz)

TRISHIA (Connie Stevens & Eddie Fisher)

TRIXIE (Jerry Garcia; Daman Wayans)

TROY (Lee Trevino)

TULIP (Tiny Tim)

TWINKA (Wayne Thiebaud)

TYLER (Molly & Roger Clinton; Barbara Gallagher & Perry Ellis; Robert Jarvik; Paul MacCready; Dana Plato; Pete Rose; Bobby Sherman)

TYNE (Hope Newell & James Daly)

TYSON (Nenah Cherry)

UNA (Nathaniel Hawthorne)

URSULA (Rudolph Serkin)

VAHE (Vartan Gregorian)

VALENTINA (Anthony Quinn)

VALERIE (Joe Cates; John D. Rockefeller)

VANESSA (Linda Ellerbee; Ray Harryhausen; Michael Redgrave; Roger Vadim & Jane Fonda; Joan Van Ark & John Marshall)

VARVARA (Rasputin)

VEEVA (Stuart Hamblen)

VENISHA (James Brown)

VERONICA (James Boswell; Dino De Laurentiis)

VICKEE (Vernon Jordan)

VICKIE (Pat Corley)

VICKY (Bud Abbott; Milton Berle)

VICTORIA (Corazon Aquino; Milton Berle; Britt Ekland & Peter Sellers; Douglas Fairbanks, Jr.; Frank Gifford; Hal Holbrook; Tommy Lee Jones; Pat Kennedy; Julia Lennon; Ray Milland; Otto Preminger; Ken Russell; Budd

Schulberg; Paul Shaffer; Roger Smith; Aaron Spelling; Les Trent; Queen Victoria; George Will)

VIOLET (Clifford Carlisle; Harold Ramis)

VIRGINIA (Galileo Galilei; Billy Graham; Ray Grey; Mario Puzo; Sissy Spacek & Jack Fisk; Giuseppe Verdi; John Warner)

VITA (Ramsey Lewis)

VITTORIA (Shelley Winters)

VYVYAN (Oscar Wilde)

WALLIS (Walter Annenberg)

WEATTA (Joe Frazier)

WENDY (Nolan Ryan; Dick Shawn; Dave Thomas; Jon Vickers; Larry Wilcox; Brian Wilson)

WHITNEY (Cindy & Steve Garvey; Cissy Houston)

WILLOW (Gabrielle Anwar)

WYNNE (Samuel Hayakawa)

WYNONNA (Naomi Judd)

YAMMA (James Brown)

YASMIN (Rita Hayworth & Aly Khan)

YASMINE (Arman)

YELENA (Mstislav Rostropovich)

YOHANCE (Dick Gregory)

YOLANDA (Coretta Scott & Martin Luther King, Jr.)

YOLANDE (Inge Hardison)

YUKIYOSHI (Seiji Ozawa)

YUVAL (Yitzhak Rabin)

YVONNE (Jamie Farr)

ZAHWA (Yasser Arafat)

ZAMIRA (Yehudi Menuhin)

ZARA (Princess Anne)

ZARINA (Zubin Mehta)

ZELDA (Robin Williams)

ZENANI (Nelson Mandela)

ZINZI (Nelson Mandela)

ZOE (Lisa Bonet & Lenny Kravitz; Laurie Metcalf; Gena Rowlands & John Cassavettes; Henry Winkler)

ZULEIKA (Charles Bronson)

---

### OR MAYBE "MELINDA LOU'S"
### DIDN'T FIT ON THE SIGN?

Dave Thomas, the founder of Wendy's, named his
business after his daughter, Wendy. Except that
Wendy's name was really Melinda Lou. "Melinda's
Biggy Fries?" I guess not.

---

## THE 81 MOST POPULAR
## CELEBRITY BABY NAMES

"Zephyr" (Robby Benson) and "Rebop" (Todd Rundgren)
notwithstanding, famous people do not seem to christen their
children with inordinately odd names. As you can see from
these lists, tradition and classic references abound. "Elizabeth" is the most popular girls name and "John" is the most
popular boys name. How retro, eh?

[NOTE: This ranking was compiled from all of the celebrity
baby names included in this volume (including those of historical personages *and* contemporary celebs). When more
than one name is listed at a specific ranking, this means that
these names were tied for popularity.]

# The Top 38 Celebrity Baby Names for Girls

1. Elizabeth
2. Mary
3. Susan
4. Jennifer
5. Sarah
6. Amy
7. Catherine; Emily
8. Barbara
9. Anne; Alexandra; Katherine
10. Lisa; Victoria
11. Kate; Margaret
12. Kelly; Laura
13. Christina; Julie; Linda
14. Maria; Melissa; Nancy
15. Jessica; Kathleen; Rachel
16. Jamie; Pamela; Patricia; Rebecca
17. Amanda; Andrea; Ashley; Jane
18. Anna; Robin; Stephanie

# The Top 43 Celebrity Baby Names for Boys

1. John
2. Michael
3. David
4. Christopher
5. James; Robert
6. William
7. Peter
8. Charles
9. Daniel; Mark
10. Matthew
11. Richard; Thomas
12. Jonathan
13. Andrew
14. Kevin
15. Anthony; Jack; Paul
16. Alexander
17. Joseph
18. Benjamin; Chris; Edward; Jeffrey
19. Eric; Steven; Timothy
20. Brian; Jason; Sean; Stephen
21. Adam; Patrick; Scott
22. Christian; George; Henry; Jamie; Nicholas
23. Billy
24. Jake

# THE MOST POPULAR BOYS & GIRLS NAMES IN ENGLAND & WALES OVER THE LAST SIX DECADES

| YEAR | BOY | GIRL |
|------|-----|------|
| 1925 | JOHN | JOAN |
| 1950 | DAVID | SUSAN |
| 1965 | PAUL | TRACEY |
| 1975 | STEPHEN | CLAIRE |
| 1981 | ANDREW | SARAH |

# Baby Names from the Movies

## BABY NAMES FROM MOVIE TITLES

This feature collects over 1,200 names from movie titles of the past fifty years or so, in separate boys and girls sections. This list is meant to be a fun look at possible baby names, and you will be surprised when looking over these monikers just how many movies use proper names in their titles.

A recent trend has been to use last names as first names. Thus, I was careful to include names from movie titles that are not technically genuine first names but upon reflection might work nicely as one.

If a name appeared *in* a movie title, the proper name, followed by the film title in parentheses, is supplied:

ADRIAN (*The List of Adrian Messenger*)
ANNIE (*Annie Hall*)
BOB (*Bob Roberts*)
BRIDEY (*The Search for Bridey Murphy*)
CONAN (*Conan the Barbarian*)
EVE (*All About Eve*)
HARRY (*When Harry Met Sally . . .*)
ROMEO (*Romeo Is Bleeding*)
SOPHIE (*Sophie's Choice*)

When a name appears by itself, it means that that is the complete name of the movie:

LAURA
ROCKY
RUBY
SIMON
ALFIE
CARRIE
FRANCES
GIGI

So warm up the VCR, sit back with *The Celebrity Baby Name Book,* and find your little one a name that is guaranteed to look good on a marquee—since it's probably already been there!

[A NOTE FOR RENTERS: All of the movie titles listed in this section were drawn from *The VideoHound's Golden Movie Retriever,* 1994 edition. This gigantic book (1,500 pages and 22,000 movies reviewed) bills itself as "The Complete Guide to Movies on Videocassette and Laserdisc" so every movie mentioned *is* definitely available on video. Some of the more obscure titles might not be in your local video store, but since they *are* all in print, you might want to either have your video people order it for you, or check out one of the mail order video rental services listed in many of the video guides published every year. Of course, you don't need to actually have seen a movie to use its title for your name selection, but it's probably a good idea to check out the type of character you're naming you're bouncing bundle of joy after! You know, just in case the title character is a diehard Republican and you've voted Democrat all your life!

## BOYS NAMES FROM MOVIE TITLES

AARON (*Aaron Loves Angela*)
ABBOTT (*Hey Abbott!*)
ABE (*Abe Lincoln in Illinois*)

ABNER (*Li'l Abner*)
ABRAHAM (*Abraham Lincoln*)
ACE (*Ace Crawford, Private Eye*)
ACHMED (*The Adventures of Prince Achmed*)
ADAM
ADRIAN (*The List of Adrian Messenger*)
AKIRA
AL (*Al Capone*)
ALADDIN
ALAN (*Alan & Naomi*)
ALBERT (*The Fat Albert Christmas Special*)
ALEX (*Alex in Wonderland*)
ALEXANDER (*Alexander Nevesky*)
ALFIE
ALFRED (*The Legend of Alfred Packer*)
ALFREDO (*Bring Me the Head of Alfredo Garcia*)
ALI (*Ali: Fear Eats the Soul*)
ALLADIN
ALLAN (*Allan Quartermain and the Lost City of Gold*)
ALVAREZ (*Alvarez Kelly*)
ALVIN (*Alvin Purple*)
AMADEUS
AMOS (*Amos and Andrew*)
ANDERSON (*The Anderson Tapes*)
ANDRÉ (*My Dinner with André*)
ANDREI (*Andrei Rubiev*)
ANDREW (*Amos and Andrew*)
ANDROCLES (*Androcles and the Lion*)
ANDY (*Andy Warhol's Bad*)
ANGELO (*Angelo My Love*)
ANTHONY (*Anthony Adverse*)
ANTOINE (*Mon Oncle Antoine*)
ANTONY (*Antony and Cleopatra*)
APARAJITO
ARCHER (*Archer: The Fugitive from the Emprie*)
ARCHIBALDO (*The Criminal Life of Archibaldo de la Cruz*)

ARNE (*The Treasure of Arne*)
ARNOLD
ARTHUR
ASTERIX (*Asterix vs. Caesar*)
ATOR (*Ator the Fighting Eagle*)
AUGUSTINE (*Augustine of Hippo*)
BABA
BABAR (*Babar: The Movie*)
BABE (*The Babe Ruth Story*)
BABU (*Hey, Babu Riba*)
BALBOA
BANDINI (*Wait Until Spring, Bandini*)
BARABBAS
BARNABY (*Barnaby and Me*)
BARNES (*Burn 'Em Up Barnes*)
BARNEY (*The Haunting of Barney Palmer*)
BARNUM
BARRY (*Barry Lyndon*)
BARTLEBY
BARTON (*Barton Fink*)
BASH (*Liberty & Bash*)
BAXTER
BEAU (*Beau Brummel*)
BECKET
BEETHOVEN
BELA (*Bela Lugosi Meets a Brooklyn Gorilla*)
BELIZAIRE (*Belizaire the Cajun*)
BELLAMY
BEN
BENJAMIN (*Private Benjamin*)
BENJI
BENNY (*Benny & Joon*)
BERNARD (*Bernard and the Genie*)
BERNHARD (*The Trial of Bernhard Goetz*)
BERNIE (*A Weekend at Bernie's*)
BERT (*Bert Rigby, You're a Fool*)
BETHUNE

BILL

BILLY (*Billy Bathgate*)

BIRD

BIRDIE (*Bye, Bye, Birdie*)

BIRDY

BLACKIE (*The Return of Boston Blackie*)

BLAISE (*Blaise Pascal*)

BLAKE (*Blake's Seven*)

BLUE (*Buckeye and Blue*)

BLUME (*Blume in Love*)

BOB (*Bob Roberts*)

BOBBY (*Aloha, Bobby and Rose*)

BOBO

BOGIE

BONNER (*Junior Bonner*)

BOOTS (*Boots Malone*)

BORIS (*Boris and Natasha: The Movie*)

BOUDU (*Boudu Saved from Drowning*)

BOURNE (*The Bourne Identity*)

BRADDOCK (*Braddock: Missing in Action 3*)

BRADFORD (*Ex-Mrs. Bradford*)

BRADY (*Brady's Escape*)

BRAM (*Bram Stocker's Dracula*)

BRANNIGAN

BRENNAN (*That Brennan Girl*)

BREWSTER (*Brewster McCloud*)

BRIAN (*Brian's Song*)

BRONSON (*Bronson Lee, Champion*)

BRUBAKER

BRUCE (*Dragon: The Bruce Lee Story*)

BUCK (*Uncle Buck*)

BUCKEYE (*Buckeye and Blue*)

BUD (*Bud and Lou*)

BUDDY (*The Buddy System*)

BUFORD (*Buford's Beach Bunnies*)

BUGSY

BULL (*Bull Durham*)

BUNYON (*Battling Bunyon*)
BURGESS (*Burgess, Philby, and MacLean: Spy Scandal of the Century*)
BURKE (*Burke & Wills*)
BUSBY (*The Busby Berkeley Disc*)
BUSTER
BUTCH (*Butch Cassidy and the Sundance Kid*)
CABLE (*The Ballad of Cable Hogue*)
CABO (*Cabo Blanca*)
CAESAR (*Asterix vs. Caesar*)
CAHILL (*Cahill: United States Marshal*)
CAIN (*Cain's Cutthroats*)
CAL
CALIGARI (*Caligari's Cure*)
CALLAHAN
CAMERON (*Cameron's Closet*)
CANDIDE
CAPONE
CARAVAGGIO
CARLTON (*Carlton Browne at the F.O.*)
CARNY
CARTOUCHE
CARUSO (*The Great Caruso*)
CASEY (*The Return of Casey Jones*)
CASH (*Tango and Cash*)
CASIMIR (*Casimir the Great*)
CASPER (*Casper the Friendly Ghost*)
CASS
CASSIDY (*Hopalong Cassidy*)
CASTILE (*Hawk and Castile*)
CESAR
CHANDU (*Chandu the Magician*)
CHANG (*Chang: A Drama of the Wilderness*)
CHAPAYEV
CHAPLIN
CHARLES (*Charles & Diana: A Palace Divided*)
CHARLEY (*Charley and the Angel*)

CHARLIE (*A Charlie Brown Christmas*)
CHARLY
CHARRO (*Charro!*)
CHATO (*Chato's Land*)
CHEECH (*Cheech and Chong's Up in Smoke*)

---

### NAMESAKE DEPARTMENT

Ron Howard and his wife Cheryl always give their children a middle name for the place (usually a hotel like The Carlyle) where the kids were conceived.

---

CHEYENNE (*Cheyenne Takes Over*)
CHINO
CHISUM
CHONG (*Cheech and Chong's Up in Smoke*)
CHRISTIAN (*Christian the Lion*)
CHRISTOPHER (*Christopher Columbus*)
CHUCK (*Chuck Berry: Hail! Hail! Rock 'n' Roll*)
CHUKA
CID (*El Cid*)
CIMARRON
CLARENCE
CLARK (*Clark & McCullough*)
CLAUDIUS (*I, Claudius*)
CLIFFORD
CLYDE (*Bonnie & Clyde*)
CODY
COFFY
COHEN (*Cohen and Tate*)
COLOSSUS (*Colossus: The Forbin Project*)
COLTER (*Kid Colter*)
COLUMBUS (*Goodbye Columbus*)
CONAGHER

CONAN (*Conan the Barbarian*)
CONRACK
COOGAN (*Coogan's Bluff*)
CORIOLANUS (*Coriolanus, Man without a Country*)

---

**NICKNAME DEPARTMENT**

Singer Sarah Vaughn's nickname to her closest
friends was "Sassy."

---

CORLEONE
CORREGIDOR
CORSAIR
COSMO (*Cosmo Jones, Crime Smasher*)
COTTER
COURTNEY (*The Courtney Affair*)
CRAIG (*Craig's Wife*)
CRESPI (*The Crime of Dr. Crespi*)
CROMWELL
CRUSOE
CUJO
CURLEY
CUSTER (*Crazy Horse and Custer: The Untold Story*)
CUTTER (*Cutter's Way*)
CYRANO (*Cyrano de Bergerac*)
DAIN (*The Dain Curse*)
DAKOTA
DAMIEN (*Damien: Omen 2*)
DAN (*The Best of Dan Aykroyd*)
DANIEL
DANNY (*Broadway Danny Rose*)
DANTE (*Dante's Inferno*)
DANTON
DANZON
DARBY (*Darby O'Gill & the Little People*)

DARYL (*D.A.R.Y.L.*)
DAVID
DaVINCI (*DaVinci's War*)
DAVY (*Davy Crockett, King of the Wild Frontier*)
DAYTON (*Dayton's Devils*)
DELANCEY (*Crossing Delancey*)
DEMETRIUS (*Demetrius and the Gladiators*)
DEMPSEY
DENNIS (*Dennis the Menace*)
DERSU (*Dersu Uzala*)
DESI (*Lucy and Desi: Before the Laughter*)
DESTRY (*Destry Rides Again*)
DEVLIN
DICK (*Dick Tracy*)
DIGBY (*Digby, the Biggest Dog in the World*)
DILLINGER
DINO
DISRAELI
DJANGO
DOMINIC (*Requiem for Dominic*)
DOMINICK (*Dominick & Eugene*)
DOMINO
DON (*The Adventures of Don Juan*)
DONALD (*The Test of Donald Norton*)
DONOVAN (*Donovan's Brain*)
DORIAN (*The Picture of Dorian Gray*)
DORRIT (*Little Dorrit, Film 1: Nobody's Fault*)
DRAKE (*The Drake Case*)
DRAW (*The Return of Draw Egan*)
DUDDY (*The Apprenticeship of Duddy Kravitz*)
DUKE (*Duke: The Films of John Wayne*)
DUMBO
DUNDEE (*Crocodile Dundee*)
DUSTY
DUTCH
EARL (*Cornbread, Earl & Me*)
ED (*Rubin & Ed*)

EDDIE (*Homer and Eddie*)
EDDY (*The Eddy Duchin Story*)
EDGAR (*The Loves of Edgar Allan Poe*)
EDISON (*Edison the Man*)
EDWARD (*Edward Scissorhands*)
EIGER (*The Eiger Sanction*)
ELFEGO (*The Nine Lives of Elfego Baca*)
ELI (*Eli Eli*)
ELLIOTT (*Calling Wild Bill Elliott*)
ELMER (*Elmer Gantry*)
ELMO (*St. Elmo's Fire*)
ELVIS (*Elvis and Me*)
EMANON
EMIL (*Emil and the Detectives*)
EMILE (*The Life of Emile Zola*)
EMILIANO (*Emiliano Zapata*)
EMILIO (*Emilio Varela vs. Camelia La Texana*)
EMMANUEL (*Mr. Emmanuel*)
ERIC
ERIK
ERNEST (*Wrestling Ernest Hemingway*)
ERNESTO
ERNIE (*Ernie Kovacs: Between the Laughter*)
ESSEX (*The Private Lives of Elizabeth & Essex*)
ETHAN (*Ethan Frome*)
EUBIE (*Eubie!*)
EUGENE (*Dominick & Eugene*)
EVEL (*Evel Knievel*)
FABIAN (*The Adventures of Captain Fabian*)
FARGO (*Fargo Express*)
FEDERICO (*Ciao Federico! Fellini Directs Satyricon*)
FELIX (*Felix the Cat: The Movie*)
FERNANDEL (*Fernandel the Dressmaker*)
FERNANDO (*The Bells of San Fernando*)
FERRIS (*Ferris Bueller's Day Off*)
FINIAN (*Finian's Rainbow*)
FINNEGAN (*Finnegan Begin Again*)

FITZCARRALDO
FLASH (*Flash & Firecat*)
FLETCH
FLETCHER (*The Ghost of Fletcher Ridge*)
FLINT (*In Like Flint*)
FORBIN (*Colossus: The Forbin Project*)
FORD (*The Adventures of Ford Fairlane*)
FORREST (*Forrest Gump*)
FOSTER (*Friday Foster*)
FOX (*Fox and His Friends*)
FRANCIS (*The Flowers of St. Francis*)
FRANCOIS (*Vincent, Francois, Paul and the Others*)
FRANK (*The Adventures of Frank and Jesse James*)
FRANKIE (*Frankie and Johnny*)
FRANKLIN (*Eleanor & Franklin*)
FRANZ
FRASIER (*Frasier the Sensuous Lion*)
FRED (*Ginger & Fred*)
FREDDY (*Freddy's Dead: The Final Nightmare*)
FREDERICK (*Ten North Frederick*)
FREEBIE (*Freebie and the Bean*)
FRENCHIE (*The Legend of Frenchie King*)
FRITZ (*Fritz the Cat*)
FROSTY (*Frosty the Snowman*)
FU (*The Fiendish Plot of Dr. Fu Manchu*)
GABBO (*The Great Gabbo*)
GABRIEL (*Gabriel Over the White House*)
GABY (*Gaby: A True Story*)
GALAHAD (*Kid Galahad*)
GALLEGHER (*Let'er Go Gallegher*)
GALYON
GAMERA (*Gamera, the Invincible*)
GANDHI
GARFIELD (*Here Comes Garfield*)
GARP (*The World According to Garp*)
GARRINGO
GATSBY (*The Great Gatsby*)

GEMINI (*Happy Birthday, Gemini*)
GENE (*The Gene Krupa Story*)
GEORGE (*The George McKenna Story*)
GERONIMO
GERVAISE
GIDEON (*Gideon's Trumpet*)
GILBERT (*What's Eating Gilbert Grape?*)
GILDERSLEEVE (*The Great Gildersleeve*)
GIORGIO (*Yes, Giorgio*)
GLEN (*Glen or Glenda*)
GLENN (*The Glenn Miller Story*)
GODFREY (*My Man Godfrey*)
GOLIATH (*Goliath Awaits*)
GORE (*Gore Vidal's Billy the Kid*)
GREGORIO (*The Ballad of Gregorio Cortez*)
GREGORY (*Gregory's Girl*)
GRIFFIN (*Griffin and Phoenix: A Love Story*)
GRIZZLY (*The Life & Times of Grizzly Adams*)
GULLIVER
GUS
HADLEY (*Hadley's Rebellion*)
HAMLET
HAMMETT
HAMSIN
HANK (*Final Shot: The Hank Gathers Story*)
HANS (*Hans Brinker*)
HANSEL (*Hansel and Gretel*)
HARE (*The Horrors of Burke & Hare*)
HARLEY
HAROLD (*Harold and Maude*)
HARPER
HARRY (*When Harry Met Sally . . .*)
HARVEY
HAWK (*Hawk and Castile*)
HAWKEN (*Hawken's Breed*)
HAWKEYE
HAWTHORNE (*Hawthorne of the USA*)

HAYES (*Nate and Hayes*)
HECTOR (*Hector's Bunyip*)
HENNESSY
HENRY (*Regarding Henry*)
HERBIE (*Herbie Goes Bananas*)
HERCULES
HEROD (*Herod the Great*)
HOBSON (*Hobson's Choice*)
HOMER (*Homer and Eddie*)
HOOCH
HOOPER
HOPPITY (*Hoppity Goes to Town*)
HOPPY (*Hoppy Serves a Writ*)
HORATIO (*Captain Horatio Hornblower*)
HORSE (*A Man Called Horse*)
HOUDINI
HOWARD (*Howard's End*)
HUCK (*The Adventures of Huck Finn*)
HUCKLEBERRY (*The Adventures of Huckleberry Finn*)
HUD
HUEY (*Baby Huey The Baby Giant*)
HUGH (*Hugh Hefner: Once Upon a Time*)
HUGO (*Hugo the Hippo*)
HUNTER
IAN (*Spymaker: The Secret Life of Ian Fleming*)
ICARUS (*Codename: Icarus*)
ICHABOD (*The Adventures of Ichabod and Mr. Toad*)
IGOR (*Igor & the Lunatics*)
IKE
IKIRU
INDIANA (*Indiana Jones and the Temple of Doom*)
INDIO
IVAN (*Ivan the Terrible*)
IVANHOE
IVES (*St. Ives*)
IZZY (*Izzy & Moe*)

**ALOHA!**

Actor Keanu Reeves's first name means "cool breeze over the mountains" in Hawaiian. (His father is from Hawaii.)

JACK (*Jack the Bear*)
JACKIE (*The Jackie Robinson Story*)
JACKO (*Jacko & Lise*)
JACKSON (*Action Jackson*)
JACOB (*Jacob's Ladder*)
JAKE (*Jake Speed*)
JAMES (*James Dean*)
JAMON (*Jamon, Jamon*)
JANUARY (*Captain January*)
JASON (*Jason Goes to Hell: The Final Friday*)
JED (*Sonny and Jed*)
JEDEDIAH (*The Legend of Jedehiah Carver*)
JEEVES (*Jeeves & Wooster: Jeeve's Arrival*)
JEREMIAH (*Jeremiah Johnson*)
JERICHO (*The Jericho Mile*)
JESSE
JIM (*Bad Jim*)
JIMMY (*Come Back to the Five & Dime, Jimmy Dean, Jimmy Dean*)
JO JO (*Jo Jo Dancer, Your Life Is Calling*)
JOB (*The Revolt of Job*)
JOCK (*Jock Peterson*)
JOE
JOEL (*The Possession of Joel Delaney*)
JOEY
JOHN (*John & Yoko: A Love Story*)
JOHNNIE (*Johnnie Gibson, F.B.I.*)
JOHNNY (*Frankie and Johnny*)

JONAH (*Jonah Who Will Be 25 in the Year 2000*)
JONATHAN (*Jonathan Livingston Seagull*)
JORY
JOSEPH (*Joseph Andrews*)
JOSEY (*The Outlaw Josey Wales*)
JOSH (*Josh and S.A.M.*)
JOSHUA (*Joshua Then and Now*)
JUAN (*The Adventures of Don Juan*)
JUAREZ
JUBAL
JUBILEE
JUD
JUDEX
JULES (*Jules and Jim*)
JULIUS (*Julius Caesar*)
JUNIOR (*Junior Bonner*)
JUNO (*Juno and the Paycock*)
KAGEMUSHA
KELLY (*Alvarez Kelly*)
KEMEK
KENNY (*Kenny Rogers as the Gambler*)
KEROUAC
KHAN (*Star Trek 2: The Wrath of Khan*)
KIPPS
KIT (*Kit Carson*)
KLEIN (*Mr. Klein*)
KIT (*The Adventures of Kit Carson*)
KNUTE (*Knute Rockne: All American*)
KOHLBERG
KOJIRO
KOLBERG
KONRAD
KOROSHI
KOTCH
KRONOS (*Captain Kronos: Vampire Hunter*)
KYRIL (*Codename Kyril*)
LAFAYETTE (*Lafayette Escadrille*)

LAI SHI (*Lai Shi: China's Last Eunuch*)
LANCELOT (*Sword of Lancelot*)
LARRY (*Dirty Mary Crazy Larry*)
LASSITER
LAWRENCE (*Lawrence of Arabia*)
LEE (*The Fate of Lee Khan*)
LENNY
LEO (*Cleo/Leo*)
LEON (*The Flustered Comedy of Leon Errol*)
LEONARD (*Leonard, Part 6*)
LEPKE
LEROY (*The Devil & Leroy Basset*)
LES (*Les Patterson Saves the World*)
LIBERTY (*The Man Who Shot Liberty Valance*)
LOGAN (*Logan's Run*)
LORENZO (*Lorenzo's Oil*)
LOU (*Bud and Lou*)
LOUIS (*Louis Armstrong: Chicago Style*)
LOYOLA (*Loyola, the Soldier Saint*)
LUCAS
LUKE (*Cool Hand Luke*)
LUPO
LUTHER
MAC
MACARIO
MacARTHUR
MACBETH
MACK (*Mack & Carole*)
MacKENNA (*MacKenna's Gold*)
MacLEAN (*Burgess, Philby, and MacLean: Spy Scandal of the Century*)
MADIGAN
MADO
MAGEE (*Magee and the Lady*)
MAHLER
MAHONEY (*Hard-Boiled Mahoney*)
MALCOLM (*Malcolm X*)

MALONE
MANDELA
MANON
MARCEL (*Edith & Marcel*)
MARCO
MARIO (*Super Mario Brothers*)
MARIUS
MARJO
MARK (*The Adventures of Mark Twain*)
MARLON (*Marlon Brando*)
MARLOWE
MARTIN
MARTY
MARVIN (*The King of Marvin Gardens*)
MASON (*Mason of the Mounted*)
MATTHEW (*The Gospel According to St. Matthew*)
MAURICE
MAX (*The Devil & Max Devlin*)
MAXIMILLIAN (*The Outside Chance of Maximillian Glick*)
MAYALUNTA
McCABE (*McCabe & Mrs. Miller*)
McCONNELL (*The McConnell Story*)
McCULLOUGH (*Clark & McCullough*)
McGINTY (*The Great McGinty*)
McGONAGALL (*The Great McGonagall*)
McKENNA (*The Challenge of McKenna*)
McLINTOCK
McQUADE (*Lone Wolf McQuade*)
MEL (*Salute to Mel Blanc*)
MELVIN (*I Love Melvin*)
MERRILL (*Merrill's Marauders*)
MICHAEL (*My Michael*)
MICKEY (*Mickey the Great*)
MIDAS (*The Midas Touch*)
MIGUEL (*And Now Miguel*)
MIKE (*Fallen Champ: The Untold Story of Mike Tyson*)
MIKEY (*Life with Mikey*)

MILLER (*Miller's Crossing*)
MILO (*The Adventures of Milo & Otis*)
MISHIMA (*Mishima: A Life in Four Chapters*)
MITCH (*Samaritan: The Mitch Snyder Story*)
MITCHELL
MOE (*Izzy & Moe*)
MOHAMMED (*Mohammed: Messenger of God*)
MONTE (*Monte Walsh*)
MORGAN (*Morgan Stewart's Coming Home*)
MOSBY (*Mosby's Marauders*)
MOSES
MOZART (*Forever Mozart*)
MURPH (*Murph the Surf*)
MURPHY (*Murphy's Romance*)
MURROW
NAPOLEON
NARCISSUS (*Black Narcissus*)
NATE (*Nate and Hayes*)
NED (*Ned Kelly*)
NEMO (*Little Nemo: Adventures in Slumberland*)
NEPTUNE (*Neptune's Daughter*)
NEVADA (*Nevada Smith*)
NEWMAN (*Captain Newman, M.D.*)
NICHOLAS (*Nicholas Nickleby*)
NICK (*Nick Knight*)
NICKY (*Mikey & Nicky*)
NIKITA (*Little Nikita*)
NOAH (*The Last Flight of Noah's Ark*)
NOEL (*Noel's Fantastic Trip*)
NORMAN (*Norman Loves Rose*)
OLIVIER (*Olivier, Olivier*)
OLLIE (*Stan Without Ollie* [series])
OMAR (*Omar Khayyam*)
ORPHEUS (*Black Orpheus*)
OSCAR
OTELLO
OTHELLO

OTIS (*The Adventures of Milo & Otis*)
OZZIE (*The Adventures of Ozzie & Harriet*)
PACO
PADDY
PANCHO (*Pancho Villa*)
PAPILLON
PARKER
PATHER (*Pather Panchali*)
PAUL (*Paul and Michelle*)
PECK (*Peck's Bad Boy*)
PEE-WEE (*Big Top Pee-Wee*)
PELLE (*Pelle the Conqueror*)
PENN (*The Courageous Mr. Penn*)
PEPE (*Pepe Le Moko*)
PERRY (*Perry Mason Returns*)
PETE (*For Pete's Sake*)
PETER (*Peter Pan*)
PHEDRE
PHIL (*Willie & Phil*)
PHILBY (*Burgess, Philby, and MacLean: Spy Scandal of the Century*)
PHILIP (*The Last of Philip Banter*)
PICASSO (*The Adventures of Picasso*)
PICCONE (*Where's Piccone*)
PIPPI (*Pippi Longstocking*)
PIPPIN
PIXOTE
POPI
PORTNOY (*Portnoy's Complaint*)
PROSPERO (*Prospero's Books*)
PULVER (*Ensign Pulver*)
PUTNEY (*Putney Swope*)
QUERELLE
QUIGLEY
QUILLER (*The Quiller Memorandum*)
QUINN (*The Mighty Quinn*)
RAFFERTY (*Rafferty & the Gold Dust Twins*)

RAMBO (*Rambo: First Blood, Part 2*)
RANDOLPH (*The Unnameable 2: The Statement of Randolph Carter*)
RANDY (*Randy Rides Alone*)
RANSON (*Ranson's Folly*)
RAOUL (*Eating Raoul*)
RAUL (*Fury to Freedom: The Life Story of Raul Ries*)
RAY (*Heart of a Champion: The Ray Mancini Story*)
RAYMOND (*The Execution of Raymond Graham*)
REBA (*Come Back Little Reba*)
RED (*Big Red*)
REGGIE (*Reggie Mixes In*)
REGINALD (*The Fall and Rise of Reginald Perrin*)
REILLY (*Reilly: Ace of Spies*)
REMBRANDT
REMO (*Remo Williams: The Adventure Begins*)
RENFREW (*Renfrew of the Royal Mounted*)
RENO (*Reno and the Doc*)
REUBEN (*Reuben, Reuben*)
REX (*The Adventures of Rex & Rinty*)
RHODES
RICCO
RICH (*Rich in Love*)
RICHARD (*Richard III*)
RICKY (*Ricky 1*)
RICHIE (*The Death of Richie*)
RIFIFI
RIKYU
RIPLEY (*Ripley's Believe It or Not*)
ROB (*Rob Roy—The Highland Rogue*)
ROBBY
ROBERT (*Robert et Robert*)
ROBIN (*Robin Hood: Prince of Thieves*)
ROBINSON (*Robinson Crusoe*)
ROCCO (*Rocco and His Brothers*)
ROCKY
RODAN

RODRIGO (*Rodrigo D.: No Future*)
ROGER (*Who Framed Roger Rabbit?*)
ROLAND (*Roland the Mighty*)
ROMEO (*Romeo Is Bleeding*)
ROMERO
RON (*Captain Ron*)
RONALD (*Bad Ronald*)
ROOSTER (*Rooster Cogburn*)
ROSS (*Glengarry Glen Ross*)
ROY (*Judge Roy Bean*)
RUBIN (*Rubin & Ed*)
RUBY
RUDOLPH (*Rudolph the Red-Nosed Reindeer*)
RUDYARD (*Rudyard Kipling's Classic Stories*)
RUPERT (*The Great Rupert*)
RYAN (*Ryan's Daughter*)
SACCO (*Sacco & Vanzetti*)
SALLAH
SAM (*Play It Again, Sam*)
SAMMY (*Sammy & Rosie Get Laid*)
SAMSON
SANSHO (*Sansho the Bailiff*)
SANTEE
SANTINI (*The Great Santini*)
SATCHEL (*Don't Look Back: The Story of Leroy "Satchel" Paige*)
SAUL (*Saul and David*)
SCARAMOUCHE
SCARLETT (*Captain Scarlett*)
SCORPIO
SCOTT (*Scott of the Antarctic*)
SEBASTIAN
SEXTON (*Meet Sexton Blake*)
SHADEY
SHANE
SHARKY (*Sharky's Machine*)
SHERLOCK (*The Adventures of Sherlock Holmes*)

SID (*Sid & Nancy*)
SIDNEY (*Sidney Sheldon's Bloodline*)
SIEGFRIED
SIGMUND (*The Secret Diary of Sigmund Freud*)
SILAS (*Silas Marner*)
SIMBA
SIMON
SIMPSON (*Sudie & Simpson*)
SINBAD (*The Adventures of Sinbad*)
SIROCCO
SLADE (*Kill Slade*)
SLATE (*Slate, Wyn & Me*)
SLEDGE (*A Man Called Sledge*)
SLOANE
SMOKEY (*Smokey and the Bandit*)
SNUFFY (*Snuffy Smith, Yard Bird*)
SOLOMON (*King Solomon's Mines*)
SOMMERSBY
SONNY (*The Education of Sonny Carson*)
SPALDING (*Spalding Gray: Terrors of Pleasure*)
SPIKE (*Spike of Bensonhurst*)
SPOCK (*Star Trek 3: The Search for Spock*)
SPRAGGUE
STAN (*Stan Without Ollie* [series])
STANLEY (*Stanley and Iris*)
STEPHEN (*The Crimes of Stephen Hawke*)
STEVE (*Steve Martin Live*)
STIGGS (*O.C. and Stiggs*)
STRIKER
STROSZEK
STRYKER
STUCKEY (*Stuckey's Last Stand*)
SUNDANCE (*Butch Cassidy and the Sundance Kid*)
SWEENEY (*Sweeney Todd: The Demon Barber of Fleet
Street*)
SWIFTY
SYLVESTER

TAFFIN
TAGGET
TANGO (*Tango and Cash*)
TARAS (*Taras Bulba*)
TARO (*Taro, the Dragon Boy*)
TARTU (*The Adventures of Tartu*)
TARTUFFE
TARZAN (The *Tarzan* series)
TATE (*Cohen and Tate*)
TCHAO (*Tchao Pantin*)
TED (*Bob & Carol & Ted & Alice*)
TEDDY (*Indomitable Teddy Roosevelt*)
TENNESSEE (*The Further Adventures of Tennessee Buck*)
TERRY (*The Terry Fox Story*)
TEVYE
TEX
THARUS (*Tharus Son of Attila*)
THEO (*Vincent & Theo*)
THOMAS (*Doubting Thomas*)
THOR (*Thor and the Amazon Women*)
TIGE (*Marvin & Tige*)
TIM
TIMOTHY (*Timothy and the Angel*)
TOBY (*Toby Tyler*)
TOM (*Tom Jones*)
TOMMY
TONI
TONIO (*Tonio Kroger*)
TONY (*Tony Rome*)
TOPPER
TRILBY
TRINIAN (*Blue Murder at St. Trinian's*)
TROILUS (*Troilus & Cressida*)
TROMBA (*Tromba, the Tiger Man*)
TUCKER (*Tucker: The Man and His Dream*)
TURNER (*Turner and Hooch*)
TURPIN (*The Eyes of Turpin Are Upon You!*)

UBU (*Ubu and the Great Gidouille*)
ULYSSES
ULZANA (*Ulzana's Raid*)
UMBERTO (*Umberto D*)
UTU
VALDEZ (*Valdez is Coming*)
VALENTINO (*The Legend of Valentino*)
VALMONT

---

### IMAGINE IF HIS NAME HAD BEEN FLOYD

The Academy Award statue is called an Oscar
because one day Margaret Herrick, the Academy of
Motion Picture Arts and Sciences librarian,
remarked that the statue looked like her uncle
Oscar—and the name stuck.

---

### BROOKES OF THE FORREST

Actor Forrest Tucker gave his two daughters Pamela
and Cynthia the same middle name: Brooke.

---

VANZETTI (*Sacco & Vanzetti*)
VERNE (*Verne Miller*)
VERNON (*The Story of Vernon and Irene Castle*)
VERONICO (*Veronico Cruz*)
VIC (*The Gospel According to Vic*)
VICTOR (*Victor/Victoria*)
VINCENT (*Monsieur Vincent*)
VINNY (*My Cousin Vinny*)
VITELLONI (*I, Vitelloni*)
VOLPONE

WALDO (*The Great Waldo Pepper*)
WALTER (*Harry & Walter Go to New York*)
WAYNE (*Wayne's World*)
WILBY (*The Wilby Conspiracy*)
WILE (*The Road Runner vs. Wile E. Coyote: Classic Chase*)
WILL (*Will Penny*)
WILLARD
WILLIAM (*The Greed of William Hart*)
WILLIE (*Tell Them Willie Boy Is Here*)
WILLS (*Burke & Wills*)
WILLY ( *Free Willy*)
WINDOM (*Windom's Way*)
WINSTON (*Young Winston*)
WITHNAIL (*Withnail and I*)
WONG (*To Wong Foo, Thanks for Everything, Julie Newmar*)
WOOSTER (*Jeeves & Wooster: Jeeves' Arrival*)
WYN (*Slate, Wyn & Me*)
YANCO
YENTL
YOR (*Yor, the Hunter from the Future*)
YORGA (*Count Yorga, Vampire*)
YOTSUYA (*The Ghost of Yotsuya*)
YURI (*Yuri Nosenko, KGB*)
ZACHARY (*The Resurrection of Zachary Wheeler*)
ZACHARIAH
ZANDY (*Zandy's Bride*)
ZIEGFIELD (*The Great Ziegfield*)
ZOLTAN (*Zoltan . . . Hound of Dracula*)
ZONTAR (*Zontar, the Thing from Venus*)
ZORBA (*Zorba the Greek*)
ZORRO (*The Mark of Zorro*)

## GIRLS NAMES FROM MOVIE TITLES

ABIGAIL (*Abigail's Party*)
ADELE (*The Story of Adele H.*)
ADELINE (*Sweet Adeline*)
AELITA (*Aelita: Queen of Mars*)
AGATHA
AGGIE (*Aggie Appleby, Maker of Men*)
AGNES (*Agnes of God*)
AIMEE (*The Disappearance of Aimee*)
ALEXA (*Alexa: A Prostitute's Own Story*)
ALEXANDRA (*Nicholas and Alexandra*)
ALEXINA (*The Mystery of Alexina*)
ALICE
ALISON (*Alison's Birthday*)
ALLISON (*The Abduction of Allison Tate*)
AMY
ANASTASIA
ANGEL
ANGELA
ANGELE
ANGIE
ANITA (*Anita, Dances of Vice*)
ANN (*The Ann Jillian Story*)
ANNA
ANNABEL (*The Affairs of Annabel*)
ANNE (*Anne of Green Gables*)
ANNIE (*Annie Hall*)
ANTONIA (*Antonia and Jane*)
ARIEL
ATALIA
ATHENA
AUDREY (*Audrey Rose*)
AZARIA (*Who Killed Baby Azaria?*)
BABETTE (*Babette's Feast*)
BAMBI

BARBARA (*Major Barbara*)
BARBARELLA
BATHSHEBA (*David and Bathsheba*)
BEATRICE
BEATRIX (*Tales of Beatrix Potter*)
BEBE (*Bebe's Kids*)
BECKY (*Becky Sharp*)
BELLE (*The Belle Starr Story*)
BELLISSIMA
BERNADETTE
BERNICE (*Bernice Bobs Her Hair*)
BERTHA (*Boxcar Bertha*)
BESS (*The Adventures of Gallant Bess*)
BETSY (*Betsy's Wedding*)
BETTY (*Betty Boop*)
BETTY LOU (*The Gun in Betty Lou's Handbag*)
BEULAH (*Beulah Land*)
BILLIE
BIRGITT (*Birgit Haas Must Be Killed*)
BLAZE
BOBBIE (*Bobbie Jo and the Outlaw*)
BOM (*Pepi, Luci, Bom and Other Girls on the Heap*)
BONNIE (*Bonnie & Clyde*)
BRENDA (*Brenda Starr*)
BRIDEY (*The Search for Bridey Murphy*)
BRIGITTE (*Dear Brigitte*)
BUFFY (*Buffy the Vampire Slayer*)
CABIRIA
CADDIE
CALLIE (*Callie and Son*)
CAMELIA
CAMILA
CAMILLE (*Camille Claudel*)
CAMORRA (*Camorra: The Naples Connection*)
CANDIDE
CANDRA (*Awakening of Candra*)
CARMELA (*Ay, Carmela!*)

CARMEN
CARMILLA
CAROL (*Bob & Carol & Ted & Alice*)
CAROLE (*Mack & Carole*)
CAROLINE (*Caroline?*)
CARRIE
CASSANDRA
CASSIE
CATHERINE (*Catherine & Co.*)
CATHY (*Cathy's Curse*)
CELESTE
CELIA (*Celia: Child of Terror*)
CHARLOTTE (*Charlotte's Web*)
CHINA (*China O'Brien*)
CHLOE (*Chloe in the Afternoon*)
CHRISTABEL
CHRISTIANE (*Christiane F.*)
CHRISTIE (*Get Christie Love!*)
CHRISTINA
CINDERELLA
CLAIRE (*Claire's Knee*)
CLARA (*Clara's Heart*)
CLAUDIA
CLEMENTINE (*My Darling Clementine*)
CLEO (*Cleo from 5 to 7*)
CLEOPATRA (*Antony and Cleopatra*)
COLETTE (*Becoming Colette*)
COOKIE
COQUETTE
CORDELIA
CORRINA (*Corrina, Corrina*)
COURTNEY (*The Courtney Affair*)
CRESSIDA (*Troilus & Cressida*)
CRIA
CRYSTAL (*Hollywood Hot Tubs 2: Educating Crystal*)
CURLY (*Curly Sue*)
CYBELE (*Sundays & Cybele*)

CYNTHIA (*30 Is a Dangerous Age, Cynthia*)
DAISY (*Driving Miss Daisy*)
DANA (*On the Edge: The Survival of Dana*)
DANIELLE (*Tatie Danielle*)
DAWN (*Dawn!*)
DEDEE (*Dedee d'Anvers*)
DELANCEY (*Crossing Delancey*)
DELILAH (*Samson and Delilah*)
DEVI
DIANA (*Charles & Diana: A Palace Divided*)
DIANE
DIVA
DIVINE
DIXIANA
DIXIE (*Dixie: Changing Habits*)
DOLLY (*Hello, Dolly!*)
DOMINIQUE (*Dominique Is Dead*)
DOMINO
DONA (*Dona Flor and Her Two Husbands*)
DOROTHY (*Dorothy in the Land of Oz*)
DOT (*Dot & the Bunny*)
DUBARRY
DUSTY
EDIE (*Edie in Ciao! Manhattan*)
EDITH (*Edith & Marcel*)
EFFI (*Effi Briest*)
EILEEN (*My Sister Eileen*)
ELEANOR (*Eleanor & Franklin*)
ELENA (*Elena and Her Men*)
ELENI
ELIZA (*Eliza's Horoscope*)
ELIZABETH (*Elizabeth, the Queen*)
ELLA (*Ella Cinders*)
ELLIE
ELSA (*Elsa, Elsa*)
ELSIE (*The Revealing of Elsie*)
ELVIRA (*Elvira Madigan*)

EMANUELLE (*Yellow Emanuelle*)
EMILIENNE
EMILY
EMMA (*Emma's Shadow*)
EMMANUELLE
ERENDIRA
EVA (*A Man Like Eva*)
EVE (*All About Eve*)
EVELYN (*The Passion of Evelyn*)
FABIOLA
FAITH
FANNY
FATTY (*Fatty Finn*)
FAUSTA (*The Story of Fausta*)
FERGIE (*Fergie & Andrew: Behind Palace Doors*)
FIFI (*Mademoiselle Fifi*)
FRAN
FRANCES
FRANKIE (*Frankie and Johnny*)
FRIDA
FRIEDA
FYRE
GABRIELA
GALAXINA
GARBO (*Garbo Talks*)
GENEVIEVE
GEORGIA (*Georgia, Georgia*)
GEORGY (*Georgy Girl*)
GERTIE (*Dirty Gertie from Harlem U.S.A.*)
GERTRUD
GIDGET
GIGI
GILDA
GINGER
GLENDA (*Glen O Glenda*)
GLORIA
GOLDA (*A Woman Called Golda*)

GOLDY (*Goldy: The Last of the Golden Bears*)
GOSTA (*The Atonement of Gosta Berling*)
GRACE (*Grace Quigley*)
GRAZUOLE
GRENDEL (*Grendel, Grendel, Grendel*)
GRETA
GRETEL (*Hansel and Gretel*)
GWENDOLINE (*The Perils of Gwendoline*)
HANNA (*Hanna K.*)
HANNAH (*Hannah and Her Sisters*)
HANNIE (*Hannie Caulder*)
HARLOW
HARRIET (*The Adventures of Ozzie & Harriet*)
HATTER (*Lost Legacy: A Girl Called Hatter Fox*)
HATTIE (*Panama Hattie*)
HAZEL (*Hazel's People*)
HEATHER (*Heathers*)
HEDDA
HEIDI
HELEN (*Max and Helen*)
HESTER (*Hester Street*)
HONEY
INGA
IPHIGENIA
IRENE (*The Story of Vernon and Irene Castle*)
IREZUMI
IRIS (*Stanley and Iris*)
IRINA (*The Loves of Irina*)
IRMA (*Irma La Douce*)
ISABELLE (*Therese & Isabelle*)
ISADORA
JACQUELINE (*Jacqueline Bouvier Kennedy*)
JANE (*Antonia and Jane*)
JANIS (*Janis: A Film*)
JAYNE (*The Jayne Mansfield Story*)
JEAN (*Jean de Florette*)
JEANNIE (*I Dream of Jeannie*)

JENNIE (*Portrait of Jennie*)
JENNIFER (*Jennifer 8*)
JENNY (*A Fight for Jenny*)
JESSE
JESSICA (*Let's Scare Jessica to Death*)
JESSIE (*Jessie's Girls*)
JEZEBEL
JILL (*Four Jacks and a Jill*)
JO (*The Ballad of Little Jo*)
JOAN (*Joan of Arc*)
JOON (*Benny & Joon*)
JONI
JOSEPHA
JOSEPHINE (*The Josephine Baker Story*)
JUDITH (*Judith of Bethulia*)
JUDY (*A Date with Judy*)
JULIA
JULIE (*To Wong Foo, Thanks for Everything, Julie Newmar*)
JULIET (*Juliet of the Spirits*)
JUNE (*Henry & June*)
JUSTINE
KARI (*The Abduction of Kari Swenson*)
KATARINA (*A Prayer of Katarina Horovitzova*)
KATE (*Kiss Me Kate*)
KATHARINA (*The Lost Honor of Katharina Blum*)
KATHERINE
KATHRYN (*The Lost Passion of Kathryn Beck*)
KATHY (*Seizure: The Story of Kathy Morris*)
KATIE (*Katie's Passion*)
KEETJE (*Keetje Tippei*)
KELLY (*Queen Kelly*)
KILMA (*Kilma, Queen of the Amazons*)
KIM
KITTY (*Kitty Foyle*)
KRIEMHILDE (*Kriemhilde's Revenge*)
LENA (*Lena's Holiday*)
LEONOR

LETTY (*Moran of the Lady Letty*)
LAURA
LIANA (*Liana, Jungle Goddess*)
LIANNA
LILITH
LILLIE
LILY (*Lily in Love*)
LISA
LISE (*Jacko & Lise*)
LOIS (*Lois Gibbs and the Love Canal*)
LOLA
LOLITA (*Lethal Lolita—Amy Fisher: My Story*)
LORRAINE (*Sweet Lorraine*)
LOUISE (*Thelma & Louise*)
LOULOU
LUCI (*Pepi, Luci, Bom and Other Girls on the Heap*)
LUCY (*Lucy and Desi: Before the Laughter*)
LULU (*Forever, Lulu*)
LUZIA
LYDIA (*Love for Lydia*)
MABEL (*Fatty and Mabel Adrift*)
MADELEINE
MADELON (*The Sin of Madelon Claudet*)
MADONNA (*Big Deal on Madonna Street*)
MAE (*Mae West*)
MAGDALENE
MAGGIE (*Say Goodbye, Maggie Cole*)
MAME
MAMELE
MANDY
MANON
MARGARET (*Double Exposure: The Story of Margaret Bourke-White*)
MARIA
MARIAN (*Robin and Marian*)
MARIANELA
MARICELA

MARIE
MARIETTA (*Naughty Marietta*)
MARJORIE (*Marjorie Morningstar*)
MARILYN
MARNIE
MARTHA (*The Strange Love of Martha Ivers*)
MARY (*Mary Poppins*)
MARY LOU (*Hello Mary Lou: Prom Night 2*)
MATA (*Mata Hari*)
MATILDA
MAUD (*My Night at Maud's*)
MAUDE (*Harold and Maude*)
MAXIE
MAYA
MEDEA
MEDUSA
MEG (*The Incredible Journey of Dr. Meg Laurel*)
MELANIE
MELODY
MESSALINA (*Messalina, Empress of Rome*)
MICKEY
MICKI (*Micki & Maude*)
MILDRED (*Mildred Pierce*)
MILLIE (*Thoroughly Modern Millie*)
MIMI
MIN (*Min & Bill*)
MIRABELLA (*Maria and Mirabella*)
MIRABELLE (*Four Adventures of Reinette and Mirabelle*)
MISTY
MOANA (*Moana, a Romance of the Golden Age*)
MOLL (*The Amorous Adventures of Moll Flanders*)
MOLLY (*Molly Maguires*)
MONA (*Mona Lisa*)
MONIKA
MONIQUE
MORELLA (*The Haunting of Morella*)
MOUCHETTE

MYRA (*Myra Breckinridge*)
MURIEL
NADIA
NADINE
NANA
NANCY (*Nancy Astor*)
NANETTE (*No, No Nanette*)
NAOMI (*Alan & Naomi*)
NARAYAMA (*The Ballad of Narayama*)
NATASHA (*Boris and Natasha: The Movie*)
NATHALIE (*Nathalie Comes of Age*)
NATTY (*The Journey of Natty Gann*)
NEA
NEFERTITI (*Nefertiti, Queen of the Nile*)
NELL
NELLIE (*The Adventures of Nellie Bly*)
NICOLE
NINOTCHKA
NOA (*Noa at Seventeen*)
NORMA
NORMA JEAN (*Goodbye, Norma Jean*)
NORMA RAE
NYOKA (*Nyoka and the Tigerman*)
OCTAVIA
ODESSA (*Little Odessa*)
OHARU (*The Life of Oharu*)
OLGA (*My Nights with Susan, Sandra, Olga, and Julie*)
OLIVIA
ONIBABA
ORIANE
OSA
PAMELA (*Mistress Pamela*)
PAT (*Pat and Mike*)
PATRICK
PATSY (*Patsy, Mi Amor*)
PATTI (*Patti Rocks*)
PATTY (*Patty Hearst*)

PAULINE (*Pauline at the Beach*)
PEG (*Peg O' My Heart*)
PEGGY (*Peggy Sue Got Married*)
PEPI (*Pepi, Luci, Bom and Other Girls on the Heap*)
PEPPER
PETRA (*The Bitter Tears of Petra von Kant*)
PETULIA
PHOENIX (*Griffin and Phoenix: A Love Story*)
POLLYANNA
PRISCILLA (*The Adventures of Priscilla, Queen of the Desert*)
QUEENIE
RACHEL (*Rachel, Rachel*)
RAPUNZEL
REBECCA
REGINA
REINETTE (*Four Adventures of Reinette and Mirabelle*)
RIKKY (*Rikky and Pete*)
RITA (*Educating Rita*)
ROBERTA
ROO (*Who Slew Auntie Roo?*)
RONA (*Rona Jaffee's Mazes & Monsters*)
ROSA (*I Love You Rosa*)
ROSALIE
ROSARITA (*The Bells of Rosarita*)
ROSE (*Aloha, Bobby and Rose*)
ROSE MARIE
ROSEMARY (*Rosemary's Baby*)
ROSIE (*Rosie: The Rosemary Clooney Story*)
ROXANNE
ROXY (*Welcome Home, Roxy Carmichael*)
RUBY
RUTH (*The Story of Ruth*)
SABRINA
SADIE (*Sadie Thompson*)
SALINA (*The Road to Salina*)
SALLY (*When Harry Met Sally . . .*)

SALOME

SAMANTHA

SANDRA (*My Nights with Susan, Sandra, Olga, and Julie*)

SARA (*Sara Dane*)

SARAFINA (*Sarafina!*)

SARAH (*The Haunting of Sarah Brady*)

SAVANNAH (*Savannah Smiles*)

SCARLETT (*Captain Scarlett*)

SHEBA (*Come Back, Little Sheba*)

SHEENA

SHEILA (*The Last of Sheila*)

SHELLEY (*Shelley Duvall's Bedtime Stories*)

SHIRLEY (*Shirley Valentine*)

SINTHIA (*Sinthia: The Devil's Doll*)

SNOW (*Snow White and the Seven Dwarfs*)

SONJA (*Red Sonja*)

SOPHIE (*Sophie's Choice*)

STACEY

STACY (*Stacy's Knights*)

STELLA (*Stella Dallas*)

STEVIE

SUDIE (*Sudie & Simpson*)

SUE (*Curly Sue*)

SUNNY

SUSAN (*Desperately Seeking Susan*)

SUSANA

SUSANNA (*Susanna Pass*)

SUSANNAH (*Oh Susannah*)

SUSIE (*If You Knew Susie*)

SUZANNE (*The Second Coming of Suzanne*)

SUZIE (*The World of Suzie Wong*)

SUZY

SYBIL

SYLVIA

SWEETIE

TAM TAM (*Princess Tam Tam*)

TAMMY (*Tammy and the Bachelor*)

TANYA (*Tanya's Island*)
TERESA (*Portrait of Teresa*)
TEREZA
TESS
THELMA (*Thelma & Louise*)
THERESE
THOMASINA (*The Three Lives of Thomasina*)
TIFFANY (*Tiffany Jones*)
TILLIE (*Pete 'n' Tillie*)
TISA (*My Girl Tisa*)
TOOTSIE
TRISTANA
ULI (*The Taking of Flight 847: The Uli Derickson Story*)
VANESSA
VANINA (*Vanina Vanini*)
VENUS (*Black Venus*)
VERA (*Little Vera*)
VERONIKA (*Veronika Voss*)
VERONIQUE (*The Double Life of Veronique*)
VICTORIA (*Victor/Victoria*)
VIOLETTE
VIRIDIANA
WANDA (*A Fish Called Wanda*)
WILLA
WILMA
YANG (*Princess Yang Kwei Fei*)
YOKO (*John & Yoko: A Love Story*)
YOLANDA (*The Secret of Yolanda*)
ZANDALEE
ZELLY (*Zelly & Me*)
ZORA (*Zora Is My Name!*)
ZOU ZOU

# Baby Names from Songs

## BABY NAMES FROM SONG TITLES:
### 759 Unique & Distinctive Names From Song Titles of the Past Hundred Years

These 759 names (289 boy's names; 470 girl's names) are all drawn from popular song titles of the past century and this massive collection comprises what is probably the most offbeat selection of names in this book. (There are some admittedly odd name suggestions here, but in a time of children named Rumer and Boston, I did not want to presume that any specific name lacked appeal for someone.)

When the song title is *only* a proper name ("Angie"), then no additional information is provided. When the song title *includes* a name ("Along Comes Mary"), then the complete title of the song is provided. When I came across the same name being used in several song titles, I went with the most popular or recognizable song.

[For complete discographic and bibliographic information about individual songs, see *Who Wrote That Song?* by Dick Jacobs and Harriet Jacobs, published in 1994 by Writer's Digest Books. This is one of the most definitive song references in print today and it is also a goldmine of musical and pop-culture information.]

# BOYS

AARON ("Aaron Loves Angela")
ABIE ("Abie's Wild Irish Rose")
ABRAHAM ("Abraham, Martin and John")
AL ("Allegheny Al")
ALADDIN ("I Wish I Were Aladdin")
ALBERT ("Uncle Albert/Admiral Halsey")
ALEXANDER ("Alexander's Ragtime Band")
ALLAH ("Allah's Holiday")
ALVIN ("Alvin's Harmonica")
AMADEUS ("Rock Me Amadeus")
AMARILLO
ANATOLE ("Anatole [of Paris]")
ANTONY ("Antony and Cleopatra Theme")
ARABY
ARIZONA
ARKANSAS ("Arkansas Traveler")
ARTHUR ("Arthur's Theme")
AUGUSTINE ("I Dreamed I Saw St. Augustine")
AVALON
AXEL ("Axel F")
BARETTA ("Baretta's Theme")
BEN
BENNIE ("Bennie and the Jets")
BERNIE ("Bernie's Tune")
BIJOU
BILL
BILLY ("Billy, Don't Be a Hero")
BLUE
BLYNKEN ("Wynken, Blynken and Nod")
BO ("Bo Diddley")
BOB ("Bob Dylan's 115th Dream")
BOBBY ("Bobby's Girl")
BOJANGLES ("Mr. Bojangles")
BONAPARTE ("Bonaparte's Retreat")

BOND ("James Bond Theme")
BOO ("Me and You and a Dog Named Boo")
BRIAN ("Brian's Song")
BRUCE ("Lenny Bruce")
BUDDY ("Wish You Were Here, Buddy")
CAESAR ("Caesar and Cleopatra Theme")
CALLAGHAN ("Meet Mister Callaghan")
CALLEY ("The Battle Hymn of Lieutenant Calley")
CANAAN ("Been to Canaan")
CAREY
CARIOCA
CASANOVA
CASEY ("Casey at the Bat")
CHARLESTON
CHARLEY ("Charley, My Boy")
CHARLIE ("Charlie Brown")
CHEROKEE
CHEYENNE

---

### "ON THE LEVEL?" DEPARTMENT

In 1994, a British fan of the group Level 42 had his name legally changed to include the titles of his favorite Level 42 songs, as well as the names of the original members of the band. After the change, Antony Hicks legally became *Ant Level Forty Two The Pursuit Of Accidents The Early Tapes Standing In The Light True Colors A Physical Presence World Machine Running In The Family Running In The Family Platinum Edition Staring At The Sun Level Best Guaranteed The Remixes Forever Now Influences Changes Mark King Mike Lindup Phil Gould Boon Gould Wally Badarou Lindup-Badarou.*

CHICK ("Chicory Chick")
CHICO ("Chico and the Man")
CHRISTIAN ("Sister Christian")
CHRISTOPHER ("Christopher Columbus")
CHUCK ("Chuck E's in Love")
CLYDE ("The Ballad of Bonnie and Clyde")
COLORADO
COLUMBO ("Crosby, Columbo, and Vallee")
CONSTANTINOPLE
CRISTOFO ("Misto Cristofo Columbo")
CROSBY ("Crosby, Columbo, and Vallee")
CURLY ("Curly Shuffle")
CUSTER ("Mr. Custer")
DANIEL
DANNY ("Danny's Song")
DAVID ("David and Lisa's Love Song")
DAVY ("The Ballad of Davy Crockett")
DAZZ
DELAWARE
DELICADO
DENNIS ("Dennis the Menace")
DETROIT
DIOGENES ("Oh, Diogenes!")
DONDI
DONEGAL ("Dear Old Donegal")
DOOLEY ("Tom Dooley")
DUKE ("Sir Duke")
EARL ("Duke of Earl")
EDDIE ("Eddie, My Love")
EDMUND ("The Wreck of the Edmund Fitzgerald")
ELI ("Eli's Coming")
ELMER ("Elmer's Tune")
ELMO ("St. Elmo's Fire")
FERDINAND ("Ferdinand the Bull")
FERNANDO
FITZGERALD ("The Wreck of the Edmund Fitzgerald")
FLOYD ("The Death of Floyd Collins")

FRANK ("Frank Mills")
FRANKIE ("The Ballad of Frankie Lee & Judas Priest")
FRANKLIN ("Franklin Shephard, Inc.")
FREDDIE ("Freddie's Dead")
FREDDY
FREE
FRIDAY ("Where Did Robinson Crusoe Go With Friday On Saturday Night")
FRISCO ("Hello Frisco Hello")
GABRIEL ("Blow, Gabriel, Blow")
GALLAGHER ("Mister Gallagher and Mister Shean")
GALVESTON
GARIBALDI ("Gid-Ap, Garibaldi")
GATOR ("The Ballad of Gator McCluskey")
GENE ("Hoppy, Gene, and Me")

---

### MY NAME'S MYKELTI. PEOPLE CALL ME MYKELTI.

*Forrest Gump* star Mykelti Williamson (pronounced "Michael-T") was given his first name by his grandfather, who was 50 percent Blackfoot Indian. The name means "spirit" or "silent friend" in the Blackfoot language.

---

GEORGE ("George Jackson")
GEORGIE ("Killing of Georgie")
GERONIMO ("Geronimo's Cadillac")
GILLIGAN ("The Ballad of Gilligan's Isle")
GONZALEZ ("Speedy Gonzalez")
GOOBER ("Goober Peas")
HAJJI ("Hajji Baba")
HALSEY ("Uncle Albert/Admiral Halsey")
HAMBONE
HAMP ("Hamp's Boogie Woogie")
HANS ("I'm Hans Christian Anderson")

HAPPY

HARDING ("John Wesley Harding")

HARRIGAN

HARRY ("Harry Truman")

HATARI

HENDERSON ("Henderson Stomp")

HENNESEY

HENRY ("I'm Henry VIII, I Am")

HERNANDEZ ("Pancho Maximilian Hernandez [The Best President We Ever Had]")

HERNANDO ("Hernando's Hideaway")

HOLLIS ("The Ballad of Hollis Brown")

HOPPY ("Hoppy, Gene, and Me")

HOUSTON

HUCKLEBERRY ("Huckleberry Duck")

IDAHO

INDIANA ("Can't Get Indiana Off My Mind")

IRA ("The Ballad of Ira Hayes")

IVAN ("Dear Ivan")

JACK ("Jumpin' Jack Flash")

JACKIE ("Did You See Jackie Robinson Hit That Ball?")

JACOB ("Jacob's Ladder")

JACQUES

JAMES ("James [Hold the Ladder Steady]")

JASCHA ("Mishca, Jascha, Toshca, Sascha")

JED ("The Ballad of Jed Clampett")

JERICHO ("Joshua Fit De Battle of Jericho")

JERU

JESSE

JESSIE

JET

JIM

JIMINY ("Jiminy Cricket")

JIMMY ("Jimmy Mack")

JOE ("Hey Joe")

JOEY

JOHN ("The Ballad of John and Yoko")

JOHNNY ("Bye Bye Johnny")
JOHNSON ("Johnson Rag")
JONAH ("Good-Bye Jonah")
JONES ("Nathan Jones")
JOSEPH ("Joseph! Joseph!")
JOSHUA ("Joshua Fit De Battle of Jericho")
JUBILO ("The Day of Jubilo")
JUD ("Poor Jud")
JUDAS ("The Ballad of Frankie Lee & Judas Priest")
JUDE ("Hey Jude")
JULIO ("Me and Julio Down by the Schoolyard")
JUNIOR ("Junior's Farm")
JUPITER ("Jupiter Forbid")
LARRY ("Hats Off to Larry")
LAWRENCE ("Lawrence of Arabia")
LEE ("Mr. Lee")
LENNY ("Lenny Bruce")
LEROY ("Bad, Bad Leroy Brown")
LEVON
LIBERTY ("Liberty Bell")
LINDY ("Lucky Lindy")
LONGFELLOW ("Longfellow Serenade")
LOU ("Blue Lou")
LOUIE ("Brother Louie")
LOUIS ("St. Louis Blues")
LUKA
MacARTHUR ("MacArthur Park")
MACK ("Mack the Knife")
MacNAMARA ("MacNamara's Band")
MALONE ("Molly Malone")
MANDALAY ("On the Road to Mandalay")
MARTIN ("Abraham, Martin and John")
MAVERICK
MAXIMILIAN ("Pancho Maximilian Hernandez [The Best President We Ever Had]")
MAXWELL ("Maxwell's Silver Hammer")
MECCA

MEMPHIS
MENDOCINO
MERCEDES ("Mercedes Boy")
MICHAEL ("Message to Michael")
MICKEY
MIKE ("I Like Mike")
MILORD
MISHCA ("Mishca, Jascha, Toshca, Sascha")
MOE ("Five Guys Named Moe")
MONK ("Blue Monk")
MONTEGO ("Montego Bay")
MONTEREY
MORGEN ("Morgen [One More Sunrise]")
MOTEN ("Moten's Blues")
NAPOLEON
NARCISSUS
NATHAN ("Nathan Jones")
NEVADA
NICCOLINI ("Papa Niccolini")
NOD ("Wynken, Blynken and Nod")
NORMAN
OHIO
OTIS ("Miss Otis Regrets")
PADRE
PALADIN ("The Battle of Paladin")
PANCHO ("Pancho Maximilian Hernandez [The Best President We Ever Had]")
PAUL ("Tall Paul")
PEN ("Uncle Pen")
PEPINO ("Pepino, the Italian Mouse")
PERCY ("Percy's Song")
PETE ("Cuban Pete")
PETER ("Peter Gunn Theme")
PIERROT ("Poor Pierrot")
POONEIL ("The Ballad of You and Me and Pooneil")
PORGY ("I Loves You Porgy")
PORTER ("King Porter Stomp")

## THE "PEOPLE WHO NEED TO GET A LIFE" DEPARTMENT

In August 1994, a woman gave birth on Max Yasgur's farm in upstate New York to a baby boy and named him Woodstock. The birth did not take place on the site of the *big* "Woodstock '94" festival (remember the "Mud People"?) but rather on the site of the *other* Woodstock concert that took place that same weekend. This other, *free* Woodstock concert happened where the *original* 1969 festival was held, Max Yasgur's farm. Little baby Woodstock was born *a week after* the concert weekend ended. At that time, there were still several *thousand* people wandering around the farm, 150 vendors still selling everything from T-shirts to soda, and bands and musical acts still showing up to play for free. Even Carlos Santana showed up, but he was told to come back later because they were in the middle of building a bigger soundstage.

QUENTIN ("Quentin's Theme")
QUINN ("The Mighty Quinn")
RAPP ("Brother Rapp")
REMUS ("Uncle Remus Said")
RICHARD ("Open the Door, Richard!")
RICO ("Rico Suave")
RINGO
RIO
ROBERT ("Doctor Robert")
ROCKY
RODGER ("Rodger Young")
ROMEO
RON ("Da-Doo Ron Ron")

RONNIE
RUDOLPH ("Rudolph the Red-Nosed Reindeer")
SAM ("Mohair Sam")
SAMSON ("Run Samson Run")
SASCHA ("Mishca, Jascha, Toshca, Sascha")
SCOTTY ("Watchin' Scotty Grow")
SHANE
SHEAN ("Mister Gallagher and Mister Shean")
SHEPHARD ("Franklin Shephard, Inc.")
SHILO
SIERRA ("Sierra Sue")
SIMON ("Simon Says")
SLOOPY ("Hang On Sloopy")
SMOKEY ("When Smokey Sings")
SOLOMON
SONNY ("Sonny Boy")
SPAIN
SPARTACUS
SPEEDY ("Speedy Gonzalez")
STORMY
STRAUSS ("By Strauss")
SUE ("A Boy Named Sue") [just a joke-sjs]
SWANEE ("Hello! Swanee, Hello!")
TAMMANY
TAMPICO
TAURUS
TEDDY
TENNESSEE
TERRY ("Terry Theme")
TIGER
TIMOTHY
TOM ("Major Tom")
TONY ("Tony's Wife")
TORERO
TOSCHA ("Mishca, Jascha, Toshca, Sascha")
TRACY
TUCKY ("Hello Tucky")

VALLEE ("Crosby, Columbo, and Vallee")
VICTORY
VINCENT
WANG ("The Wang Wang Blues")
WASHINGTON ("Washington and Lee Swing")
WENCESLAS ("Good King Wenceslas")
WESLEY ("John Wesley Harding")
WILLIAM ("William Tell Overture")
WILLY ("Little Willy")
WOODY ("Woody Woodpecker Theme")
WYNKEN ("Wynken, Blynken and Nod")
YEHOODI ("Who's Yehoodi")
YOUNG ("Rodger Young")
YUBA ("When Yuba Plays the Rumba On His Tuba")
ZARATHUSTRA ("Also Spake Zarathustra")
ZONKY
ZORBA ("[Theme from] Zorba the Greek")

## BUT NONE OF THESE GUYS IS *EVER* CONFUSED WITH WHITNEY HOUSTON

The August 12, 1994 *Entertainment Weekly* reported that film director Whit Stillman (*Metropolitan, Barcelona*) is constantly mistaken for country legend Slim Whitman because of the similarities of their names. Slim Whitman (whose real name is Otis Dewey Whitman) on the other hand, reported that he is often mistaken for country singer Montana Slim. Slim Whitman's record company hated his real name so much that they took it upon themselves to christen him "Slim" for his first album and it stuck. Auteur Whit Stillman's real name is John Whitney Stillman.

# GIRLS

ABILENE
ADELAIDE
ADELINE ("Sweet Adeline")
ALFIE
ALICE ("Alice's Restaurant")
ALISON
ALLISON ("Allison's Theme from *Parrish*")
ALOUETTE
AMANDA
AMAPOLA ("Amapola [Pretty Little Poppy]")
AMBER ("Forever Amber")
AMELIA
ANASTASIA
ANGEL
ANGELA ("Aaron Loves Angela")
ANGELIA
ANGELINA ("Farewell, Angelina")
ANGIE
ANITRA ("Anitra's Dance")
ANNA
ANNABELLE
ANNIE ("Annie's Song")
ANNIE LAURIE
APRIL ("April Showers")
AQUARIUS
ASIA ("Asia Minor")
ATHENA
ATLANTA ("The Burning of Atlanta")
ATLANTIS
AUBREY
AURA LEE
AURORA
BAIA
BAMBALINA

BAMBINA ("Ciao, Ciao, Bambino")
BARBARA ("Please Don't Ask About Barbara")
BARBARA ANN
BARCELONA
BEAUTY ("Black Beauty")
BELLA ("Bella Bella Marie")
BELLE ("Belle of the Ball")
BERMUDA
BERNADETTE
BERNADINE
BERTHA ("The Bertha Butt Boogie")
BESS ("Bess, You Is My Woman")
BESSIE ("Barrelhouse Bessie from Basin Street")
BETH
BETTE ("Bette Davis Eyes")
BETTY ("Betty Co-Ed")
BIANCA
BILL ("My Girl Bill")
BILLIE
BILLIE JEAN
BLANCA ("Paloma Blanca")
BLONDY
BONITA ("La Isla Bonita")
BONNIE ("The Ballad of Bonnie and Clyde")
BONNIE JEAN ("I'll Go Home With Bonnie Jean")
BRANDY ("Brandy [You're a Fine Girl]")
BUTTERCUP ("Build Me Up, Buttercup")
CALCUTTA
CALDONIA ("Caldonia [What Makes Your Big Head So
Hard?]")
CANDIDA
CANDY
CAPRI ("Isle of Capri")
CARA ("Cara Mia")
CAREY
CARIOCA
CAROL

CAROLINA ("Carolina in the Pines")
CAROLINE ("Caroline, No")
CAROLYN
CARRIE
CARRIE-ANNE
CAT ("The Ballad of Cat Ballou")
CATERINA
CATHY ("Cathy's Clown")
CECILIA
CELIE ("Miss Celie's Blues")
CERVEZA
CHANSON ("Chanson D'Amour")
CHARLOTTE ("Hush Hush, Sweet Charlotte")
CHARMAINE
CHELSEA ("Chelsea Morning")
CHERIE
CHERISH
CHERRY
CHEYENNE
CHINA ("China Grove")
CHIQUITA
CHLOE
CHRISTINE ("Christine Sixteen")
CINDERELLA
CINDY ("Cindy, Oh Cindy")
CLAIR
CLARA ("Oh, Donna Clara")
CLAWDY ("Lawdy Miss Clawdy")
CLEMENTINE
CLEOPATRA ("Caesar and Cleopatra Theme")
COD'INE
COLUMBIA ("Columbia, the Gem of the Ocean")
CONCHITA ("Conchita Marquita Lolita Pepita Rosita
Juanita Lopez")
COOKIE ("[Lookie, Lookie, Lookie] Here Comes Cookie")
COPPELIA ("Waltz Coppelia")
COQUETTE

CORAZON
CORRINA ("Corrine, Corrina")
CORRINE ("Corrine, Corrina")
CUPID
CYNTHIA ("Cynthia's in Love")
DAISY ("Daisy Bell")
DAISY JANE
DANDELION
DANDY
DARDANELLA
DAWN
DEANIE ("Hey Deanie")
DEDE ("Dede Dinah")
DELILAH
DELTA ("Delta Dawn")
DENISE
DESIREE
DIANA
DIANE ("Jack and Diane")
DINAH
DIXIE ("The Night They Drove Old Dixie Down")
DOLLY ("Dolly Dagger")
DOMINIQUE
DOMINO
DONNA

---

### AND I SUPPOSE THE VEGETARIAN THING IS A LIE TOO, RIGHT?

Paul McCartney's wife Linda Eastman McCartney is *not*—contrary to a widely disseminated (and wholly believed) rumor—an Eastman-Kodak heiress (even though, ironically, she *is* a professional photographer). Her father Lee changed his name from Epstein to Eastman.

DONNA LEE
DUNA
EADIE ("Eadie Was a Lady")
EILEEN
ELEANOR ("Eleanor Rigby")
ELENA
ELENORE
ELISA ("I Still See Elisa")
ELLA ("Egyptian Ella")
ELOISE ("Sweet Eloise")
ELVIRA
EMALINE
EMILY
EMMA
EVANGELINE
EVELINA
FAITH
FANCY
FANNIE ("Fan Tan Fannie")
FANNY
FATIMA ("Our Lady of Fatima")
FIFI
FINI
FINLANDIA
FLO ("Frisco Flo")
FREE
FRESHIE
FROSTY ("Frosty the Snow Man")
GARDENIA ("Blue Gardenia")
GEGETTA
GENEVIEVE ("Sweet Genevieve")
GEORGETTE
GEORGIA ("Georgia On My Mind")
GEORGIE ("Killing of Georgie")
GEORGY ("Georgy Girl")
GIANNINA ("Giannina Mia")
GIDGET

GIGI
GINA
GINGER ("Ginger Bread")
GINNY ("Ginny Come Lately")
GLENDORA
GLORIA
GODIVA ("Lady Godiva")
GOLONDRINA ("La Golondrina")
GRANADA
GUANTANAMERA
GUENEVERE
GYPSY ("Tell Me, Little Gypsy")
HANNAH ("Hard Hearted Hannah, the Vamp of Savannah")
HAPPY
HARMONY
HARRIET
HATTIE ("Lonesome Death of Hattie Carroll")
HAVANA ("A Weekend in Havana")
HAZEL ("Hooray for Hazel")
HEATHER ("Heather Honey")
HEAVEN
HEAVENLY
HELEN ("Helen Wheels")
HOLLY ("Holly Holy")
HONEY
HUGUETTE ("Waltz Huguette/or the Vagabond King Waltz")
HYSTERIA
IDA ("Ida, Sweet As Apple Cider")
IESHA
ILONA
INDIA ("Song of India")
INDIANA ("Can't Get Indiana Off My Mind")
INEZ ("Mama Inez")
IRENE
IRMA ("Irma La Douce")
ISLA ("La Isla Bonita")

IVY
JACKIE ("Jackie Blue")
JAMAICA ("Jamaica Farewell")
JAMIE
JANE ("Baby Jane")
JANIE ("Janie's Got a Gun")
JASCHA ("Mischa, Jascha, Toscha, Sascha")
JEAN
JEANIE ("I Dream of Jeanie With the Light Brown Hair")
JEANNIE ("Little Jeannie")
JEANNINE ("Jeannine, I Dream of Lilac Time")
JENIFER ("Jenifer Juniper")
JENNIE ("Sweet Jennie Lee")
JENNY ("867–5309/Jenny")
JERU
JESSE
JESSIE
JET
JEZEBEL
JILL ("The House That Jack Built for Jill")
JO-ANN
JOANNA
JOANNE
JOHANNA
JOSEPHINE
JOSIE
JUANITA ("Conchita Marquita Lolita Pepita Rosita Juanita Lopez")
JUDE ("Hey Jude")
JUDY ("Judy in Disguise")
JULIA
JULIE ("Oh Julie")
JULIET ("[Just Like] Romeo and Juliet")
JUNE ("It Was a Night in June")
JUNIPER ("Jenifer Juniper")
KATE ("I Wish I Could Shimmy Like My Sister Kate")
KATHARINA ("O, Katharina!")

KATHLEEN ("I'll Take You Home Again Kathleen")
KATHY ("The Death of Little Kathy Fiscus")
KATIE ("Katie Went to Haiti")
KATINKITSCHKA
KATY ("K-K-K-Katy")
KOOKIE ("Kookie, Kookie, Lend Me Your Comb")
LADYBIRD
LAGUNA ("Lily of Laguna")
LARA ("Lara's Theme")
LARK ("Up With the Lark")
LASSIE ("My Bonnie Lassie")
LAURA
LAURIE ("Laurie [Strange Things Happen]")
LAYLA
LEE ("Miss Annabelle Lee")
LEILANI ("Sweet Leilani")
LENA ("Bald Headed Lena")
LIDA ("Lida Rose")
LILLI ("Lilli Marlene")
LILY ("Lily Belle")
LINDA
LING ("Ling Ting Tong")
LISA ("I'm Not Lisa")
LIZA ("Liza [All the Clouds'll Roll Away]")
LOLA
LOLITA
LORELEI
LORNA ("Lorna's Here")
LORRAINE ("Sweet Lorraine")
LOUISA ("I Love Louisa")
LOUISE
LOUISIANA
LU ("Little Latin Lupe Lu")
LUCILLE
LUCY ("Lucy in the Sky With Diamonds")
LULU ("Don't Bring Lulu")
LYDIA ("Lydia, the Tattooed Lady")

LYGIA
MADELIN ("Paddlin' Madelin Home")
MADELON
MADONNA ("Lady Madonna")
MAGGIE ("Maggie May")
MALAGUENA
MAME
MAMIE ("Flamin' Mamie")
MANDY
MANTECA
MARCHETA
MARGIE
MARGOT
MARIA
MARIAN ("Marian the Librarian")
MARIANNE
MARIE
MARINA
MARLENE ("Lilli Marlene")
MARMALADE ("Lady Marmalade")
MARQUITA ("Conchita Marquita Lolita Pepita Rosita
Juanita Lopez")
MARTA
MARTHA ("Martha My Dear")
MARY ("Along Comes Mary")
MARY LOU ("Hello, Mary Lou")
MATELOT
MATILDA ("Waltzing Matilda")
MAUDE ("And Then There's Maude")
MAXIM ("Maxim's)
MAXIXE ("Boogie Woogie Maxixe")
MAY ("Maggie May")
MAYBELLENE
MECCA
MEDINA ("Funky Cold Medina")
MELINDA
MELODIE ("Melodie D'Amour")

MELODY ("Melody of Love")
MERCEDES ("Mercedes Boy")
MERCY
MIA ("Cara Mia")
MICHELLE
MICKEY
MILLIE ("Thoroughly Modern Millie")
MIMI
MINNIE ("Minnie the Moocher")
MIRA ("Mira [Can You Imagine That?]")
MIRABELLE
MISHCA ("Mishca, Jascha, Toshca, Sascha")
MISIRLOU
MISTY
MOLLY ("Good Golly, Miss Molly")
MONA ("Mona Lisa")
MONTEREY
MORGEN ("Morgen [One More Sunrise]")
MORITAT
MOTEN ("Moten's Blues")
MUSETTA ("Musetta's Waltz")
NADIA ("Nadia's Theme")
NADINE ("Nadine [Is It You?]")
NANCY ("Nancy [With the Laughing Face]")
NANETTE ("No, No, Nanette")
NASTY
NEIANI
NEVADA
NICCOLINI ("Papa Niccolini")
NIGHTINGALE
NIKI ("Niki Hoeky")
NIKITA
NINA
NINEVAH ("Not Since Ninevah")
NOLA
OCARINA ("[Dance to the Music of] The Ocarina")
OTIS ("Miss Otis Regrets")

PALESTEENA
PALOMA ("Paloma Blanca")
PAM ("Polythene Pam")
PANAMA ("Visit Panama")
PAREE ("Take My Hand, Paree")
PATIENCE
PATRICIA
PATTY ("The Patty Duke Theme")
PAULA ("Hey, Paula")
PEARL ("Black Pearl")
PEG
PEGGY ("Peggy Sue")
PENNINAH ("Walkin' With Penninah")
PEPITA ("Conchita Marquita Lolita Pepita Rosita Juanita Lopez")
PERFIDIA
PINTA ("Nina, the Pinta, the Santa Maria")
PRUDENCE ("Dear Prudence")
PURLIE
RAMONA
RAQUEL ("Bells of San Raquel")
RENEE ("Walk Away, Renee")
RHIANNON ("Rhiannon [Will You Ever Win]")
RHONDA ("Help Me, Rhonda")
RITA ("Lovely Rita")
ROBIN ("Fly, Robin, Fly")
ROLENE
ROMA ("Arrivederci, Roma")
RONI
RONNIE
ROSALIE
ROSALITA ("Rosalita [Come Out Tonight]")
ROSANNA
ROSE ("Broadway Rose")
ROSE MARIE
ROSETTA
ROSIE ("Cracklin' Rosie")

ROSIE LEE

ROSITA ("Conchita Marquita Lolita Pepita Rosita Juanita Lopez")

RUBY

RUSSIA ("And Russia Is Her Name")

SADIE ("Sexy Sadie")

SAL ("My Gal Sal")

SALLY ("Lay Down Sally")

SAMANTHA ("I Love You, Samantha")

SANDY

SARA

SASCHA ("Mishca, Jascha, Toshca, Sascha")

SATANI ("Ave Satani")

SAVANNAH

SEAGULL ("Song to a Seagull")

SHANNON

SHARONA ("My Sharona")

SHEILA

SHERRIE ("Oh, Sherrie")

SHERRY

SHILO

SIERRA ("Sierra Sue")

SIMILAU

SIMPATICA

SKOKIAAN

SKYLARK

SONATA

SONGBIRD

SPAIN

SPOOKY

STAR

STELLA ("Stella by Starlight")

STORMY

SUAVECITO

SUE ("Runaround Sue")

SUGAR ("Sugar, Sugar")

SUKIYAKI

SUNNY
SUSAN ("Black-Eyed Susan Brown")
SUSANNA ("Oh! Susanna")
SUSIE ("Wake up, Little Susie")
SUZANNA ("Oh Suzanna [Dust Off That Old Pianna]")
SUZANNE
SUZI ("Doing the Suzi-Q")
SUZY ("Suzy Snowflake")
SYLVIA ("Sylvia's Mother")
TABOO
TALLULAH ("I'll Take Tallulah")
TAMIKO ("A Girl Named Tamiko")
TAMMANY
TAMMY
TAMPICO
TANGERINE
TEQUILA
TERRY ("Terry Theme")
TESS ("Tess's Torch Song [I Had a Man]")
THERESA ("St. Theresa of the Roses")
THUMBELINA
TICO ("Tico Tico")
TIGER
TINA ("Tina Marie")
TOOTSIE ("Toot Toot Tootsie")
TOPSY
TOSHCA ("Mishca, Jascha, Toshca, Sascha")
TRACY
TZENA ("Tzena, Tzena, Tzena")
VAHEVELA
VALENCIA
VALENTINE
VALERIE
VALLERI
VANESSA
VANITY
VENICE

VENUS
VIENI
VIENNA
VILIA
VIOLETTA ("Hear My Song, Violetta")
VIRGINIA
WENDY
XANADU
YOKO ("The Ballad of John and Yoko")
ZSA ZSA

# Channeling: Baby Names from Favorite TV Shows

Don't you just love those interviews where people are asked what they watch on TV? *TV Guide* asks celebrities that question in every issue. All the stars seem to watch is CNN, PBS, sports, and the Discovery Channel.

Few people are willing to admit what they *really* watch: *Beavis and Butt-head, Wheel of Fortune, The Bikini Carwash Company II* on HBO, and an *I Love Lucy* marathon on Nick at Nite.

Americans don't just *like* television. In the good ol' U.S. of A., we *love* the one-eyed potentate who sits in the corner of almost every room in the house.

And with cable and the ubiquitousness of remote-control TVs, a new phrase has entered the vernacular: *channel-surfing.* There is nothing as heady or mind-numbing as flipping through sixty channels during a thirty-second commercial, and then using the Jump button to fly back to Home Base and make sure you don't miss any of *Roseanne.* (And people want to know why kids today have shorter attention spans!)

This feature allows all you TV aficionados out there to consider almost 1,200 names from 217 of your favorite TV shows of the past forty years.

From *The A Team* to *Zorro,* all your favorites are here.

From **ALAN** Kinkaid (*The Partridge Family*) and **ALEX** Keating (*Family Ties*) to **WILL** Robinson (*Lost in Space*) and **ZEB** Walton (*The Waltons*); the boys list collects over 670 unique names.

And from **ALEXIS** Carrington (*Dynasty*) and **ALICE** Kramden (*The Honeymooners*) to **VANESSA** Huxtable (*The Cosby Show*) and **WEDNESDAY** Addams (*The Addams Family*), the girls list offers over 500 distinctive names.

Rather than put the actual names of the TV shows after each name, to save space, the names are followed by the last name of the character and then a code number, which refers you to the following master list of numbered TV series (which also provides the network and the year the show first aired). For instance, if you like the name "Alister," you'll notice that it's followed by the last name "Mundy" and then the number 103, which you'll see is the show *It Takes a Thief* on the master list. This system will allow you to track down the TV series in which your favorite names appear.

[**A NOTE TO VIEWERS:** All of the characters listed were drawn from cast lists in *TV Guide* magazine and the book, *The Complete Directory to Prime Time Network TV Shows* by Tim Brooks and Earle Marsh (Ballantine Books). This book is exhaustive and should answer any questions you might have about a particular show of the past four decades. *All* serious TV buffs should have this book on the table next to the recliner. (Just slide the remote over a little and it should fit nicely.)]

## The Shows

1. *The A-Team* (NBC; 1983)
2. *Adam 12* (NBC; 1968)
3. *The Addams Family* (ABC; 1964)
4. *The Adventures of Rin Tin Tin* (ABC; 1954)
5. *The Adventures of Superman* (SYNDICATED, 1951)
6. *ALF* (NBC; 1986)
7. *Alice* (CBS; 1976)
8. *All in the Family* (CBS; 1971)
9. *Amos 'N' Andy* (CBS; 1951)
10. *The Andy Griffith Show* (CBS; 1960)
11. *The Avengers* (ABC; 1966)
12. *Bachelor Father* (CBS, NBC, ABC; 1957)
13. *Baretta* (ABC; 1975)
14. *Barnaby Jones* (CBS; 1973)
15. *Barney Miller* (ABC; 1975)
16. *Batman* (ABC; 1966)
17. *Battlestar Galactica* (ABC; 1978)
18. *Beauty and the Beast* (CBS; 1987)
19. *Ben Casey* (ABC; 1961)
20. *Benson* (ABC; 1979)
21. *The Beverly Hillbillies* (CBS; 1962)
22. *Bewitched* (ABC; 1964)
23. *The Big Valley* (ABC; 1965)
24. *The Bill Cosby Show* (NBC; 1969)
25. *The Bionic Woman* (ABC, NBC; 1976)
26. *The Bob Newhart Show* (CBS; 1972)
27. *Bosom Buddies* (ABC, NBC; 1980)
28. *The Brady Bunch* (ABC; 1969)
29. *Branded* (NBC; 1965)
30. *Bridget Loves Bernie* (CBS; 1972)
31. *Burke's Law* (ABC; 1963; CBS; 1993)
32. *C.P.O. Sharkey* (NBC; 1976)
33. *Cagney & Lacey* (CBS; 1982)
34. *Car 54, Where Are You?* (NBC; 1961)
35. *Centennial* (NBC; 1978)
36. *Charlie's Angels* (ABC; 1976)
37. *Cheers* (NBC; 1982)
38. *CHiPS* (NBC; 1977)
39. *The Colbys* (ABC; 1985)

40. *Combat* (NBC; 1971)
41. *The Cosby Show* (NBC; 1984)
42. *The Courtship of Eddie's Father* (ABC; 1969)
43. *Dallas* (CBS; 1978)
44. *The Days and Nights of Molly Dodd* (NBC; 1987)
45. *Dennis the Menace* (CBS; 1959)
46. *Designing Women* (CBS; 1986)
47. *The Dick Van Dyke Show* (CBS; 1961)
48. *Diff'rent Strokes* (NBC, ABC; 1978)
49. *A Different World* (NBC; 1987)
50. *Dr. Kildare* (NBC; 1961)
51. *The Donna Reed Show* (ABC; 1958)
52. *Dragnet* (NBC; 1952)

53. *The Dukes of Hazzard* (CBS; 1979)
54. *Dynasty* (ABC; 1981)
55. *Eight Is Enough* (ABC; 1977)
56. *F Troop* (ABC; 1965)
57. *The Facts of Life* (NBC; 1979)
58. *Falcon Crest* (CBS; 1981)
59. *Fame* (NBC; 1982)
60. *Family Affair* (CBS; 1966)
61. *Family Ties* (NBC; 1982)
62. *Fantasy Island* (ABC; 1978)
63. *The Farmer's Daughter* (ABC; 1963)
64. *Father Knows Best* (CBS, NBC, ABC; 1954)
65. *Fernwood 2-Night* (SYNDICATED, 1977)
66. *Flipper* (NBC; 1964)

67. *The Flying Nun* (ABC; 1967)
68. *Frasier* (NBC; 1993)
69. *The Fugitive* (ABC; 1963)
70. *Full House* (ABC; 1987)
71. *Gentle Ben* (CBS; 1967)
72. *The George Burns and Gracie Allen Show* (CBS; 1950)
73. *Get Smart* (NBC, CBS; 1965)
74. *The Ghost and Mrs. Muir* (NBC, ABC; 1968)
75. *Gidget* (ABC; 1965)
76. *Gilligan's Island* (CBS; 1964)
77. *The Girl from U.N.C.L.E.* (NBC; 1966)
78. *The Golden Girls* (NBC; 1985)
79. *Gomer Pyle, U.S.M.C.* (CBS; 1964)

80. *Grace Under Fire* (ABC; 1993)
81. *Green Acres* (CBS; 1965)
82. *The Green Hornet* (ABC; 1966)
83. *Growing Pains* (ABC; 1985)
84. *Gunsmoke* (CBS; 1955)
85. *Happy Days* (ABC; 1974)
86. *Hart to Hart* (ABC; 1979)
87. *Have Gun Will Travel* (CBS; 1957)
88. *Hawaii Five-O* (CBS; 1968)
89. *Hazel* (NBC, CBS; 1961)
90. *Highway to Heaven* (NBC: 1984)
91. *Hill Street Blues* (NBC; 1981)
92. *Hogan's Heroes* (CBS; 1965)
93. *Home Improvement* (ABC; 1991)
94. *The Honeymooners* (CBS; 1955)
95. *Hotel* (ABC; 1983)
96. *How the West Was Won* (ABC; 1978)
97. *I Dream of Jeannie* (NBC: 1965)
98. *I Love Lucy* (CBS; 1951)
99. *I Spy* (NBC; 1965)
100. *I'm Dickens—He's Fenster* (ABC; 1962)
101. *The Incredible Hulk* (CBS; 1978)
102. *Ironside* (NBC; 1967)
103. *It Takes a Thief* (ABC; 1968)
104. *It's Gary Shandling's Show* (FOX; 1988)
105. *Jake and the Fatman* (CBS; 1987)
106. *The Jeffersons* (CBS; 1975)
107. *The Jetsons* (ABC; 1962)
108. *Judd, For the Defense* (ABC; 1967)
109. *Kate & Allie* (CBS; 1984)
110. *Knight Rider* (NBC 1982)
111. *Knots Landing* (CBS; 1979)
112. *Kojak* (CBS; 1973)
113. *L.A. Law* (NBC; 1986)
114. *Lassie* (CBS; 1954)
115. *Laverne & Shirley* (ABC; 1976)
116. *Leave It to Beaver* (CBS, ABC; 1957)
117. *The Life and Times of Grizzly Adams* (NBC; 1977)
118. *The Life of Riley* (NBC; 1949)
119. *Life with Father* (CBS; 1953)
120. *Little House on the Prairie* (NBC; 1974)

121. *Logan's Run* (CBS; 1977)
122. *The Lone Ranger* (ABC 1949)
123. *Lost in Space* (CBS; 1965)
124. *Lou Grant* (CBS; 1977)
125. *The Love Boat* (ABC; 1977)
126. *The Lucy Show* (CBS; 1962)
127. *M*A*S*H* (CBS; 1972)
128. *The Man from U.N.C.L.E.* (NBC; 1964)
129. *Mannix* (CBS; 1967)
130. *The Many Loves of Dobie Gillis* (CBS; 1959)
131. *Marcus Welby, M.D.* (ABC; 1969)
132. *Married . . . With Children* (FOX; 1987)
133. *Mary Hartman, Mary Hartman* (SYNDICATED; 1975)
134. *The Mary Tyler Moore Show* (CBS; 1970)
135. *Matlock* (NBC; 1986)
136. *Maude* (CBS; 1972)
137. *Maverick* (ABC; 1957)
138. *Max Headroom* (ABC; 1987)
139. *McHale's Navy* (ABC; 1962)
140. *McMillan and Wife* (NBC; 1971)
141. *Miami Vice* (NBC; 1984)
142. *Mission: Impossible* (CBS; 1966)
143. *Mr. Ed* (CBS; 1961)
144. *The Mod Squad* (ABC; 1968)
145. *The Monkees* (NBC; 1966)
146. *Moonlighting* (ABC; 1985)
147. *Mork & Mindy* (ABC; 1978)
148. *The Munsters* (CBS; 1964)
149. *Murder, She Wrote* (CBS; 1984)
150. *Murphy Brown* (CBS; 1988)
151. *My Favorite Martian* (CBS; 1963)
152. *My Little Margie* (CBS, NBC; 1952)
153. *My Mother the Car* (NBC; 1965)
154. *My Three Sons* (ABC, CBS; 1960)
155. *Nanny and the Professor* (ABC; 1970)
156. *Newhart* (CBS; 1982)
157. *Night Court* (NBC; 1984)
158. *9 to 5* (ABC; 1982)
159. *Northern Exposure* (CBS; 1990)
160. *N.Y.P.D. Blue* (ABC; 1994)
161. *The Odd Couple* (ABC; 1970)
162. *One Day at a Time* (CBS; 1975)

163. *Operation Petticoat* (ABC; 1977)

164. *Our Miss Brooks* (CBS; 1952)

165. *Owen Marshall, Counselor at Law* (ABC; 1971)

166. *The Paper Chase* (CBS, CABLE; 1978; 1983)

167. *The Partridge Family* (ABC; 1970)

168. *The Patty Duke Show* (ABC; 1963)

169. *Perry Mason* (CBS; 1957)

170. *Petticoat Junction* (CBS; 1963)

171. *Peyton Place* (ABC; 1964)

172. *The Planet of the Apes* (CBS; 1974)

173. *Quincy, M.E.* (NBC; 1976)

174. *Rawhide* (CBS; 1959)

175. *The Real McCoys* (ABC, CBS; 1957)

176. *Remington Steele* (NBC; 1982)

177. *Rhoda* (CBS; 1974)

178. *Rich Man, Poor Man* (ABC; 1976)

179. *The Rifleman* (ABC; 1958)

180. *The Rockford Files* (NBC; 1974)

181. *The Rookies* (ABC; 1972)

182. *Room 222* (ABC; 1969)

183. *Roots* (ABC; 1977)

184. *Roseanne* (ABC; 1988)

185. *Route 66* (CBS; 1960)

186. *St. Elsewhere* (NBC; 1982)

187. *Sanford and Son* (NBC; 1972)

188. *The Scarecrow and Mrs. King* (CBS; 1983)

189. *Second City TV* (SYNDICATED; 1977)

190. *Secret Agent* (CBS; 1965)

191. *Seinfeld* (NBC; 1992)

192. *77 Sunset Strip* (ABC; 1958)

193. *The Simpsons* (FOX; 1990)

194. *The Six Million Dollar Man* (ABC; 1974)

195. *Soap* (ABC; 1977)

196. *Spenser: For Hire* (ABC; 1985)

197. *Star Trek* (NBC; 1966)

198. *Star Trek: The Next Generation* (SYNDICATED; 1987)

199. *Starsky and Hutch* (ABC; 1975)

200. *The Streets of San Francisco* (ABC; 1972)

201. *Taxi* (ABC, NBC; 1978)

202. *That Girl* (ABC; 1966)

203. *Thirtysomething* (ABC; 1987)

## BOYS NAMES FROM TV SHOWS

ABE (159)

ABNER (Kravitz, 22)

ACE (Evans, 125)

ADAM (159; Bricker, 125; Carrington, 42; Greer, 144; Kendall, 120; Stephens, 22; Tobias, 129; Wilson, 124)

AH (Chew, 187)

AL (93; Baker, 111; Barber, 178; Bundy, 132; Corassa, 33; Cowley, 182; Craven, 157; Fanducci, 178; Hurley, 58)

ALAN (Beam, 43; Brady, 47; Caldwell, 58; Wachtel, 91; Kinkaid, 167; Posner, 195; Virdon, 172)

ALBERT (Ingalls, 120)

ALEX (Diehl, 180; Handris, 162; Hayes, 146; Keaton, 61; Rieger, 201; Stone, 51; Ward, 43)

ALEXANDER (McKeag, 35; Mundy, 103; Scott, 99; Waverly, 77; Waverly, 128)

ALF (Chesley, 91; Monroe, 81)

ALFRED (Bellows, 97; Delvecchio, 85; Pennyworth, 16)

ALGONQUIN (Calhoun, 9)

ALISTER (Mundy, 103)
ALLAN (Willis, 106)
ALMANZO (Wilder, 120)
AMOS (Burke, 31; Jones, 9; McCoy, 175; Tupper, 149)
ANDREW (Brown, 9; Keaton, 61; Laird, 54; Rush, 206; Squiggman, 115)
ANDY (7; 80; Garvey, 120; Moffet, 57; Renko, 91; Sipowicz, 160; Taylor, 10; Travis, 212)
ANGELO (Martelli, 59)
ANGUS (Crock, 189)
ANTHONY (Bouvier, 46)
ANTONIO (211)
ARCH (Fenster, 100)
ARCHIE (Bunker, 8)
ARLINGTON (Jones, 214)
ARMANDO (Sidoni, 43)
ARNIE (Becker, 113)
ARNOLD (85; Horshack, 215; Jackson, 48; Simms, 178)
ART (157; Donovan, 124)
ARTHUR (22; Carlson, 212; Cates, 39; Dietrich, 15; Falconetti, 178; Fonzarelli, 85; Harmon, 136; Raymond, 178; Trogg, 169; Wainwright, 206)
ARTIE (7)
ASHER (Berg, 178)
ASHLEY (Evans, 125)
ASHWELL (138)
AXEL (Dumire, 35; Jordache, 178)
BARNABY (Jones, 14; West, 213)
BARNEY (84; Collier, 142; Fife, 10; Hefner, 8; Miller, 15)
BART (Maverick, 137; Simpson, 193)
BARTH (Gimble, 65)
BARTON (Stuart, 170)
BAT (2)
BEAU (De Labarre, 215)
BEAUREGARD (Maverick, 137)
BEAVER (Cleaver, 116)
BEN (Caldwell, 108; Carrington, 42; Casey, 19; Cheviot,

138; Gibson, 111; Kokua, 88; Romero, 52; Samuels, 186; Seaver, 83; Stivers, 43; Walton, 214)

BENJAMIN (Matlock, 135; Pierce, 126; Shorofsky, 59)

BENNY (Goodwin, 177; Romero, 164; Stulwicz, 113)

BENSON (195; DuBois, 20)

BENTLEY (Gregg, 12)

BERNARD (Stevens, 159)

BERNIE (182; Steinberg, 30; Tupperman, 26)

BERT (Beasley, 136; Munson, 8; Samuels, 33; Smedley, 170)

BIFF (O'Hara, 4)

BILL (Brennan, 151; Davis, 60; Denton, 178; Gannon, 52; Goodwin, 72; Hawks, 213)

BILLY (178; Griffin, 95; Melrose, 188; Nelson, 40; Tate, 195; Truman, 13)

BINZER (209)

BLAIR (Sullivan, 43)

BLAKE (Carrington, 42)

BO (Duke, 53)

BOB (Barsky, 109; Brooks, 135; Campbell, 195; Dyrenforth, 59; Erickson, 114; Hartley, 26)

BOBBY (Borso, 209; Brady, 28; Crocker, 112; Ewing, 43; Gibson, 111; Hill, 91; Nelson, 38; Wheeler, 201)

BOOMER (Bates, 114)

BOXEY (17)

BRAD (Knight, 178)

BRADY (York, 43)

BRANDON (Clayton, 127)

BRENT (Maverick, 137)

BRET (Maverick, 137)

BRETT (Lomax, 43)

BRIAN (7; 211; Cunningham, 111; Kincaid, 24; Tanner, 6)

BRITT (Reid, 82)

BRUCE (8; 38; Harvey, 43; Wayne, 16)

BRUNO (Martelli, 59)

BRYCE (Lynch, 138)

BUB (O'Casey, 154)

BUBBA (Hoover, 187)
BUCK (Buckner, 32; Fallmont, 54)
BUD (156; Bundy, 132; Coleman, 158; Ricks, 66)
BUDDY (Sorrell, 47)
BUFE (Coker, 35)
BULL (Shannon, 157)
BURL (Smith, 125)
BURT (Campbell, 195)
BUTCH (Everett, 155)
BUZ (Murdock, 185)
CADDY (Cadron, 49)
CAJE (Cadron, 40)
CAL (Mitchell, 12)
CALVIN (Dudley, 118)
CAM (Allison, 208)
CARL (Levitt, 15; Reese, 102)
CARLO (Agretti, 58)
CARLOS (111; Ramirez, 67; Valdez, 195)
CARLSON (73)
CARLTON (177)
CARMINE (Ragusa, 115)
CASEY (Clark, 57; Denault, 43)
CASH (Cassidy, 39)
CECIL (7; Colby, 54)
CHACHI (Arcola, 85)
CHANO (Amenguale, 15)
CHARLES (30; 54; Arcola, 85; Cabot, 95; Eccles, 43;
    Enright, 140; Estep, 178; Kingsfield, 166; Lowell, 109;
    Parker, 57; Parker, 139; Raymond,; Ingalls, 120; Winches-
    ter, 127)
CHARLEY (O'Casey, 154)
CHARLIE (7; 106; 48; 152; Fong, 12; Haggers, 133; Hume,
    124; Pratt, 170; Townsend, 36; Wade, 43; Wooster, 213)
CHARMIN (Cunningham, 158)
CHASE (Gioberti, 58)
CHATSWORTH (Osborne, Jr., 130)
CHE (Fong, 88)

CHESTER (Goode, 84; Riley, 118; Tate, 195; Wanamaker, 156)

CHET (Kincaid, 24)

CHIN HO (Kelly, 88)

CHIP (Douglas, 154; Lowell, 109; Morton, 210; Roberts, 111; Saunders, 40)

CHRIS (136; Deegan, 54; Owens, 181; Stevens, 159; Webber, 171)

CHRISTOPHER (58; Donlon, 59; Ewing, 43; Hale, 213; Partridge, 167)

CHRISTY (Christopher, 139)

CHUCK (7; Boyle, 79; Campbell, 195; Cunningham, 85)

CLARENCE (Day, 119; Rutherford, 116)

CLARK (Kent, 5)

CLAUDE (Messner, 64; Tinker, 178)

CLAY (Fallmont, 54; Forrester, 174)

CLAYMORE (Gregg, 74)

CLAYTON (Endicott III, 20; Farlow, 43; Greenwood, 84)

CLETUS (53)

CLIFF (57; Barnes, 43; Clavin, 37; Huxtable, 41)

CLINT (Albright, 164; Ogden, 43)

CLINTON (Judd, 108)

COLE (Gioberti, 58)

CONRAD (Siegfried, 73)

COOPER (63; Smith, 213)

COOTER (53)

COREY (Stuart, 114)

COSMO (Topper, 207)

COY (Duke, 53)

CRAIG (Carter, 126; Stewart, 43)

CULLY (Wilson, 114)

CURLEY (Jones, 210)

CURTIS (Willard, 214)

DALE (Mitchell, 114)

DAN (Connors, 184; Fielding, 157; Fixx, 58; Robbins, 200; Tanna, 209)

ANDY (Dandridge, 43)

DANIEL (Auschlander, 186; Briggs, 142; Freeland, 19; Gregg, 74; Reece, 54)

DANNY (7; Amatullo, 59; Carrington, 42; Dallas, 195; Morley, 63; Partridge, 167; Paterno, 165; Tanner, 70; Tovo, 173; Williams, 88)

DARRIN (Stephens, 22)

DARRYL (156; Clayton, 58)

DASH (Riprock, 21)

DATA (198)

DAVE (159; Crabtree, 153; Culver, 43; Kelsey, 51; Kendall, 95; Starsky, 199; Stratton, 43; Welch, 154)

DAVEY (Gillis, 130)

DAVID (Addison, 146; Banner, 101; Baxter, 134; Bradford, 55; Gideon, 169; Kane, 162; Keeler, 33; Miller, 15; Nelson, 209; Reardon, 59; Zorba, 19)

DAVY (145)

DEAN (Raymond Bailey, 130)

DENNIS (Becker, 180; Foley, 133; Mitchell, 45; Phillips, 195; Price, 124; Randall, 102; Widmer, 44)

DENNY (41)

DEREK (Mitchell, 105)

DEVON (Miles, 110)

DEX (Dexter, 54)

DICK (Grayson, 16; Loudon, 156)

DIGBY (O'Dell, 118)

DINO (Baroni, 139)

DOBIE (Gillis, 130)

DON (Marshall, 118; Roberts, 1; West, 123)

DONALD (Westphall, 186)

DONNY (Gerard, 177)

DOPLOS (163)

DORY (McKenna, 33)

DOUG (7; 142; Chapman, 180; Phillips, 205)

DOUGLAS (Brackman, Jr., 113; Channing, 58; Harrigan, 139)

DOYLE (Hobbs, 64)

DUDLEY (Ramsey, 48)

DUKE (Lukela, 88; Shannon, 213; Slater, 79)
DUNCAN (Calderwood, 178; Gillis, 130)
DUSTY (Farlow, 43)
DUTCH (195)
DWAYNE (Cooley, 58; Schneider, 162; Wayne, 49)
DWIGHT (59)
EARL (Camembert, 189; Hicks, 7; Trent, 111)
EB (Dawson, 81; Dawson, 170)
EBENEZER (Sprague, 120)
ED (Brown, 102; Chigliak, 159; Davis, 64; Jacobs, 52;
  Norton, 94; O'Connor, 84; Swanson, 8; Wells, 2)
EDDIE (83; 173; Corbett, 42; Cronin, 43; Haskell, 116;
  Jacks, 171; Munster, 148; Ryker, 181)
EDGAR (Randolph, 43)
EDISON (Carter, 138)
EDWARD (Gray, 79)
EGBERT (Gillis, 118)
ELI (Carson, 171)
ELIOT (Ness, 208; Novak, 7)
ELLIOT (Axelrod, 186; Carlin, 26; Gabler, 156; Weston,
  203)
ELLIOTT (Carson, 171)
ELROY (Carpenter, 139; Jetson, 107)
ELVIN (Tibideaux, 41)
EMERY (Potter, 53)
EMMETT (Clark, 10)
ENOS (Strate, 53)
ENRICO (Rossi, 208)
EP (Bridges, 214)
ERIC (159; Fairgate, 111; Lloyd, 95; Russell, 183; Stavros,
  58)
ERNIE (166; Douglas, 154; Fields, 55; Pantusso, 37)
EUGENE (147; Bullock, 43)
EVAN (Brent, 183; Drake, 37)
EXIDOR (147)
FARNSWORTH (Dexter, 54)
FATS (13)

FELIX (Unger, 161)

FERGUS (Douglas, 154)

FESTER (Frump, 3)

FESTUS (Haggen, 84)

FLETCHER (Daniels, 91)

FLINT (McCullough, 213)

FLIP (Phillips, 85)

FLOYD (Lawson, 10; Smoot, 170)

FRANCIS (121; Mulcahy, 126; Muldoon, 34)

FRANK (150; Belson, 196; Burns, 127; De Fazio, 115; Elliot, 111; Furillo, 91; Lorenzo, 8; Luger, 15; McNeil, 112; Monahan, 173; Nitti, 208; Poncherello, 38; Smith, 52; Williams, 111)

FRANKIE (20; Lombardi, 79; Sanchez, 1)

FRANKLIN (Bickley, 147; Hart, 158)

FRANZ (Kafka, 159)

FRASIER (Crane, 37)

FRED (Dodd, 44; Johnson, 69; Mertz, 98; Russell, 171; Rutherford, 116; Sanford, 187; Wilkinson, 58; Ziffel, 81)

FREDDIE (Washington, 215; Wilson, 152)

FREDERICK (McConnell, 147)

FUJI (Kobiaji, 139)

GABE (Kotter, 215)

GAGARIAN (166)

GALEN (172; Adams, 84)

GARRETT (Boydston, 39; Boydston, 54)

GARTH (58; Gimble, 65; Gimble, 133)

GARY (Ewing, 43; Ewing, 111; Levy, 177; Rabinowitz, 8; Shandling, 104; Shepherd, 203)

GASPAR (Gormento, 67)

GENE (Fritz, 38; Talbot, 164)

GEOFFREY (Wells, 216)

GEORDI (La Forge, 198)

GEORGE (183; Anderson, 171; Baxter, 89; Burnett, 57; Burns, 72; Christopher, 139; Descenzo, 191; Honeywell, 152; Jefferson, 8; Jefferson, 106; Jetson, 107; Kerby, 207;

MacMichael, 175; Lester, 202; Shumway, 133; Stevens, 9;
Utley, 156; Wilson, 45)
GERALD (Kookson, 192)
GERARD (54)
GIL (Favor, 174; Hanley, 40)
GILBERT (Bates, 116; Slater, 79)
GILES (French, 60)
GILLIGAN (76)
GLEN (Morley, 63)
GOMER (Pyle, 10; Pyle, 79)
GOMEZ (Addams, 3)
GOOBER (Pyle, 10)
GOPHER (Smith, 125)
GORDON (Howard, 134; Kirkwood, 143; Sims, 212; Wales,
54)
GORDY (Howard, 134)
GRADY (Fletcher, 149; Wilson, 187)
GRANT (Schumaker, 104)
GREG (Brady, 28; Howard, 175; Maxwell, 55; Reardon, 58)
GREGORY (49; Sumner, 111)
GRILL (183)
GRIZZLY (Adams, 117)
GUNTHER (Toody, 34)
GUS (Chernak, 171; Nunouz, 58)
GUSTAV (Riebmann, 58)
GUY (Caballero, 189; Stafford, 58)
HAL (Brubaker, 13; Everett, 155)
HALLIGAN (84)

---

### I GUESS "TINY HERB"
### DIDN'T SOUND RIGHT, EH?

Eccentric "singer" Tiny Tim's real name is Herbert
Khuarty.

HAMILTON (Burger, 169)

HANK (84; Buchanan, 214; Ferguson, 154; Kimball, 81; Pivnik, 8)

HANNIBAL (Dobbs, 56; Smith, 1)

HANS (Brumbaugh, 35; Schultz, 92)

HAP (Gorman, 66)

HAPPY (187; Haines, 139; Kyne, 65)

HARKNESS (Mushgrove, 174)

HARLAN (38; Day, 119)

HARLEY (Estin, 156)

HARMON (Farinella, 133)

HAROLD (Baxter, 89; Dobey, 199; Dyer, 111)

HARRIMAN (Nelson, 210)

HARRISON (Bell, 139; Carter, 126)

HARRY (95; Bentley, 106; Burns, 151; Conners, 126; Dickens, 100; Garibaldi, 91; Miles, 53; Morton, 72; Nussbaum, 158; Snowden, 8; Stone, 157; Thompson, 89; Von Zell, 72)

HARVE (Smithfield, 43)

HARVEY (Griffin, 89; Lacey, 33; Peck, 202)

HAWK (196)

HEATH (Barkley, 23)

HENDERSON (Palmer, 39)

HENRY (7; Ames, 31; Blake, 127; Boomhauer, 71; Desmond, 27; Evans, 136; Goldblume, 91; Harrison, 43; Jefferson, 8; Mitchell, 45; Pearson, 154; Rush, 206)

HERB (Tarlek, 212)

---

### YEAH, BUT IN ENGLISH, IT MEANS "CANCELED"

Arsenio Hall once told *The Hollywood Reporter* that he used to open his act by telling the audience, "Hi, I'm Arsenio. A very unique name for a black man. In Greek, it means 'Leroy.'"

HERBERT (Gillis, 130; Johnson, 89; Molumphrey, 163; Viola, 146)

HERMAN (Munster, 148)

HEY SOOS (Patines, 174)

HEYWOOD (Kirk, 2050

HOLLING (Vincour, 159)

HOMER (Bedloe, 170; Simpson, 193)

HOWARD (57; Borden, 26; Cunningham, 85; Everett, 155; Hunter, 91; Meechim, 12; Sprague, 10;

HOWIE (84)

HUGGY BEAR (199)

HUGH (Beale, 186)

HUNT (Stockwell, 1)

HUTCH (Corrigan, 39; Hutchinson, 199)

HYMIE (73)

IAN (Cabot, 174; Ware, 59)

IGOR (127)

IKE (Godsey, 214)

ILYA (Kuryakin, 128)

IRWIN (Bernstein, 91; Handelman, 61)

ISAAC (Washington, 125)

ISAIAH (Edwards, 120)

ITT (3)

IZZY (Moreno, 141)

JACK (Arnold, 217; Chandler, 171; Doyle, 177; Ewing, 43; McGee, 101; Morrison, 186; North, 58; Tripper, 204)

JACKIE (Devereaux, 54)

JAKE (Pasquinel, 35; Styles, 105)

JAMES (158; 183; Adams, 117; Carew, 88; Cooper, 120; Crockett, 141; Gatling, 20; Hart, 166; Kildare, 50; T. Kirk, 197; Kinchloe, 92; Phelps, 142)

JAMIE (King, 188)

JARRETT (McLeish, 43)

JARROD (Barkley, 23)

JASON (7; Allen, 182; Avery, 111; Carter, 120; Colby, 39; McCabe, 105; McCord, 29; Seaver, 83; Walton, 214)

JASPER (DePew, 21)

JAY (Spence, 58)

JEAN-LUC (Picard, 198)

JEB (Amos, 43; Carter, 120)

JED (Clampett, 21; Colby, 174)

JEDEDIAH (Jones, 14)

JEFF (Colby, 39; Colby, 54; Farraday, 43; Spencer, 192; Stone, 51; Wainwright, 58; Williams, 57)

JEFFERSON (Hogg, 53)

JEFFREY (Burton, 214; DeVito, 133)

JEMMY (Brent, 183)

JEREMY (Andretti, 55; Wendell, 43)

JERRY (7; Bauman, 202; Carmichael, 126; Davenport, 162; Fuchs, 91; Helper, 47; Hubbard, 65; Kenderson, 43; Seinfeld, 191; Walters, 2)

JESS (Brandon, 165)

JESSE (Cochran, 70; Duke, 53; Nash, 216; Valesquez, 59)

JESUS (Martinez, 91)

JETHRO (Bodine, 21)

JIM (Anderson, 64; Elgin, 25; Gillis, 118; Ignatowski, 201; Lloyd, 35; Quince, 174; Reed, 2; Rockford, 180; Westmont, 111)

JIM-BOB (Walton, 214)

JIMMY (Olson, 5)

JIMMY JOE (Jeter, 133)

JOCK (Ewing, 43)

JODY (60)

JOE (211; Carson, 170; Chernak, 171; Coffey, 91; Cooper, 111; Friday, 52; Gerard, 177; Getraer, 38; Mannix, 129; Rossi, 124; Rossi, 171; Scarlett, 174; Taylor, 14)

JOEL (Abrigore, 54; Fleischman, 159; McCarthy, 58)

JOEY (Gladstone, 70; McDonald, 45; Quales, 178)

JOHN (Biddle, 14; Bosley, 36; Brewster, 21; Burns, 201; Carter, 120; Coblentz, 111; Cooper, 75; Cooper, 180; Costello, 58; Day, 119; Drake, 190; Fowler, 171; Franklin, 178; Gideon, 186; Kelly, 160; Manicote, 88; McIntosh, 35; McIntyre, 127; Moretti, 39; Mulcahy, 127; Reid, 122;

Reynolds, 183; Smith, 1; Taylor, 20; Walton, 214; Wilson, 45)

JOHN BOY (Walton, 214)

JOHNNY (Fever, 212; LaRue, 91; LaRue, 189; Rourke, 111; Venture, 177)

JON (Baker, 38)

JONAH (Newman, 33)

JONAS (Grumby [The Skipper], 76)

JONATHAN (Bower, 216; Brooks, 166; Garvey, 120; Hart, 86; Muir, 74; Rollins, 113; Smith, 90; Steed, 11)

JORDAN (Lee, 43)

JOSÉ (8)

JOSEPH (Anders, 54; Gioberti, 58; Haines, 139; Rockford, 180)

JOSH (Macahan, 96)

JOSHUA (Rush, 111)

JUAN (Epstein, 215)

JUD (Crowley, 10)

JULIAN (Roberts, 58)

JULIO (Fuentes, 187)

JUNIOR (118)

JUSTIN (183; Culp, 177; Quigley, 8)

KADI (Touray, 183)

KATO (82)

KEI (95)

KEITH (Holden, 114; Partridge, 167)

KELLY (Robinson, 99)

KEN (Hutchinson, 199; Valere, 186)

KENNY (41; Ward, 111)

KEVIN (Arnold, 217)

KIMO (Carew, 88)

KING (Galen, 54)

KINTANGO (183)

KIP (Wilson, 27)

KIPPER (18)

KIPPY (Watkins, 64)

KIRK (Devane, 156)

KIT (159)
KOLYA (Rostov, 39)
KONO (Kalakaua, 88)
KOOKIE (Kookson, 192)
KRAMER (191)
KUNTA (Kinte, 183)
LAME BEAVER (35)
LAMONT (Sanford, 187)
LANCE (124; Cumson, 58; White, 180)
LARRABEE (120)
LARRY (79; 156; 182;) Bondurant, 26; Dallas, 204;
   Mondello, 116; Tate, 22; Zito, 141
LARS (Hanson, 120)
LATKA (Gravas, 201)
LAWRENCE (62; Chapman, 21)
LEANDER (Pomfritt, 130)
LEE (Crane, 210; Hobson, 208; Stetson, 188; Webber, 171)
LELAND (McKenzie, 113)
LENNY (Kosnowski, 115)
LEO (Schnitz, 91)
LEON (157; 184; Bessemer, 202)
LEONARD (Gillespie, 50; McCoy, 197; Smith, 104)
LEROY (Johnson, 59)
LES (Crowley, 43; Hart, 31; Nessman, 212)
LESTER (Gruber, 139; Hummel, 79)
LEVI (Zandt, 35)
LEW (Miles, 171; Vernor, 35)
LEWIS (183)
LINC (Case, 185; Hayes, 144)
LIONEL (Jefferson, 8; Jefferson, 106)
LITTLEJOHN (40)
LLOYD (Burgess, 135)
LOGAN (121)
LOU (Grant, 124; Grant, 134; Mackie, 59; Mallory, 179;
   Marie, 202; Martin, 178; Wickersham, 129)
LOUIE (De Palma, 201; Pheers, 84)
LOUIS (LeBeau, 92; )

LOWELL (211)

LUCAS (Carter, 39; McCain, 179)

LUIS (Rueda, 43)

LUKE (Duke, 53; Fuller, 54; Macahan, 96; McCoy, 175)

LUMPY (Rutherford, 116)

LURCH (3)

LUTHER (Hawkes, 186

MAC (Robinson, 157; Slattery, 133)

MACE (Mobrey, 159)

MANNY (Esposito, 33; Vasquez, 111)

MARC (173)

MARCELLO (67; 189)

MARCUS (Garvey, 106; Welby, 131)

MARIO (58; Lugatto, 139)

MARK (93; Craig, 186; Danning, 95; Gordon, 90; Graison, 43; Jennings, 54; McCain, 179; Petrie, 33; Royer, 162; Sanger, 102; Slate, 77; St. Claire, 111; Templeton, 21; Wedloe, 71)

MARSH (Goodwin, 178)

MARTIN (151; Block, 34; Castillo, 141; Crane, 68; Flaherty, 208; Lane, 168; Morgenstern, 177; Peterson, 97; Peyton, 171; Quirk, 196)

MATT (Brockway, 114; Cantrell, 43; Dillon, 84)

MATTHEW (Blaisdel, 54; Fordwick, 214; Sherman, 163; Swain, 171)

MAURICE (22; Minnifield, 159)

MAX (86; Hartman, 58; Headroom, 138; Horvath, 162; Vincent, 178; Waltz, 24)

MAXWELL (Klinger, 127; Mercy, 35; Smart, 73)

MAYNARD (Krebs, 130)

MEARTH (147)

MEL (Beach, 133; Cooley, 47; Sharples, 7; Warshaw, 100)

MELVIN (187)

MERLE (Jeeter, 133; Stockwell, 55)

MERRILL (Stubing, 125)

MERVIN (Wendell, 35)

MICAH (Torrance, 179)

MICHAEL (Culhane, 54; Fairgate, 111; Harris, 156; Henderson, 158; Knight, 110; Kuzak, 113; Lacey, 33; O'Casey, 154; Ranson, 58; Ridley, 186; Rossi, 171; Steadman, 203; Torrance, 54; Woodman, 215)

MICK (Belker, 91)

MICKEY (Trotter, 43)

MICKY (145)

MIKE (7; 145; 204; Axford, 82; Bender, 163; Brady, 28; Danko, 181; Douglas, 154; Fitzgerald, 30; Gambit, 11; Holden, 114; Monroe, 159; Pasquinel, 35; Rogers, 19; Seaver, 83; Stivic, 8; Stone, 200)

MILBURN (Drysdale, 21)

MILES (150; Colby, 39; Sternhagen, 147)

MILTIE (Horowitz, 59)

MILTON (Armitage, 130)

MINGO (183)

MITCH (Aames, 7; Cooper, 43)

MITCHELL (Casey, 111)

MOE (Green, 189; Plotnick, 30)

MONROE (Ficus, 206)

MONTGOMERY (MacNeil, 59; Scott, 197)

MORGAN (158; O'Rourke, 56; Wendell, 35)

MORK (147)

MOSS (Goodman, 44)

MOUSE (18)

MURPHY (Michaels, 176)

MURRAY (138; 215; Greshner, 161; Klein, 8; Slaughter, 134)

MYRON (Bannister, 100)

NACHO (35)

NAKUMA (117)

NAPOLEON (Solo, 128)

NATE (Grossman, 768; Person, 35)

NATHAN (Burke, 84)

NEAL (McVane, 54; Washington, 91)

NED (Svenborg, 159)

NEIL (Kittredge, 39)

## LAST NAME FIRST . . .

In the chapter on names from TV characters, you will find nine character names listed from the popular seventies series *Quincy, M.E.,* but you will *not* find a name for the Jack Klugman character, Quincy himself. Why? Because, like Columbo, Quincy's first name was never mentioned on the show, although it seems he *did* have one. In one episode, the doc's business card is briefly visible and it reads, "Dr. R. Quincy." Does the surname "Quincy" work as a first name? I guess it depends on how much you love the show, right?

*The Young and the Restless* star J. Eddie Peck said that he and his wife discussed several names for their soon-to-be-arriving son before they finally settled on Dalton. "Dalton is a name I thought of years ago when we were coming up with names for [our first son] Austin," said Peck. "It was similar to other names we were considering: 'Dayton,' 'Clayton,' 'Damon'—those two-syllable, last name-sounding names. Dalton won out this time around."

NELS (Oleson, 120)
NELSON (Flavor, 147)
NEWLY (O'Brien, 84)
NEWT (Kiley, 81)
NICHOLAS (43; Bradford, 55; Pearce, 43; Stone, 7)
NICK (Barkley, 23; Guccinello, 79; Handris, 162; Hogan, 58; Holden, 163; Kanavaras, 19; Kimball, 54; Moore, 61; Morrison, 111; Toscanni, 54; Yemana, 15)
NIKOLAI (Rostov, 39)
NILES (Crane, 68)
NOAH (183; Bain, 103)

NORM (Green, 2; Peterson, 37)

NORMAN (Buntz, 91; Curtis, 170; Harrington, 171; Tinker, 42)

NORTON (Crane, 58)

OLIVER (Wendell Douglas, 81; Munsey, 164)

OMORO (183)

OPIE (Taylor, 10)

ORDELL (183)

ORRIN (Pike, 170)

ORSON (147)

OSCAR (Goldman, 25; Goldman, 194; Madison, 161)

OSGOOD (Conklin, 164)

OTIS (Campbell, 10; Foster, 30)

OTTO (Schmidlap, 188; Sharkey, 32)

OWEN (Marshall, 165)

OZWALD (Valentine, 43)

OZZIE (Cleveland, 91)

PADGETT (58)

PALADIN (87)

PARIS (142)

PATRICK (Flaherty, 91; MacKenzie, 111)

PAUL (Drake, 169; Galveston, 111; Garrett, 35; Hanley, 171; La Guardia, 33; Martin, 114; Morgan, 43; Pfeiffer, 217; Seeger, 59)

PAVEL (Chekhov, 197)

PEPINO (Garcia, 175)

PERCIVAL (Dalton, 120)

PERCY (Crump, 84)

PERRY (Mason, 169; White, 5)

PETE (Adams, 43; Burke, 172; Cochran, 144; Dixon, 182; Downey, 20; Malloy, 2; Nolan, 174; Schumaker, 104; Tierney, 178)

PETER (145; 150; Brady, 28; Campbell, 195; Chiara, 41; de Vilbis, 54; Hollister, 111; McDermott, 95; Newkirk, 92; Richards, 43; Stavros, 58; Stone, 75; Tong, 12; White, 186)

PETRIE (Martin, 114)

PHIL (150; 157; Esterhaus, 91; Fish, 15; Greenberg, 178; McGee, 178; Porter, 131)

PHILIP (Boynton, 164; Drummond, 48; Gerard, 69; Grey, 88; King, 188; Roth, 209; Wendell, 35)

PHILLIP (136; Chandler, 186; Colby, 39; Erickson, 58)

POPESCO (133)

PORKY (Brockway, 114)

PORTER (Ricks, 66)

PUGSLEY (Addams, 3)

QUENTIN (Kelly, 80; Morloch, 59)

QUINT (Asper, 84)

QUINTON (McHale, 139; Shively, 46)

RALEIGH (7)

RALPH (7; 106; Furley, 204; Kramden, 94; Little, 64; Malph, 85; Ramsey, 98)

RAMÓN (Diaz, 177; Gallardo, 163)

RANDOLPH (Agarn, 56)

RANDY (93; Crabtree, 153)

RAOUL (8)

RAVENSWOOD (21)

RAY (Calletano, 91; Dwyer, 178; Geary, 111; Krebbs, 43)

RAYMOND (91; Larkin, 133; Swain, 205)

REESE (Watson, 46)

REGINALD (Cornelius III, 110)

REM (121)

REMINGTON (Steele, 176)

REMO (DaVinci, 147)

REUBEN (Kincaid, 167)

REX (Randolph, 192)

RICARDO (Tubbs, 141)

RICHARD (116; Avery, 111; Baker, 92; Channing, 58; Cooksey, 135; Harrison, 168; Kimble, 69; Stabone, 83)

RICHIE (Cunningham, 85; Lane, 182)

RICK (Bonner, 57)

RICKY (Ricardo, 98; Stevens, 167; Valasca, 164)

RIFF (Ryan, 130)

---

**NAMESAKE DEPARTMENT**

The character of Roz Doyle on the TV hit sitcom *Frasier* was named after a producer named Roz, who, before her early death from breast cancer at forty-nine in 1991, had been a well-liked figure in the TV industry. The real Roz had helped make the series *Wings* a success and after she died, her friends on *Frasier* wanted to do something in honor of her memory.

---

RILEY (Wicker, 58)
RIP (Masters, 4)
RITCHIE (Petrie, 47)
ROB (Petrie, 47)
ROBBIE (Cartman, 117; Douglas, 154; Jason, 48)
ROBERT (Alden, 120; Astin, 173; Caldwell, 186; Hogan, 92; Ironside, 102; Morton, 171)
ROCKY (Rockford, 180)
RODERICK (Decker, 1)
RODNEY (Harrington, 171)
ROGER (161; Addison, 143; Healey, 97; Landon, 39; Lawson, 187; Phillips, 85)
ROLAND (Saunders, 58)
ROLLIN (Hand, 142)
ROLLO (Larson, 187)
RON (159; Harris, 15; Holden, 114; Johnson, 49)
RONALD (Coleman, 33)
RONNIE (Burns, 72)
ROOSTER (13)
ROSCOE (192; Coltrane, 53)
ROSEMONT (58)
ROSS (Lane, 168)
ROWDY (Yates, 174)

ROY (127; 161; 211; Hinkley [The Professor], 76; Lance, 111; Ralston, 43)
RUDY (Jordache, 178; Wells, 25; Wells, 194)
RUSS (Gehring, 171; Lawrence, 75; Merman, 158)
RUSSELL (Huxtable, 41)
RUSTY (4)
RYAN (Thomas, 95)
SACHA (Malenkov, 39)
SAM (84; Bennett, 183; Drucker, 81; Drucker, 170; Fujiyama, 173; Malone, 37; McKinney, 48; Royer, 162; Steinberg, 30)
SANDY (Ricks, 66)
SCOOTER (Warren, 111)
SCOTT (Turner, 114)
SCOTTY (178; Demarest, 43)
SEAN (McAllister, 39; Rowan, 54)
SETH (Adams, 213; Griffin, 186; Hazlitt, 149)
SEYMOUR (45; Kaufman, 182; Schwimmer, 202)
SHERMAN (Bagley, 126; Potter, 127)
SHIFTY (Shafer, 21)
SHORTY (Kellems, 21)
SID (Fairgate, 111; Gossett, 178; Thurston, 91)
SIDDO (75)
SILAS (23)
SIMON (Agurski, 50)
SKIPPY (Handelman, 61)
SMITTY (51; 178; 187)
SNAKE (Robinson, 57)
SOLOMON (King, 174)
SONNY (Crockett, 141; Drysdale, 21; Lumet, 27; St. Jacques, 115)
SPEED (161)
SPENSER (196)
SPHEERIS (58)
SPIROS (Koralis, 39)
SPOCK (197)
STAN (Switek, 141)

---

### "AKA" DEPARTMENT

Ben Kingsley's real name is Krishna Bhanji: He was born in Britain, but he is the son of an Indian physician, thus the traditional Indian name.

---

STANISLAUS (Jablonski, 91)

STANLEY (Roper, 204; Wojohowicz, 15)

STEPHEN (Bennett, 183)

STEVE (2; Austin, 194; Baxter, 89; DiMaggio, 140; Douglas, 154; Drumm, 169; Elliott, 170; Keaton, 61; Keller, 200; McGarrett, 88; Morley, 63)

STEVEN (Bradley, 57; Carrington, 42; Cord, 171; Kiley, 131)

STEWART (McMillan, 140)

STRETCH (Cunningham, 8; Snodgrass, 164)

STU (Riley, 210)

STUART (Bailey, 192; Markowitz, 113)

SUDSY (Pfeiffer, 154)

SULU (197)

SWEENEY (179)

SYLVESTER (Brockway, 114)

TATTOO (62)

TED (Bartelo, 109; Baxter, 134; Hoffman, 19; McCovey, 124; Ramsey, 48; Warrick, 165)

TEDDY (Boylan, 178)

TEMPLETON (Smith, 1)

TERRENCE (Clay, 169)

TERRY (McDaniel, 19; Webster, 181)

THADDEUS (73)

THEO (Kojak, 112)

THEODORE (Cleaver, 116; Dowell, 171; Huxtable, 41; Mooney, 45; Mooney, 126)

THOMAS (Anderson, 166; Gerson, 50)

THORNTON (McLeish, 43)

THURSTON (Howell III, 76)

TIM (93; O'Hara, 151; Tilson, 31)

TIMMY (114)

TIMOTHY (Flotsky, 195)

TINKER (Bell, 139)

TOBY (183)

TOD (Stiles, 185)

TODD (Ludlow, 215)

TOM (183; Basil, 33; Bradford, 55; Corbett, 42; Hartman, 133; Jordache, 178; Moore, 183; Pezik, 111; Wedloe, 71; Willis, 106; Winter, 171)

TOMMY (158; Anderson, 45; Bradford, 55; Hyatt, 7; Kelsey, 8)

TONTO (122)

TONY (43; Banta, 201; Baretta, 13; Cumson, 58; Micelli, 216; Nelson, 97; Newman, 205; Roletti, 65)

TRANQUILINO (35)

TREVOR (Ochmonek, 6)

TRUCK (Kealoha, 88)

TURK (Tobias, 58)

TYLER (Hudson, 135)

URKO (172)

VANCE (Duke, 53)

VAUGHN (Leland, 43)

VENUS (Flytrap, 212)

VERNE (Rowe, 65)

VERNON (Albright, 152)

VICTOR (Ehrlich, 186; Isbecki, 33; Sifuentes, 113)

VINCE (Caproni, 58; Carter, 79; Karlotti, 58)

VINCENT (18; Markham, 171)

VINNIE (161; Barbarino, 215; Day, 119)

VIRGIL (Edwards, 139; Sims, 65)

VIRGINIA (Calderwood, 178)

WALDO (Binney, 118)

WALLACE (Binghampton, 139)

WALLIE (Powers, 103)

WALLY (Cleaver, 116)

WALT (Driscoll, 43; Fitzgerald, 30)

WALTER (Denton, 164; Findlay, 136; Lanakershim, 54; Oakes, 49; O'Reilly, 127; Steward, 88)

WARD (Cleaver, 116)

WARREN (Coolidge, 186; Dawson, 12; Ferguson, 10; Weber, 85)

WAYNE (Arnold, 217; Fiscus, 186; Harkness, 111; Masterson, 39)

WENDELL (Gibbs, 170)

WES (Parmalee, 43)

WESLEY (178; Crusher, 198)

WHITEY (Whitney, 116)

WHITNEY (Day, 119)

WILBUR (Post, 143)

WILHELM (Klink, 92)

WILL (Robinson, 123)

WILLARD (Barnes, 43)

WILLIAM (Coleman, 158; Henderson, 5; Kirby, 40; Reynolds, 183; Riker, 198; Youngfellow, 208)

WILLIE (71; Abbott, 178; Armitage, 142; Garr, 43; Gillis, 181; Oleson, 120; Tanner, 6)

WILLIS (Bell, 166; Jackson, 48)

WILLY (Moss, 139)

WILTON (Parmenter, 56)

WINFIELD (Schaeffer, 97)

WINGARD (Stone, 97)

WISHBONE (174)

WOODY (Anderson, 187; Boyd, 37)

WORF (198)

XAVIER (17)

YANCY (Tucker, 214)

ZACHARY (Powers, 39; Smith, 123)

ZAIUS (172)

ZEB (Macahan, 96; Walton, 214)

---

### NAME CHANGE DEPARTMENT

When Native-American princess Pocahontas
converted to Christianity, she renounced her
ancestral name in favor of the Christian
name Rebecca.

U.S. Representative Leo Ryan was slain in Guyana
by followers of cult leader Jim Jones. Later, his
daughter Shannon Jo changed her name to Ma
Prem Amrita after she joined an ashram of the
Bhagwam Sheree Rajneesh.

Thea Vidale, star of the TV sitcom *Thea*, tells
people that she has four children, Hellfire,
Damnation, Pestilence, and Scurvy, and that "those
are their Christian names."

The Indians' name for George Armstrong Custer
was "Yellow Hair."

---

## GIRLS NAMES FROM TV SHOWS

ABBY (Ewing, 111)
ADA (Jacks, 171)
ADELAIDE (Brubaker, 48; Mitchell, 12)
ADRIENNE (Cassidy, 39; Van Leyden, 171)
AFTON (Cooper, 43)
AGATHA (140; Morley, 63)
AGGIE (Larkin, 175)
AGNES (Dipesto, 146)
ALEX (211)
ALEXIS (Carrington, 42)

ALICE (195; Barth, 177; Garvey, 120; Hyatt, 7; Johnson, 182; Kramden, 94; Lacey, 33; Mitchell, 45; Nelson, 28)

ALLIE (Lowell, 109)

ALLISON (49; 58; Mackenzie, 171)

ALMA (Miles, 171)

AMANDA (Bellows, 97; Carrington, 42; King, 188)

AMY (111; 125; Allen, 1; Cassidy, 27; Fitzgerald, 30)

ANA (67; 111)

ANGEL (Martin, 180)

ANGELA (164; Bower, 216; Brown, 151; Channing, 58)

ANGELICA (Nero, 43)

ANGIE (Globagoski, 215; Turner, 209)

ANN (Howard, 171; MacGregor, 205; Marie, 202; Romano, 162)

ANNA (Huxtable, 41; Rossini, 58; Rostov, 39)

ANNABELLE (133)

ANNE (183; Cooper, 75; Matheson, 111)

ANNIE (Adams, 178; Cavanero, 186; Horvath, 162; O'Connell, 60)

APOLLONIA (58)

APRIL (Adams, 64; Curtis, 110; Dancer, 77; Rush, 206; Stevens, 43)

ARLISS (Cooper, 43)

ASHELEY (Brooks, 166)

ASHLEY (Pfister, 85)

ATHENA (17)

AUDRA (Barkley, 23)

BABS (118)

BAILEY (Quarters, 212)

BARBARA (111; Baxter, 89; Cooper, 162; Crabtree, 153; Douglas, 154; Duran, 163; Gordon, 16)

BEATRICE (Travis, 209)

BEE (Taylor, 10)

BELL (183)

BELLA (Archer, 209)

BELLE (Dudley, 118; Dupree, 7)

BERNICE (Fish, 15; Foxe, 176)

BERTRILLE (67)
BESS (Lindstrom, 134)
BETH (Davenport, 180)
BETSY (Gibson, 111)
BETTY (43; Anderson, 64; Harrington, 171; Jones, 14;
    Ramsey, 98; Wheeler, 163)
BETTY JO (Bradley, 170)
BEV (Dutton, 156)
BEVERLEY (Faverty, 33)
BEVERLY (Crusher, 198)
BEVERLY ANN (Stickle, 57)
BILLIE (Bunker, 8; Newman, 124)
BILLIE JO (Bradley, 170)
BINTA (183)
BLAIR (Warner, 57)
BLANCHE (Devereaux, 78; Madison, 161; Morton, 72)
BLISS (Colby, 39)
BLOSSOM (Kenney, 130)
BOBBIE JO (Bradley, 170)
BONNIE (216; Barstow, 110; Clark, 38; Robertson, 43)
BONNIE SUE (McAfee, 72)
BRENDA (Morgenstern, 177)
BRIDGET (Steinberg, 30)
BRIMA (Cesay, 183)
BUFFY (60; 27)
BUNNY (79)
CAITLIN (Davies, 141)
CANDICE (Muir, 74)
CARESS (Morell, 54)
CARLA (1; Mardigian, 124; Tortelli, 37)
CARLY (Fixx, 58)
CAROL (111; 136; 166; Bondurant, 26; Brady, 28; David,
    195; Novino, 186; Post, 143; Seaver, 83)
CAROLINE (Ingalls, 120)
CAROLYN (Muir, 74; Russell, 171)
CARRIE (Ingalls, 120; Sharples, 7)
CASEY (142; Case, 82)

CASSANDRA (Cooper, 120; Wilder, 58)
CASSIE (Phillips, 135)
CASSIOPEA (17)
CATHERINE (18)
CATHY (Lane, 168; Martin, 186; Rush, 111; Shumway, 133)
CECILY (Pigeon, 161)
CELESTE (Patterson, 91)
CHANNING (Colby, 39)
CHARLENE (DuPrey, 48; Matlock, 135; Winston, 46)
CHARLOTTE (Lloyd, 35; Miller, 59)
CHERYL (Dolan, 95)
CHRIS (Cagney, 33; Carmichael, 126)
CHRISSY (Snow, 204)
CHRISTINE (Chapel, 197; Francis, 95; Sullivan, 157)
CHRISTMAS (Snow, 204)
CIJI (Dunne, 111)
CINAMMON (Carter, 142)
CINDY (Brady, 28; Crabtree, 153; Devane, 156; Snow, 204;
  Walton, 214; Webster, 57)
CISSY (60)
CLAIR (158; Huxtable, 41)
CLAIRE (195; Estep, 178; Morton, 171; Reed, 163)
CLARA (22; Edwards, 10)
CLARICE (Armitage, 130)
CLAUDIA (Blaisdel, 54; Shively, 46)
CLAY (Basket, 35)
CLEMMA (35)
CLEO (Hewitt, 59)
CLOTHILDE (178)
COCO (Hernandez, 59)
CONNIE (12; 43; Brooks, 164; Giannini, 58)
CONSTANCE (Colby, 39; Mackenzie/Carson, 171)
CONSUELO (Lopez, 131)
CORA (Hudson, 147)
CORABETH (Godsey, 214)
CORENE (Powers, 58)
CORKY (Sherwood Forest, 150)

CORRINE (Tate, 195)
CRISSY (Comstock, 147)
DAISY (Duke, 53; Enright, 164; Maxwell, 55; Moses, 21)
DANA (Carrington, 42; Lambert, 142)
DAPHNE (Moon, 68)
DARLENE (184; Wheeler, 81)
DEANNA (Troi, 198)
DEBBIE (83)
DEIDRE (Thompson, 89)
DELLA (Street, 169)
DENISE (Huxtable, 41; Huxtable, 49; Stevens, 20)
DIANA (Fairgate, 111; Hunter, 58; Sanger, 102)
DIANE (173; Chambers, 37; Hartford, 20; Porter, 178)
DINA (Wells, 58)
DODIE (Douglas, 154)
DOLORES (Crandell, 163)
DOMINIQUE (138)
DONNA (55; Harris, 187; Krebs, 43; Stone, 51; Taft, 69)
DONNA JO (70)
DORALEE (Brooks, 158)
DORIS (Schuster, 171; Schwartz, 59; Ziffel, 81)
DOROTHY (Baxter, 89; Halligan, 6; Ramsey, 57; Zbornak, 78)
DOTTY (Snow, 64; West, 188)
DUSTY (Tyler, 59)
EDIE (18; Grant, 134)
EDITH (Bunker, 8; Prickly, 189)
EDITY (65)
EDNA (De Fazio, 115; Garrett, 48; Garrett, 57; Howard, 163)
EDYTHE (Brewster, 21)
EILEEN (168)
ELAINE (Benes, 191; Lefkowitz, 195; Meechim, 12; Nardo, 201; Shulman, 159)
ELEANOR (Ewing, 43; Major, 133)
ELIZA JANE (Wilder, 120)

ELIZABETH (Bradford, 55; Cabot, 95; Logan, 166; Miller, 15; Sherwood, 59; Walton, 214)

ELLEN (Canby, 8; Craig, 186; Hartley, 26; Miller, 114; Reed, 61; Wedloe, 71)

ELLIE (Walker, 10)

ELLY (Zahn, 35)

ELLY MAY (Clampett, 21)

ELLYN (203)

ELOISE (Wilson, 45)

ELVERNA (Bradshaw, 21)

ELYSE (Keaton, 61)

EMILY (Baldwin, 214; Fallmont, 54; Hanover, 173; Hartley, 26; Humes, 186; Mahoney, 57; Turner, 60)

EMMA (Channing, 58; McArdle, 109; Peel, 11; Tisdale, 53)

ENDORA (22)

ERIN (Jones, 58; Walton, 214)

ESMERALDA (22)

ESTHER (187; Cathcart, 45; Walton, 214)

ETHEL (187; Mertz, 98)

ETTA (Plum, 120)

EUNICE (Tate, 195)

EVA (Simms, 120)

EVE (159; Whitfield, 102)

EVELYN (Martin, 180)

FALLON (Carrington, 42; Colby, 39)

FANTA (183)

FAY (211; Furillo, 91)

FLO (Castleberry, 7; Shafer, 21)

FLORA (MacMichael, 175)

FLORENCE (Bickford, 44; Castleberry, 7; Fowler, 155; Johnston, 106; Kleiner, 157; Pearson, 154)

FLORIDA (Evans, 136)

FLOSSIE (Brimmer, 214)

FRAN (Belding, 102; Crowley, 12)

FRANCESCA (Colby, 39; Gioberti, 58)

FRANCINE (Desmond, 188; Fowler, 155; Lawrence, 75; Webster, 162)

FRIEDA (Krause, 165)
GABRIELLE (Short, 58)
GEORGETTE (Baxter, 134)
GERI (Warner, 57)
GERTRUDE (105; Berg, 59; Lade, 169)
GIDGET (Lawrence, 75)
GINA (Calabrese, 141)
GINGER (Ballis, 127; Farrell/Loomis/Mitchell, 12; Grant, 76; Ward, 111)
GINNY (Wrobliki, 162)
GLADYS (Kravitz, 22)
GLENDA FAYE (Comstock, 147)
GLORIA (49; 85; 168; Bartley, 178; Buckles, 21; Bunker, 8; Unger, 161)
GRACE (43; Edwards, 120; Gardner, 91; Kelly, 80)
GRACIE (Allen, 72)
GRETCHEN (Kraus, 20)
GWENDOLYN (Cooper, 217; Pigeon, 161)
HANNAH (84; 192; Cord, 171)
HARRIET (Conklin, 164; Cooper, 16; Johnson, 89; Oleson, 120)
HASSIE (175)
HATTIE (Denton, 179)
HAZEL (Burke, 89)
HEATHER (Hartman, 133; Pfister, 85)
HELEN (211; Crump, 10; Elgin, 25; Loomis, 182; Marie, 202; Rosenthal, 186; Roper, 204; Thompson, 21; Willis, 106)
HELGA (92)
HENRIETTA (155; Plout, 170; Topper, 207)
HESTER SUE (Terhune, 120)
HILDA (92)
HILDEGARDE (27)
HOLLY (Harwood, 43; Laird, 59)
HONEYBEE (Gillis, 118)
HOPE (Steadman, 203; Stinson, 206)
IDA (Morgenstern, 177)

IRENE (183; Goodwin, 178; Lorenzo, 8; Sawyer, 135)
IRIS (Martin, 206)
ISABELLE (27)
JACKIE ( 184; Rush, 206; Schumaker, 104)
JACQUELINE (67; Perrault, 58; Wade, 186)
JAIME (Sommers, 25)
JALEESA (Vinson, 49)
JAMIE (Ewing, 43; Hamilton, 17)
JAN (Brady, 28)
JANE (56; 125; Hathaway, 21; Jetson, 107; Sumner, 111)
JANET (Baines, 111; Blake, 131; Craig, 170; Fields, 55; Lawson, 187; Trego, 21; Wood, 204)
JANICE (Rand, 197; Wentworth, 15)
JEAN (DaVinci, 147; Hackney, 111; Pearson, 154)
JEANNIE (97)
JENNA (Wade, 43)
JENNIE (Lowell, 109)
JENNIFER (Hart, 86; Keaton, 61; Marlowe, 212)
JENNY (85; Jefferson, 106; Sherman, 88; Wilder, 120)
JESSICA (121; Fletcher, 149; Jefferson, 106; Montford, 43; Tate, 195)
JESSIE (Macahan, 96)
JETHRENE (Bodine, 21)
JILL (93; Bennett, 111; Danko, 181; Munroe, 36; Smith/ Rossi, 171)
JILLIAN (Beckett, 59)
JO (Nelson, 8; Polniaczek, 57)
JOAN (Bradford, 55; Halloran, 186)
JOANIE (Cunningham, 85)
JOANNA (Loudon, 156)
JOANNIE (Bradford, 55)
JODIE (Dallas, 195)
JODY (Campbell, 111)
JOLENE (Hunnicut, 7)
JORDAN (Roberts, 58)
JOSIE (33)
JOY (Devine, 21)

JOYCE (Davenport, 91; Kendall, 64)

JUANITA (10)

JUDY (Bernly, 158; Bessemer, 202; Borden, 215; Jetson, 107; McCoy, 125; Robinson, 123; Trent, 111)

JULIA (Cumson, 58; Sugarbaker, 46)

JULIE (62; Anderson, 171; Barnes, 144; Cooper, 162; Gilette, 95; Grey, 43; Jordache, 178; March, 135; McCoy, 125; Miller, 59; Rogers, 36; Williams, 111)

JUNE (Cleaver, 116)

KAREN (Arnold, 217; Atkinson, 54; Fairgate, 111; Holmby, 51)

KATE (Bradley, 170; Dickens, 100; Jordache, 178; McArdle, 109; McCoy, 175 Riley, 59; Tanner, 6)

KATHERINE (O'Hara, 163; Romano, 162; Wentworth, 43)

KATHLEEN (Faverty, 131)

KATHY (Anderson, 64; Linahan, 38)

KATHY JO (Elliott, 170)

KATIE (207; Douglas, 154; Gatling, 20)

KATRIN (Holstrum, 63)

KATY (Holstrum, 63)

KAY (Addison, 143; Lloyd, 43)

KELLY (Affinado, 57; Bundy, 132; Garrett, 36; Gregg, 12)

KELLYE (127)

KIM (Carter, 126; Schuster, 171)

KIMBERLY (Cryder, 43; Drummond, 48)

KIRBY (54)

KIT (Marlowe, 58)

KITTEN (Anderson, 64)

KITTY (Devereaux, 12; Russell, 84)

KIZZY (183)

KRIS (Munroe, 36)

KRISTIN (Shephard, 43)

KRYSTINA (Carrington, 42)

KRYSTLE (Carrington, 42)

LANA (Shields, 204; Wagner, 157)

LARUE (75)

LAURA (Holt, 176; Ingalls, 120; Macahan, 96; Mackie, 59; Petrie, 47; Sumner, 111)

LAUREL (Ellis, 43)

LAUREN (138; Miller, 61)

LAURIE (Partridge, 167)

LAVERNE (53; De Fazio, 155)

LEE (Potter, 173)

LENORE (Case, 82)

LESLIE (Carrington, 42; Harrington, 171; Scorch, 127; Stewart, 43; Vanderkellen, 156; Walker, 195)

LETTIE (Bostic, 49)

LIBBY (80)

LIL (Trotter, 43)

LILITH (Sternin, 37)

LILLIAN (Carlson, 212)

LILLIMAE (Clements, 111)

LILLY (Sinclair, 27)

LINDA (8; 124; Barry, 65; Bowman, 158; Caproni, 58; Martin, 111; Quales, 178; Striker, 111)

LINDSAY (Blaisdel, 54)

LISA (Alden, 43; Bockweiss, 35; Douglas, 81; Flores, 206; Hayes, 48; Rogers, 128)

LIZ (Craig, 43; McIntyre, 182; Williams, 157)

LOIS (Lane, 5)

LOLA (Heatherton, 189)

LORELEI (Brown, 151)

LORETTA (Haggers, 133)

LORI (Stevens, 58; Wilson, 88)

LORI BETH (85)

LORNA (Minelli, 189)

LORRAINE (Prescott, 58)

LOUELLA (43)

LOUISE (Anderson, 127; Howard, 175; Jefferson, 8; Jefferson, 106; Tate, 22)

LOVEY (Howell, 76)

LUANA (88)

LUCILLE (Bates, 91)

MARY JANE (Lewis, 126)
MARY JO (Shively, 46)
MARY MARGARET (O'Connell, 159)
MARY-FRANCES (Sumner, 111)
MATHILDA (183)
MAUDE (Findlay, 136; Gormsely, 214; Wendell, 35)
MAUREEN (Robinson, 123)
MAVIS (Anderson, 43)
MAXIE (59)
MAY (88)
MEGAN (Kendall, 95)
MELISSA (Cumson, 58; Frome, 130; Marshall, 165;
Steadman, 203; Stone, 97)
MEREDITH (Braxton, 58)
MICHELLE (70; Nardo, 26; Thomas, 135)
MIDGE (Kelsey, 51)
MILDRED (140; Krebs, 176)
MILLIE (49; 195; Ballard, 89; Helper, 47)
MILLY (Scott, 179)
MIMI (142)
MINDY (McConnell, 147)
MIRIAM (Welby, 161)
MISSY (183)
MISSY ANNE (183)
MOLLY (Culhane, 96; Dodd, 44; Earl, 189; Parker, 57;
Turner, 139)
MONA (161; Robinson, 216; Williams, 89)
MONICA (Colby, 39)
MORTICIA (Addams, 3)
MURIEL (Rush, 206)
MURPHY (Brown, 150)
MYRA (Sherwood, 131)
MYRNA (Morgenstern, 177; Turner, 161)
MYRTLE (Davis, 64)
NADINE (80)
NANCY (184; Bancroft, 104; Bradford, 55; Cunningham,
161; Griffin, 217; Oleson, 120; Olson, 57; Weston, 203)

RITA (Fiori, 196; Mackenzie, 171)
ROBERTA (Townsend, 152)
ROBIN (Agretti, 58; Tataglia, 91)
ROSA (Giovanni, 139)
ROSALIE (Totzie, 215)
ROSE (Burton, 214; Kincaid, 24; Nylund, 78)
ROSEANNE (Connors, 184)
ROSEMARY (Fordwick, 214)
ROSIE (89; Greenbaum, 115)
ROXANNE (Turner, 186)
ROZ (168; Keith, 158; Russell, 157)
RUDY (Huxtable, 41)
RUTH (Adams, 130; Bauman, 202; Colfax, 163; Dunbar, 27; Galveston, 111; Martin, 114)
RUTH-ANNE (Miller, 159)
SABLE (Colby, 39)
SABRINA (Duncan, 36)
SALLY (159; 195; McMillan, 139; Rogers, 47; Gallagher, 177; Welden, 19)
SALLY ANN (Douglas, 154)
SAMANTHA (Crawford, 137; Micelli, 216; Stephens, 22)
SAMMY JO (Dean, 54)
SANDRA SUE (Bradford, 55)
SANDY (Porter, 131; Webber, 171)
SAPPHIRE (Stevens, 9)
SARA (183; Rush, 206)
SARAH (Carter, 120; Curtis, 54)
SELMA (Hacker, 157; Plout, 170)
SERENA (22; 43; Burton, 214)
SHEBA (17)
SHEILA (125; Fisher, 111)
SHELLEY (83)
SHELLY (Vincour, 159)
SHIRLEY (Daniels, 186; Fenny, 115; Partridge, 167)
SIDNEY (Enderman, 35)
SIMKA (Graves, 201)
SINDY (Cahill, 38)

SIXTO (67)
SLY (43)
SOFIA (Stavros, 58)
SONDRA (Huxtable, 41)
SOON-LEE (127)
SOPHIA (48; Petrillo, 78)
SOPHIE (Steinberg, 30)
STARLIGHT (125)
STELLA (Chernak, 171)
STEPHANIE (70; Mills, 8; Vanderkellen, 156)
SUE (Lambert, 114; Prescott, 178)
SUE ANN (Nivens, 134; Weaver, 57)
SUE ELLEN (168; Ewing, 43)
SUSAN (Bradford, 55; Deigh, 50; Graham, 21; Silverman, 196; Winter, 171)
SUSIE (125; Baxter, 89)
SUZANNE (Collins, 12; Fabray, 192; Sugarbaker, 46)
SYLVIA (Lean, 111; Schnauser, 34)
SYLVIE (111)
TABITHA (Stephens, 22)
TARA (King, 11)
TASHA (Yar, 198)
TAWNIA (Baker, 1)
TERESA (Betancourt, 8; Sanjoro, 178)
TERRI (Alden, 204; Dowling, 154; Valere, 186)
TERRY (Ranson, 58)
THALIA (Menninger, 130)
THELMA (Lou, 10)
THEORA (Jones, 138)
TIFFANY (Welles, 36)
TINA (111; Molinari, 177; Rickels, 42; Russo, 91)
TONI (Hazleton, 214)
TOOTIE (Ramsey, 57)
TRACY (Kendall, 54; Partridge, 167)
TRISHA (Stone, 51)
TRIXIE (Norton, 94)
TRUDY (85; Joplin, 141)

UHURA (197)
ULLA (Norstrand, 66)
VALENE (Ewing, 43; Ewing, 111)
VALERIE (58)
VANESSA (Huxtable, 41)
VERA (Gorman, 7)
VERDIE (Foster, 214)
VERNA (Jordan, 33; Kincaid, 24)
VERNA JEAN (215)
VERONICA (Rooney, 8)
VICKI (Stubing, 125)
VICKIE (12)
VICTORIA (Barkley, 23; Butterfield, 136; Cabot, 95; Cannon, 167; Stavros, 58)
VIOLET (Newstead, 158)
VIRGINIA (Calderwood, 178; Hayes, 146)
VIVIAN (Bagley, 126; Harmon, 136)
WANDA (80; Jeeter, 133)
WEDNESDAY (Addams, 3)
WENDY (85; Armstrong, 186)
WHITLEY (Gilbert, 49)
WINIFRED (Gillis, 130; Jordan, 175)
WINNIE (Cooper, 217; Gillis, 130; Kirkwood, 143)
ZELDA (Gilroy, 130)
ZOE (Lawton, 50)

# Presidential Baby Names

## 125 PRESIDENTIAL BABY NAMES

This feature collects the 84 names of all 125 children of the U.S. Presidents, from George Washington's two adopted children, John and Martha, through Bill Clinton's daughter Chelsea.

The "Boys" (48 names) and "Girls" (36 names) lists provide the child's name, followed by the name of the parent President.

(If you don't find a particular President, it's because he and his wife did not have any biological *or* adopted children. The adopted children of Presidents are included but not specifically identified as adopted.)

**FYI:** "John" is the most popular Presidential boy's name, with 13 lads named John; while "Mary" is the most popular girl's name, with 10 lasses named Mary.

## BOYS

ABRAHAM (Martin Van Buren)
ABRAM (James A. Garfield)
ALLAN (Herbert Hoover)
ANDREW (Andrew Jackson; Andrew Johnson)
ARCHIBALD (Theodore Roosevelt)
BENJAMIN (William Henry Harrison; Franklin Pierce)
BIRCHARD (Rutherford B. Hayes)

CALVIN (Calvin Coolidge)
CHARLES (John Adams; Andrew Jackson; William Howard Taft)
CHESTER (Chester A. Arthur)
DAVID (John Tyler)
DONNELL (Jimmy Carter))

## PRESIDENTIAL PROPAGATIONS

The most fecund President was John Tyler, who was father to fourteen children. Second place goes to William Henry Harrison with nine children and, running a distant third, is Teddy Roosevelt, with six.

ELLIOT (Franklin D. Roosevelt)
FRANCIS (Grover Cleveland)
FRANKLIN (Franklin D. Roosevelt)
FREDERICK (Ulysses S. Grant)
GEORGE (John Quincy Adams; George Bush)
HARRY (James A. Garfield)
HERBERT (Herbert Hoover)
IRVIN (James A. Garfield)
JAMES (Rutherford B. Hayes; James A. Garfield; Franklin D. Roosevelt; Jimmy Carter)
JEFFREY (Jimmy Carter))
JESSE (Ulysses S. Grant)
JOHN (George Washington; John Adams; John Quincy Adams; Martin Van Buren; William Henry Harrison; John Tyler; Calvin Coolidge; Franklin D. Roosevelt; Dwight D. Eisenhower; John F. Kennedy; Gerald R. Ford; Jimmy Carter; George Bush)
KERMIT (Theodore Roosevelt)
LACHLAN (John Tyler)
LYON (John Tyler)
MARTIN (Martin Van Buren)

MARVIN (George Bush)
MICHAEL (Gerald R. Ford; Ronald Reagan)
MILLARD (Millard Fillmore)
NEIL (George Bush)
QUENTIN (Theodore Roosevelt)
RICHARD (Zachary Taylor; Grover Cleveland)
ROBERT (John Tyler; Abraham Lincoln; Andrew Johnson; William Howard Taft)
RONALD (Ronald Reagan)
RUSSELL (Benjamin Harrison)
RUTHERFORD (Rutherford B. Hayes)
SARDIS (Rutherford B. Hayes)
SCOTT (Rutherford B. Hayes)
SMITH (Martin Van Buren)
STEVEN (Gerald R. Ford)
TAZEWELL (John Tyler)
THEODORE (Theodore Roosevelt)
THOMAS (John Adams; Abraham Lincoln)
ULYSSES (Ulysses S. Grant)
WEBB (Rutherford B. Hayes)
WILLIAM (William Henry Harrison; Abraham Lincoln)

# GIRLS

ABIGAIL (John Adams)
ALICE (John Tyler; Theodore Roosevelt)
AMY (Jimmy Carter)
ANN (Zachary Taylor)
ANNA (William Henry Harrison; Franklin D. Roosevelt)
CAROLINE (John F. Kennedy)
CHELSEA (Bill Clinton)
DOROTHY (George Bush)
ELEANOR (Woodrow Wilson)
ELIZA (James Monroe)
ELIZABETH (William Henry Harrison; Benjamin Harrison; Warren G. Harding)

ELLEN (Ulysses S. Grant; Chester A. Arthur)
ESTHER (Grover Cleveland)
ETHEL (Theodore Roosevelt)
FRANCES (Rutherford B. Hayes)
HELEN (William Howard Taft)
IDA (William McKinley)
JESSIE (Woodrow Wilson)
JULIA (John Tyler)
JULIE (Richard M. Nixon)
KATHERINE (William McKinley)
LETITIA (John Tyler)
LUCI (Lyndon B. Johnson)
LUCY (William Henry Harrison)
LYNDA (Lyndon B. Johnson)
MARGARET (Woodrow Wilson; Harry S Truman)
MARIA (James Monroe)
MARION (Grover Cleveland)
MARTHA (George Washington; Thomas Jefferson; Andrew Jackson)
MARY (Thomas Jefferson; William Henry Harrison; John Tyler; Zachary Taylor; Millard Fillmore; Andrew Johnson; James A. Garfield; Benjamin Harrison; Harry S Truman)
MAUREEN (Ronald Reagan)
PATRICIA (Richard M. Nixon)
PATTI (Ronald Reagan)
PEARL (John Tyler)
RUTH (Grover Cleveland)
SARAH (Zachary Taylor)

# THE CELEBRITIES

# The Celebrity Master Index

This Celebrity Index lists close to 2,500 celebrities and over 5,500 of their children, organized alphabetically by celebrity. For each celebrity, the children's names included in the Boys and Girls sections are also in alphabetical order. (When the child is also a celebrity, their last name is provided in brackets following their first name.]

[A NOTE TO NAME HUNTERS: As mentioned, the celebrities are listed alphabetically. The profession noted for each celeb is the field in which they either established themselves, or for which they are best known. The children for each celebrity are listed in alphabetical order and, as noted in "Read Me First" (you did read it first now, didn't you?), the list may not include *every* child the celeb may have.

My sources for all the names and biographical information in this book were *Who's Who,* Gale Research's annual *Newsmaker* series, *People* magazine, *US* magazine, *The Star, The National Enquirer* (don't laugh: They may sensationalize stories but they are amazingly accurate when it comes to family info about celebrities); newspapers from all over the country spanning the past forty years; *Earl Blackwell's Entertainment Celebrity Register; The Hollywood Reporter; Daily Variety; Rolling Stone; Playboy;* CNN; countless other periodicals and TV programs, as well as a whole range of reference works including *Lives of the Poets, How Did They Die?* and better than a dozen "name" books and dictionaries, many of the best of which are published by Penguin USA.

When information from one source contradicted another, I usually tried to get verification from a third source. In the rare cases where accurate information simply wasn't available, I either left the baby name out of this book or, in cases where the name was so intriguing that I just couldn't bear omitting it, I resorted to an educated guess. Most of the time, though, I was able to nail down correct spellings and/or genders for the celeb children.

If a particular name is especially interesting to you, you might want to go further and check out the meaning of the moniker in one of the aforementioned Penguin name dictionaries.]

## A

**AARON, HANK (Baseball Legend)**
Ceci
Dorinda
Gaile [aka Gail]
Gary
Henry [aka Hank]
Larry [aka Lary]

**ABBOTT, BUD (Comic)**
Bud
Vicki

**ABBOTT, DIAHNNE (Actress)**
Drina
Raphael Eugene

**ABERNATHY, THE REVEREND RALPH DAVID (Clergyman)**
Donzaleigh
Jaundalynn
Kwamae Luthuli
Ralph David

**ABRAHAMS, JIM (Director)**
Jamie

**ABZUG, BELLA (Politician)**
Eve Gail
Isobel Jo

**ACUFF, ROY (Country Singer)**
Roy Neil

**ADAIR, RED (Oil Well Fire Fighter)**
Jimmy
Robyn

**ADAMS, DON (Actor)**
Beige Dawn

**ADJANI, ISABELLE (Actress)**
Barnabe Said

**ADLER, ALFRED (Austrian Psychoanalyst)**
Alexandra
Kurt

**AGAR, JOHN (Actor)**

Linda Susan

**AIELLO, DANNY (Actor)**
Danny
Jaime
Rick
Stacy

**AINGE, DANNY
(Professional Basketball
Player)**
Ashlee
Austin
Tanner

**AKIHITO (Emperor of
Japan)**
Aya
Hiro
Nori

**AL-ASSAD, HAFEZ
(President of Syria)**
Bashar
Basil
Bushra
Mahir
Majd

**ALBERT, EDDIE (Actor)**
Edward

**ALBERT, MARV
(Sportscaster)**
Brian
Denise
Jackie
Kenny

**ALDA, ALAN (Actor &
Director)**
Beatrice
Elizabeth
Eve

**ALDA, ROBERT (Actor)**
Alan [Alda]
Antony

**ALEXANDER, JANE
(Actress)**
Jason

**ALEXANDER, POPE (VI)
(Pontiff)**
Cesare

**ALEXIS, KIM
(Supermodel)**
Noah

**ALI, MUHAMMAD
(Former Professional
Boxer)**
Hana
Ibn
Jamillah
Maryum
Rasheeda
Reeshemah

**ALLEN, ADRIENNE
(Actress)**
Daniel [Massey]

**ALLEN, BOB (Chairman
of AT&T)**
Amy Susan
Ann Elizabeth
Daniel Scott
Jay Robert
Katherine Louise

**ALLEN, DEBBIE
(Director &
Choreographer)**
Norm

**ALLEN, GRACIE
(Comedienne)**

Ronald John [Burns] [aka
Ronnie]
**ALLEN, REX (Country
Singer)**
Bonita
Curtis
Mark
Rex
**ALLEN, STEVE (Writer,
Actor, & Songwriter)**
Brian
David
Stephen
**ALLEN, TIM (Actor &
Comedian)**
Kady
Kathryn
**ALLEN, WOODY
(Director, Writer, & Actor)**
Moses
Dylan
Satchel
**ALLEY, KIRSTIE
(Actress)**
William True Parker
**ALLMAN, GREG (Singer,
Songwriter, and Actor)**
Delilah
**ALTMAN, ROBERT
(Director)**
Christine
Matthew
Michael
Robert
Stephen
**AMES, LOUISE BATES
(Child Psychologist)**

Joan
**AMURRI, FRANCO
(Writer & Director)**
Eva Maria Livia
**ANDERSON, HARRY
(Actor & Comedian)**
Dashiell
Eva Fay
**ANDERSON, JACK
(Newspaper Columnist)**
Bryan
Cheri
Kevin
Lance
Laurie
Randy
Rodney
Tanya
Tina
**ANDERSON, LIZ
(Country Singer)**
Lynn Rene
**ANDERSON, LONI
(Actress)**
Deidra
Quinton Anderson
**ANDERSON, LYNN
(Country Singer)**
Lisa
**ANDRES, JO
(Choreographer)**
Lucian
**ANDRESS, URSULA
(Actress)**
Dmitri
**ANDRETTI, MARIO
(Race Car Driver)**

Barbra Dee
Jeffrey Louis
Michael Mario [Andretti]
**ANDREW, PRINCE (British Royalty)**
Eugenie
Beatrice [aka Bea]
**ANDREWS, JULIE (Actress)**
Emma
**ANGELOU, MAYA (Writer)**
Guy
**ANISTON, JOHN (Actor, *Days of Our Lives*)**
Jennifer [Aniston]
**ANKA, PAUL (Singer/ Songwriter)**
Alexandra
Alicia
Amanda
Amelia
Anthea
**ANNE, PRINCESS (British Royalty)**
Peter
Zara
**ANNENBERG, WALTER (Publisher)**
Wallis
**ANSPACH, SUSAN (Actress)**
Caleb
**ANTHONY, EARL (Professional Bowler)**
Jeri Ann
Michael

Tracy
**ANTONY (Almost-Ruler of the Roman Empire)**
Alexander Helios
Cleopatra Selene
Ptolemy Philadelphus
**ANWAR, GABRIELLE (Actress)**
Willow
**AOKI, ROCKY (Sportsman & Restaurateur)**
Grace
Kevin
**AQUINO, CORAZON (Philippine Politician)**
Aurora
Benigno
Kristina Bernadette
Maria Elena
Victoria Elisa
**ARAFAT, YASSER (P.L.O. Leader)**
Zahwa
**ARCHER, ANNE (Actress)**
Jeffrey
Thomas
**ARCHER, JOHN (Actor)**
Anne [Archer]
**ARIAS SANCHEZ, OSCAR (Former President, Costa Rica)**
Oscar Felipe
Sylvia Eugenia
**ARIYOSHI, GEORGE (Former Governor of Hawaii)**

Donn Ryoji
Lynn Miye
Todd Ryozo
**ARKIN, ALAN (Actor)**
Adam [Arkin]
Anthony
Matthew
**ARLEDGE, ROONE (TV Executive)**
Elizabeth Ann
Patricia Lu
Roone Pinckney
Susan Lee
**ARLEN, HAROLD (Songwriter)**
Samuel
**ARMAN (Artist)**
Anne
Francoise
Philippe
Yasmine
Yves
**ARNAZ, DESI (Actor)**
Desiderio Alberto
Lucie Desiree
**ARNOLD, EDDY (Country Singer)**
Dickie
Jo Ann
**ARPEL, ADRIEN (Cosmetics Mogul)**
Lauren
**ARQUETTE, LEWIS (Actor & Director)**
Patricia [Arquette]
Rosanna [Arquette]

**ARQUETTE, PATRICIA (Actress)**
Enzo
**ARRAU, CLAUDIO (Concert Pianist)**
Carmen
Christopher
Mario
**ASHBROOK, DAPHNE (Actress)**
Paton Lee
**ASHE, ARTHUR (Tennis Pro)**
Camera Elizabeth
**ASHER, JANE (Actress)**
Alexander
Kate
**ASHFORD, EVELYN (Sprinter)**
Raina Ashley
**ASHKENAZY, VLADIMIR (Concert Pianist)**
Alexandra Inga
Dimitri Thor
Nadia Liza
Sonia Edda
Vladimir Stefan
**ASHLEY, ELIZABETH (Actress)**
Christian Moore
**ASHWORTH, ERNIE (Country Singer)**
Mark Paul
Mike
Rebecca Gail
**ASIMOV, ISAAC (Writer)**

## "FAMILY TIES"

Actress Patricia Arquette (*True Romance*) is the granddaughter of actor Cliff "Charlie Weaver" Arquette.

David
Robyn Joan
**ASNER, ED (Actor)**
Charles
Kathryn
Liza
Matthew
**ASSANTE, ARMAND (Actor)**
Alessandra
Anya
**ASTAIRE, FRED (Dancer & Actor)**
Ava
Fred
Peter
**ASTIN, JOHN (Actor)**
Allen
David
Mackenzie [Astin]
Sean [Astin]
Thomas
**ASTOR, CAROLINE (New York Society Matron)**
Charlotte
Emily
John Jacob
**ASTOR, JOHN JACOB**
**(Financier & Mogul)**
John
Vincent
**ATCHER, BOB (Country Singer)**
Cecily Ann
Mary Christopher
Robert
**ATKINS, CHET (Country Singer)**
Merle
**ATWATER, LEE (Former Chairman, Republican National Committee)**
Ashley Page
Sarah Lee
**AUBREY, JAMES (Former President, CBS)**
Skye [Aubrey]
**AUCHINCLOSS, KENNETH (Editor, *Newsweek*)**
Emily
Grant
Malcolm
**AUGUSTUS, CAESAR (Ruler of the Roman Empire)**

Julia

**AVEDON, RICHARD (Photographer)**
John

**AVILDSEN, JOHN (Director)**
Anthony
Jonathan-Rufus

**AXTON, HOYT (Country Singer)**
April Laura
Matthew Christopher
Michael Stephen

**AYERS, VIVIAN (Poet)**
Debbie [Allen]
Phylicia [Rashsad]
Tex

**AYKROYD, DAN (Actor)**
Belle Kingston
Lloyd
Mark
Oscar

# B

**BABBITT, BRUCE (Secretary of the Interior)**
Christopher
Thomas Jeffrey [also reported as Timothy]

**BACALL, LAUREN (Actress)**
Leslie
Sam
Stephen

**BACH, CATHERINE (Actress)**
Michael

**BACH, JOHANN SEBASTIAN (Composer)**
Carl Philipp Emanuel
Johann Christian
Wilhelm

**BACH, PAMELA (Actress)**
Hayley

**BACHARACH, BURT (Pianist & Composer)**
Christopher Elton
Lea Nikki [aka Nikki]

**BACON, KEVIN (Actor)**
Sosie Ruth
Travis Sedg

**BAEZ, JOAN (Singer/ Songwriter)**
Gabriel Earl

**BAILEY, FRANCIS LEE (Attorney)**
Scott Frederic

**BAILEY, PEARL (Entertainer)**
Dee Dee
Tony

**BAIN, CONRAD (Actor)**
Jennifer Jean
Kent Stafford
Mark Alexander

**BAKA, NAOMI (Artist)**
Joseph Jeremiah [aka Joey]

**BAKER, ANITA (Singer)**
Eddie
Walter

**BAKER, BILL (Lead Singer, The Five Satins)**
Nathaniel

Tammi
**BAKER, CARROLL**
**(Actress)**
Blanche [Baker]
**BAKER, DAVID (Jazz**
**Musician)**
April Elaine
**BAKER, HOWARD**
**(Former U.S. Senator)**
Cynthia
Darek
**BAKER, JOSEPHINE**
**(Singer & Actress)**
Jean-Claude
**BAKER, RUSSELL**
**(Writer)**
Allen
Kathleen Leland
Michael Lee
**BAKKER, JIM (Disgraced**
**Televangelist)**
Jamie
Tammy Sue
**BAKSH, SHAKIRA (Miss**
**Guyana) [SEE Michael**
**Caine and "Natasha" name**
**entry]**
Natasha
**BAKULA, SCOTT (Actor)**
Chelsy
**BALDESSARI, JOHN**
**(Artist)**
Annamarie
Tony
**BALDRIDGE,**
**MALCOLM (U.S.**
**Secretary of Commerce)**

Mary
Megan
**BALL, LUCILLE**
**(Actress)**
Desiderio Alberto
Lucie Desiree
**BANCROFT, ANNE**
**(Actress)**
Maximillian
**BANKS, ERNIE (Baseball**
**Coach)**
Jan
Jerry
Joey
**BARAKA, IMAMU**
**AMIRI [LEROI JONES]**
**(Poet, Playwright, Essayist**
**& Activist)**
Amiri Seku Musa
Asia
Maisha
Obalaji Malik Ali
RasJua Al Aziz
Shani Isis Makeda
**BARBEAU, ADRIENNE**
**(Actress)**
John Cody
**BARBERA, JOSEPH**
**(Film and TV Producer &**
**Cartoonist)**
Jayne Earl
Lynne Meredith
Neal Francis
**BARE, BOBBY (Country**
**Singer)**
Carla
Robert

---

### "FAMILY TIES"

Actress Drew Barrymore (*E.T.—The Extraterrestrial, Poison Ivy, Boys on the Side*) is the granddaughter of John Barrymore (*Dinner at Eight*); and the daughter of John Barrymore, Jr. (*High School Confidential*).

---

**BARKIN, ELLEN (Actress)**
Jack Daniel
Romy Marion
**BARNES, CLIVE (Drama Critic)**
Christopher John
Joanna Rosemary
**BARNUM, P.T. (Circus Mogul)**
Caroline
Pauline
**BARRETO, BRUNO (Director)**
Gabriel
**BARRY, DAVE (Writer & Humorist)**
Robby
**BARRY, GENE (Actor)**
Fredric James
Liza
Michael Lewis [Barry]
**BARRY, MARION (Mayor, Washington, D.C.)**
Marion Christopher
**BARRYMORE, JOHN,**

**JR. (Actor)**
Drew
**BARRYMORE, JOHN, SR. (Actor)**
Diana [Barrymore]
John [Barrymore, Jr.]
**BARRYMORE, MAURICE (Actor)**
Ethel [Barrymore]
John [Barrymore, Sr.]
Lionel [Barrymore]
**BARTH, JOHN (Writer)**
Christine Anne
Daniel Stephen
John
**BARTLING, JIM (Romance Novel Cover Model)**
Dylan
Nile
**BARYSHNIKOV, MIKHAIL (Ballet Dancer)**
Alexandra [also reported as Aleksandra]
Anna Katerina
Peter Andrew

**BARZUN, JACQUES**
**(Writer)**
Isabel
James
Roger Martin
**BATEMAN, KENT**
**(Theatrical Producer)**
Jason [Bateman]
Justine [Bateman]
**BATES, ALAN (Actor)**
Benedick
Tristan
**BAUER, STEVEN (Actor)**
Alexander
**BAXTER, ANNE (Actress)**
Katrina
Melissa
**BAXTER, MEREDITH**
**(Actress)**
Eva
Kate
Mollie [also reported as
Molly]
Peter
Ted
**BEALS, VAUGHN**
**(Harley-Davidson**
**Executive)**
Laurie Jean
Susan Lynn
**BEAN, ALAN L.**
**(Astronaut & Artist)**
Amy Sue
Clay
**BEATTY, WARREN**
**(Actor)**
Jack

Kathlyn
**BECK, MARILYN**
**(Columnist)**
Andrea
Mark Elliott
**BECKER, BORIS (Tennis**
**Pro)**
Noah Gabriel
**BECKER, WALTER**
**(Musician, Steely Dan)**
Kawai
Sayan
**BEERY, NOAH (Actor)**
Noah [Beery, Jr.]
**BEGLEY, ED, SR. (Actor)**
Ed [Begley, Jr.]
**BEL GEDDES,**
**BARBARA (Actress)**
Betsy
Susan
**BELAFONTE, HARRY**
**(Singer & Actor)**
Adrienne
David
Gina
Shari
**BELEW, CARL (Country**
**Singer)**
Robert Gene
**BELL, BRAD (Head**
**Writer, *The Bold and the***
***Beautiful*)**
Brad
**BELLAMY, RALPH**
**(Actor)**
Lynn
Willard

**BELLI, MELVIN**
**(Attorney & Writer)**
Caesar Melvin
Jean
Melia
Melvin
Richard
Susan
**BELLOW, SAUL (Writer)**
Adam
Daniel
Gregory
**BELUSHI, JIM (Actor)**
Robert
**BENARD, MAURICE**
**(Actor, *General Hospital*)**
Jessie
**BENATAR, PAT (Singer/**
**Songwriter)**
Haley
**BENCHLEY, PETER**
**(Writer)**
Christopher
Clayton [aka Clay]
Tracy
**BENING, ANNETTE**
**(Actress)**
Jack
Kathlyn
**BENITZ, JELLYBEAN**
**(Music Producer)**
Layla
Reya
**BENJAMIN, RICHARD**
**(Actor & Director)**
Russ Thomas

**BENNETT, RICHARD**
**(Actor)**
Constance [Bennett]
**BENNETT, TONY**
**(Singer)**
Antonia
D'Andrea
Daegal
Joanna
**BENSON, ANN (Actress)**
Robby [Benson]
**BENSON, ROBBY (Actor)**
Lyric
Zephyr
**BENTSEN, LLOYD (U.S.**
**Secretary of the Treasury)**
Lan
Lloyd
Tina
**BERENGER, TOM**
**(Actor)**
Allison
Chelsea
Chloe
Patrick
**BERENSON, MARISA**
**(Actress)**
Starlite Melody
**BERGEN, CANDICE**
**(Actress)**
Chloe
**BERGEN, EDGAR**
**(Comedian)**
Candice [Bergen]
**BERGEN, POLLY**
**(Actress)**
Kathy

Peter
**BERGMAN, INGMAR**
**(Director)**
Linn
**BERGMAN, INGRID**
**(Actress)**
Isabella [Rossellini]
**BERLE, MILTON**
**(Comedian)**
Billy
Victoria [aka Vicky]
**BERLIN, IRVING**
**(Composer)**
Elizabeth
Linda
Mary Ellin
**BERNARDI, HERSCHEL**
**(Actor)**
Adam
Beryl
Michael
Robin
**BERNHARDT, SARAH**
**(Actress)**
Maurice
**BERNSEN, CORBIN**
**(Actor)**
Angus Moore
Henry
Oliver
**BERNSTEIN, CARL**
**(Writer & Journalist)**
Jacob
Max
**BERNSTEIN, ELMER**
**(Composer & Conductor)**
Elizabeth

Emily
Eve
Gregory
Peter Matthew
**BERNSTEIN, LEONARD**
**(Composer & Conductor)**
Alexander
Jamie
Nina
**BERRA, YOGI (Baseball**
**Player)**
Dale Anthony
Lawrence
Timothy Thomas
**BERTINELLI, VALERIE**
**(Actress)**
Wolfgang
**BESCH, BIBI (Actress)**
Samantha [Mathis]
**BETTELHEIM, BRUNO**
**(Psychologist & Writer)**
Eric
Naomi
Ruth
**BEUYS, JOSEPH**
**(Sculptor)**
Jessyka
Wenzel
**BIDEN, JOSEPH (U.S.**
**Senator)**
Ashley Blazer
Joseph [aka Beau]
Naomi Christina
Robert Hunter [aka Hunt]
**BIEHN, MICHAEL**
**(Actor)**
Gaelan Michael

**BIERCE, AMBROSE (Writer)**
Helen
**BILL, TONY (Director)**
Peter
**BINOCHE, JULIETTE (Actress)**
Raphaël
**BIRD, LARRY (Professional Basketball Player)**
Corrie
**BIRNEY, DAVID (Actor)**
Mollie [also reported as Molly]
Peter
**BIXBY, BILL (Actor)**
Christopher
**BLACK, KAREN (Actress)**
Celine
Hunter Minor Norman
**BLACK, SHIRLEY TEMPLE (Former Ambassador & Retired Actress)**
Charles Alden
Linda Susan
Lori Alden
**BLACKMUN, HARRY (U.S. Supreme Court Justice)**
Nancy
Sally Ann
Susan
**BLAKE, WHITNEY (Actress)**
Meredith [Baxter]

**BLATTY, WILLIAM PETER (Writer)**
Christine Ann
Mary Joanne
Michael Peter
**BLEY, CARLA (Jazz Composer)**
Karen
**BLOCH, HENRY (Founder, H&R Block)**
Elizabeth Ann
Mary Jo
Robert
Thomas
**BLOCH, ROBERT (Writer)**
Sally Ann
**BLOCKER, DAN (Actor)**
Dirk [Blocker]
**BLOOM, CLAIRE (Actress)**
Anna
**BLUFORD, GUION (Astronaut)**
Guion Stewart
James Trevor
**BLUME, JUDY (Writer)**
Lawrence Andrew
Randy Lee
**BLY, ROBERT (Poet & Writer)**
Bridget
Mary
Micah
Noah
**BOBBITT, JOHN WAYNE**

**(Sexual Assault Victim & Actor)**
Andrew
**BOCHCO, STEVEN (TV Producer)**
Jesse
Melissa
**BOGART, HUMPHREY (Actor)**
Stephen
Leslie
**BOGDANOVICH, PETER (Director)**
Alexandra
Antonia
**BOGGS, JAMES (Writer)**
Donald
Ernestine
Jacqueline
James
Thomasine
Wayman
**BOGGS, WADE (Professional Baseball Player)**
Brett
Meagann
**BOGOSIAN, ERIC (Performance Artist & Writer)**
Harris Wolf
**BOHAN, MARC (Fashion Designer)**
Marie Anne
**BOHR, NIELS (Nobel Prize-Winning Physicist)**
Aage

Christian
Erik
Ernest
Hans
**BOHRINGER, RICHARD (Screenwriter)**
Romane
**BOLEYN, ANNE (2nd Wife of Henry VIII)**
Elizabeth
**BOLL, HEINRICH (Writer)**
Christoph
Raimund
René
Vincent
**BOLTON, MICHAEL (Singer/Songwriter)**
Isa
Holly
Taryn [also reported as Tarin]
**BOMBECK, ERMA (Writer)**
Andrew
Betsy
Matthew
**BON JOVI, JON (Rock Musician)**
Stephanie Rose
**BOND, JULIAN (Legislator)**
Horace
Jane
Jeffrey
Julia
Michael

Phyllis

**BONDS, BARRY
(Professional Baseball
Player)**

Nikolai

Shikari

**BONDS, BOBBY
(Professional Baseball
Coach)**

Barry [Bonds]

**BONET, LISA (Actress)**

Zoe

**BONHAM, JOHN
(Drummer, Led Zeppelin)**

Jason [Bonham]

**BONILLA, BOBBY
(Professional Baseball
Player)**

Danielle

**BONO (Singer/Songwriter,
U2)**

Eve

Jordan

**BONO, SONNY (Politician
& Former Pop Singer)**

Chastity

Chesare Elan

Chianna Maria

Christine [aka Christy]

**BOONE, DANIEL
(Frontiersman)**

Nathan

**BOONE, PAT (Singer &
Actor)**

Cheryl Lynn [aka Cherry]

Deborah Ann [aka Debby]

Laura Gene

Linda Lee

**BOORMAN, JOHN
(Director)**

Charley [Boorman]

**BOORSTIN, DANIEL J.
(Writer)**

David West

Jonathan

Paul Terry

**BOOZER, BRENDA
(Opera Singer)**

Alexander Stewart

**BORG, BJORN (Tennis
Pro)**

Robin

**BORGE, VICTOR
(Comedian & Pianist)**

Frederikke

Janet

Ronald

Sanna

Victor

**BORGLUM, GUTZON
(Sculptor of Mount
Rushmore)**

Lincoln

**BORMAN, FRANK
(Airline Executive &
Former Astronaut)**

Edwin

Frederick

**BOSWELL, JAMES
(Samuel Johnson's
Biographer)**

Alexander

Euphemia

James

Veronica
**BOWE, RIDDICK (Professional Boxer)**
Brenda
Riddick
Ridicia
**BOWIE, ANGELA (Writer)**
Zowie
**BOWIE, DAVID (Singer/ Songwriter)**
Zowie
**BOXER, BARBARA (U.S. Senator)**
Nicole
**BOYER, CHARLES (Actor)**
Michael
**BRACCO, LORRAINE (Actress)**
Margaux
Stella
**BRADBURY, RAY (Writer)**
Alexandra
Bettina
Ramona
Susan Marguerite
**BRADBURY, ROBERT NORTH (Silents Director)**
Bob [Steele]
**BRADLEE, BEN (Journalist)**
Benjamin
Dominic
Marina
Quinn

**BRADLEY, BILL (Former U.S. Senator)**
Theresa Anne
**BRADLEY, TOM (Mayor of Los Angeles)**
Lorraine
Phyllis
**BRADSHAW, JOHN (Family Counselor & Writer)**
Brad
Brenda
John Elliot
**BRADY, JIM (Gun Control Activist & Former White House Press Secretary)**
James Scott
**BRADY, SARAH (Gun Control Activist)**
James Scott
**BRAEDEN, ERIC (Actor, _The Young and the Restless_)**
Christian
**BRAINE, TIM (TV Producer) [SEE Judith Ivey and "Maggie" entry]**
Maggie
**BRAMLETT, BONNIE (Singer)**
Bekka
**BRANDAUER, KLAUS MARIA (Actor)**
Christian
**BRANDO, MARLON (Actor)**

Christian Devi
Miko
Ninna Priscilla
Rebecca
Simon Teihotu [aka Teihotu]
Tarita Cheyenne [aka Cheyenne]
**BRANSON, RICHARD (Founder, Virgin Records)**
Holly
**BRANT, PETER (Owner, *Interview* Magazine) [SEE Stephanie Seymour and "Peter" entry]**
Peter
**BRAUN, CAROL MOSELEY (Politician)**
Matthew
**BREGMAN, TRACEY E. (Actress, *The Young and the Restless*)**
Austin
**BREITSCHWERDT, WERNER (Daimler-Benz Executive)**
Claudia
Udo
**BREMEN, BARRY (Professional "Impostor")**
Adam
Erin
Noah
**BRENNAN, EILEEN (Actress)**
Patrick Oliver
Samuel John
**BRENNAN, WILLIAM JOSEPH (U.S. Supreme Court Justice)**
Hugh Leonard
Nancy
William Joseph
**BRENNER, DAVID (Comic)**
Cole
**BRESLIN, JIMMY (Writer)**
Christopher
Daniel
Emily
James
Kelly
Kevin
Lucy
Patrick
Rosemary
**BREYER, STEPHEN (U.S. Supreme Court Justice)**
Chloe
Michael
Nell
**BRICKELL, EDIE (Singer/Songwriter)**
Adrian Edward
**BRIDGES, BEAU (Actor)**
Casey
Dylan
Emily
Ezekiel
Jordan
**BRIDGES, JEFF (Actor)**
Hayley Rose
**BRIDGES, LLOYD (Actor)**

Beau [Bridges]
Jeff [Bridges]
Lucinda
**BRINKLEY, CHRISTIE**
**(Supermodel)**
Alexa Ray
Jack Paris
**BRINKLEY, DAVID (News**
**Commentator)**
Alan
Joel
John
**BRINKMAN, BO**
**(Director & Writer)**
Dakota Paul Mayi
**BROCCOLI, ALBERT**
**(Movie Producer)**
Anthony
Barbara
Christina
Michael
**BRODERICK, JAMES**
**(Actor)**
Matthew [Broderick]
**BRODY, JANE (Writer)**
Lee Erik
Lorin Michael
**BROKAW, TOM (TV**
**Anchor)**
Andrea Brooks
Jennifer Jean
Sarah
**BROLIN, JAMES (Actor)**
Jess
Josh James
Molly Elizabeth

**BRONSON, CHARLES**
**(Actor)**
Zuleika
**BROOK, CLIVE (Actor)**
Faith [Brook]
Lyndon [Brook]
**BROOKS, DIANA D.**
**(Executive, Sotheby's)**
Carter
Christopher
**BROOKS, GARTH**
**(Singer/Songwriter)**
August Anna
Taylor Mayne Pearl
**BROOKS, GWENDOLYN**
**(Poet)**
Henry
Nora
**BROOKS, JAMES L.**
**(Screenwriter & Director)**
Amy Lorraine
**BROOKS, MEL (Director,**
**Writer, and Actor)**
Edward
Maximillian
Nicky
Stefanie
**BROOKS, RICHARD**
**(Director)**
Kate
**BROSNAN, PIERCE**
**(Actor)**
Charlotte
Christopher
Sean William
**BROTHERS, DR. JOYCE**
**(Psychologist)**

Lisa Robin
**BROUSSARD, REBECCA**
**(Actress) [SEE Jack**
**Nicholson and name**
**entries]**
Lorraine Broussard
Raymond Nicholas
**BROWN, BOBBY (Singer)**
**[SEE Whitney Houston**
**and "Bobbi" entry]**
Bobbi Kristina
**BROWN, GEORG**
**STANFORD (Actor)**
Alyxandra
Elizabeth
Katherine [also reported as
Kathryne]
**BROWN, JAMES (Singer/**
**Songwriter)**
Daryl
Deanna
Teddy
Terry
Venisha
Yamma
**BROWN, JIM (Retired**
**Pro Football Player)**
Jim
Kevin
Kim
**BROWN, JIM ED**
**(Country Singer)**
James Edward
**BROWN, JOHN (Former**
**Governor of Kentucky)**
**[SEE Phyllis George and**
**name entries]**

Lincoln Tyler
Pamela
**BROWN, JULIE (Actress**
**& Comedian)**
Walker
**BROWN, KIMBERLIN**
**(Actress, *The Bold and the***
***Beautiful*)**
Alexes Marie
**BROWN, RON**
**(Chairman, Democratic**
**National Committee)**
Michael
Tracey Lynn
**BROWN, TINA (Magazine**
**Editor)**
George Frederick
Isabel Harriet
**BROWN, TONY**
**(Educator & TV Host)**
Byron
**BROWNE, JACKSON**
**(Singer/Songwriter)**
Ethan
**BROWNING, ROBERT**
**(Poet)**
Pen
**BRUBECK, DAVE (Jazz**
**Pianist & Composer)**
Catherine
Christopher
Daniel
Darius
David
Matthew
Michael

---

**DAVE'S TRIBUTE**

"Take 5" jazz composer Dave Brubeck named his son Darius in honor of composer Darius Milhaud, one of the Paris "Six." Milhaud combined Brazilian elements, polytonality, and jazz in his works, and is best known for the ballet *The Creation of the Earth*.

---

**BRYER, STEPHEN (U.S. Supreme Court Justice)**
Chloe

**BRYNNER, YUL (Actor)**
Rock

**BRZEZINSKI, ZBIGNIEW (Political Scientist & Writer)**
Ian
Mark
Mike

**BUCHANAN, JENSEN (Actress, *Another World*)**
John Connor

**BUCKLEY, CHRISTOPHER (Writer)**
Caitlin

**BUCKLEY, WILLIAM F. (Writer)**
Christopher

**BUFFETT, JIMMY (Singer/Songwriter & Novelist)**
Savannah

**BUJOLD, GENEVIEVE (Actress)**

Matthew James

**BUKOWSKI, CHARLES (Poet)**
Marina Louise

**BUMPERS, DALE (U.S. Senator)**
Dale Brent
Margaret Brooke
William Mark

**BURKE, SOLOMON (Preacher & Soul Singer)**
Selassie

**BURNETT, CAROL (Actress & Singer)**
Carrie Louise
Erin Kate
Jody Ann

**BURNS, GEORGE (Comedian & Actor)**
Ronald John [Burns] [aka Ronnie]
Sandra Jean

**BURNS, ROBERT (Poet)**
Elizabeth
Jean
Maxwell

Robert
**BURROUGHS, WILLIAM (Writer)**
William Seward
**BURROWS, ABE (Playwright)**
James [Burrows]
**BURROWS, JAMES (Writer, Producer, & Director)**
Elizabeth
Katherine
Margaret
**BURSTYN, ELLEN (Actress)**
Jefferson
**BURTON, LeVAR (Actor)**
Michaela Jean
**BUSCEMI, STEVE (Actor)**
Lucian
**BUSEY, GARY (Actor)**
Jake
**BUSH, GEORGE &**
**BARBARA BUSH (Former U.S. President & First Lady)**
Dorothy Walker [aka Doro]
George Walker
John Ellis
Marvin Pierce
Neil Mallon
**BUSS, JERRY (Owner, Los Angeles Lakers)**
Janie
Jeanie
Jim
John
**BUTKUS, DICK (Former Pro Football Player)**
Matthew
Nicole
Richard
**BUTLER, CARL (Country Singer)**
Carla
**BUTLER, PEARL LEE (Country Singer)**

---

## BYRON'S BYTES

Ada Byron, Lord Byron's daughter, wrote a set of technical notes that were ultimately considered to be "the world's first explanation of computer programming," according to her biographer, Joan Baum. In 1980, when the Department of Defense developed and began using a new computer programming language, they named the language ADA in her honor.

Carla
**BUTTERFIELD, PAUL (Musician)**
Gabriel
Lee
**BYRD, ADMIRAL RICHARD (South Pole Explorer)**
Richard
**BYRNE, ANN (Actress)**
Jenna
Karina
**BYRNE, DAVID (Rock Musician)**
Malu Valentine
**BYRNE, GABRIEL (Actor)**
Jack Daniel
Romy Marion
**BYRON, LORD (Poet)**
Ada

# C

**CAAN, JAMES (Actor)**
Alexander James
Scott Andrew
Tara
**CAESAR, ADOLPH (Actor)**
Alexandria
Justin
Tiffany
**CAESAR, SID (Comedian & Actor)**
Karen
Michele

Richard
**CAGE, NICHOLAS (Actor)**
Weston
**CAGNEY, JAMES (Actor)**
Cathleen
James
**CAINE, MICHAEL (Actor)**
Dominique
Natasha
**CALLAHAN, DANIEL (Institute Director & Writer)**
David Lee
John Vincent
Mark Sidney
Peter Thorn
Sarah Elisabeth
Stephen Daniel
**CALLOWAY, CAB (Bandleader & Musician)**
Cabella
**CAMERON, JAMES (Director & Writer)**
Josephine
**CAMPBELL, ARCHIE (Country Singer)**
Philip Edward Lee
Stephen Archie
**CAMPBELL, GLEN (Singer)**
Ashley Noel
Cal
Debby
Dillon
Kane

Kelli Glyn
Nicklaus
Shannon
William Travis [aka Travis]
**CAMPBELL, VALERIE (Model)**
Naomi
Pierre
**CAMPEAU, ROBERT (Canadian Entrepreneur)**
Daniel
Giselle
Jacques
Jean Paul
Rachel
Robert
**CAMUS, ALBERT (Writer)**
Catherine
**CANDY, JOHN (Actor)**
Christopher Michael
Jennifer Anne
**CANNON, DYAN (Actress)**
Jennifer
**CANOVA, JUDY (Actress)**
Diana [Canova]
**CAPONE, AL "SCARFACE" (1920s Crime Lord)**
Al
**CAPSHAW, KATE (Actress)**
Sasha
Sawyer
Theo
**CAPUTO, PHILIP (Writer)**

Geoffrey Jacob
Marc Anthony
**CARAY, HARRY (Sports Announcer)**
Christopher
Elizabeth
Harry
Michelle
Patricia
**CAREY, HARRY (Cowboy Actor)**
Harry [Carey, Jr.]
**CARLIN, GEORGE (Comedian & Actor)**
Kelly
**CARLISLE, BILL (Country Singer)**
Billy
Sheila
**CARLISLE, CLIFFORD (Country Singer)**
Thomas
Violet
**CARNEY, ART (Actor)**
Brian
Eileen
Paul
**CAROLINE, PRINCESS (Royalty)**
Andrea
Charlotte
Pierre
**CARON, LESLIE (Actress)**
Christopher John
Jennifer

**CARPENTER, JOHN
(Director)**
John Cody
**CARRADINE, DAVID
(Actor)**
Free [later changed to Tom]
**CARRADINE, JOHN
(Actor)**
Bruce John
Christopher John
David [Carradine]
John Arthur
Keith Ian
Robert
**CARREY, JIM (Actor)**
Jane
**CARROLL, COLLEEN
(Country Singer)**
Garth [Brooks]
**CARROLL, DIAHANN
(Actress)**
Suzanne Ottilie
**CARSON, JOHNNY
(Retired TV Host)**
Chris
Cory
Jody
Ricky
**CARSON, MARTHA LOU
(Country Singer)**
Paul
Rene
**CARTER, BETTY (Jazz
Singer/Songwriter)**
Kagle
Myles
**CARTER, GARY**

**(Professional Baseball
Player)**
Christy
Douglas
Kimberly
**CARTER, JIMMY
(Former U.S. President)**
Amy Lynn
Donnel Jeffrey
James Earl
John William
**CARTER, LYNDA
(Actress)**
James Clifford [aka Jamie]
Jessica
**CARTER, MAYBELLE
(Country Singer)**
Anita [Carter]
Helen [Carter]
Janette [Carter]
June [Carter]
**CARTER, RON (Jazz
Bassist)**
Miles
Ronald
**CARTER, ROSALYNN
(Former U.S. First Lady)**
Amy Lynn
Donnel Jeffrey
James Earl
John William
**CARTERIS, GABRIELLE
(Actress, *Beverly Hills
90210*)**
Kelsey Rose
**CARTLAND, BARBARA
(Writer)**

Glen
Ian
Raine
**CARUSO, DAVID (Actor)**
Greta
**CARUSO, ENRICO (Operatic Tenor)**
Gloria
**CARVEY, DANA (Actor)**
Dex
Thomas
**CASANOVA, GIACOMO (Paramour & Writer)**
Leonilda
**CASEY, WILLIAM (Former Director CIA)**
Bernadette
**CASH, JOHNNY (Country Singer)**
Cindy
John
Kathleen
Rosanne [Cash]
Tara
**CASH, TOMMY (Country Singer)**
Mark Alan
Paula Jean
**CASPER, BILLY (Professional Golfer)**
Billy
Bobby
Byron
Charles
David
Jennifer
Judith

Julia
Linda
Sarah Beth
Tommy
**CASPER, GERHARD (President, Stanford University)**
Hanna
**CASSAVETTES, JOHN (Actor)**
Alexandra
Nicholas
Zoe
**CASSIDY, JACK (Actor)**
David [Cassidy]
**CASSIDY, SHAUN (Actor)**
Caitlin
Jake
**CASSINI, OLEG (Fashion Designer)**
Christina
Daria
**CASTRO, FIDEL (Head of State of Cuba)**
Fidel
**CATES, JOE (Hollywood Impressario)**
Alexandra
Philip
Phoebe [Cates]
Valerie
**CATES, PHOEBE (Actress)**
Owen Joseph
**CATHERINE OF ARAGON (1st wife of Henry VIII)**

Mary
**CATHERINE THE
GREAT (Russian Empress)**
Paul
**CHANCELLOR, JOHN
(TV News Correspondent)**
Barnaby
Laura
Mary
**CHANEY, LON (Actor)**
Lon [Chaney, Jr.]
Ron
**CHANNING, CAROL
(Actress)**
Channing George
**CHAPLIN, CHARLIE
(Actor & Director)**
Charles [Chaplin]
Sidney [Chaplin]
Geraldine [Chaplin]
**CHARLEMAGNE
(Emperor)**
Bertha
Louis
Rotrud
**CHARLES V (Roman
Emperor)**
Margaret
**CHARLES, PRINCE
(British Royalty)**
Henry Charles Albert David
William Arthur Philip Louis
**CHARLES, RAY
(Entertainer)**
David
Ray
Robert

**CHARLES, VISCOUNT
ALTHROP (Royalty)**
Eliza
Katya
Kitty Eleanor
**CHARTOFF, ROBERT
IRWIN (Film Producer)**
Charley
Jenifer
Julie
William
**CHASE, CHEVY (Actor)**
Caley Leigh
Cydney Cathalene
Emily Evelyn
**CHAST, ROZ (Cartoonist)**
Ian
Nina
**CHATHAM, RUSSELL
(Artist)**
Georgina Romy
Lea Irene
Rebecca
**CHAVIS, BENJAMIN
(Civil Rights Activist)**
Benjamin
Michele
Paula
**CHEEVER, JOHN
(Writer)**
Susan
**CHENEY, DICK & LYNN
CHENEY (Former U.S.
Secretary of Defense &
Head of the National
Endowment for the
Humanities)**

Elizabeth

Mary

**CHER (Actress & Singer)**

Chastity

Elijah Blue

**CHERRY, NENAH (Singer)**

Tyson

**CHILES, LAWTON (Former U.S. Senator)**

Edward

Lawton

Rhea Gay

Tandy

**CHONG, RAE DAWN (Actress)**

Morgan

**CHONG, TOMMY (Actor & Comedian)**

Rae Dawn

**CHRISTO (Artist)**

Cyril

**CHURCHILL, WINSTON (British Prime Minister)**

Randolph

Sarah [Churchill]

**CICCIOLINA (Italian Porn Star)**

Ludwig Maximillian

**CILENTO, DIANE (Actress)**

Jason [Connery]

**CIMBER, MATT (Director)**

Tony

**CISNEROS, HENRY**

**(Secretary of Housing & Urban Development)**

John Paul

Mercedes Christina

Teresa Angelica

**CLAIBORNE, LIZ (Fashion Designer)**

Alexander

**CLAPTON, ERIC (Singer/ Songwriter)**

Conor

**CLARK, DICK (TV Entertainer & Producer)**

Cindy

Duane

Richard

**CLARK, RAMSEY (Lawyer)**

Ronda Kathleen

Thomas Campbell

**CLAVELL, JAMES (Writer)**

Holly

Michaela

**CLAY, ANDREW DICE (Comic & Actor)**

Maxwell

**CLAYBURGH, JILL (Actress)**

Lily

**CLEESE, JOHN (Actor & Writer)**

Camilla

Cynthia

**CLEMENS, ROGER (Professional Baseball Player)**

Koby
Kory
**CLEOPATRA (Queen of Egypt)**
Alexander Helios
Cleopatra Selene
Ptolemy Philadelphus
**CLINTON, BILL (U.S. President)**
Chelsea
**CLINTON, GEORGE (Funk Musician)**
Darryl
Donna
Georgie
**CLINTON, HILLARY RODHAM (U.S. First Lady)**
Chelsea
**CLINTON, ROGER (Singer & President's Brother)**
Tyler Cassidy
**CLOONEY, ROSEMARY (Singer)**
Gabriel
Maria
Miguel José
Monsita Teresa
Rafael
**CLOSE, GLENN (Actress)**
Annie Maude
**COBAIN, KURT (Singer/Songwriter, Nirvana)**
Frances Bean
**COBB, LEE J. (Actor)**
Julie

**COBURN, JAMES (Actor)**
James
Lisa
**COFFIN, WILLIAM SLOANE (Clergyman & Activist)**
Alexander Sloane
Amy Elizabeth
David Andrew
**COHEN, ALEXANDER (Theatrical & Television Producer)**
Barbara Ann
Christopher Alexander
Gerald Parks
**COHEN, BENNETT (Ben of "Ben & Jerry" Ice Cream)**
Aretha
**COLE, NAT KING (Singer)**
Natalie [Cole]
Timolin
**COLE, NATALIE (Singer)**
Elizabeth
Kyle
Robert Adam
**COLEMAN, DABNEY (Actor)**
Kelly
Mary
Randolph
**COLERIDGE, SAMUEL (Poet)**
Hartley
Sara

**COLES, ROBERT (Child Psychiatrist & Writer)**
Daniel
Michael
Robert
**COLLINS, ALANA (Actress)**
Ashley [Hamilton]
**COLLINS, GARY (TV Host)**
Mary Clancy
**COLLINS, JOAN (Actress)**
Katy
Sasha [also spelled Sacha]
Tara Cynara
**COLLINS, JUDY (Singer/Songwriter)**
Clark Taylor
**COLLINS, MARVA (Educator)**
Cynthia
Eric
Patrick
**COLLINS, PHIL (Singer/Songwriter)**
Joely
Lily
Simon
**COMMONER, BARRY (Biologist & Writer)**
Frederic Gordon
Lucy Alison
**CONFUCIUS (Chinese Philosopher)**
Po-Yu

**CONNALLY, JOHN (Lawyer)**
John
Mark
Sharon
**CONNER, DENNIS (Yachtsman)**
Julie
Shanna
**CONNERY, SEAN (Actor)**
Giovanna
Jason [Connery]
**CONNORS, JIMMY (Professional Tennis Player)**
Brett David
**CONRAD, JOSEPH (Writer)**
Borys
**CONRAD, KIMBERLEY (Model)**
Cooper Bradford
**CONVY, BERT (TV Host & Actor)**
Jennifer
Jona
Joshua
**COOGAN, JACKIE (Actor)**
Leslie
**COOKE, ALISTAIR (Journalist & Broadcaster)**
John
Susan
**COOLIDGE, RITA (Singer/Songwriter)**
Casey

**COOPER, GARY (Actor)**
Maria
**COOPER, JEANNE
(Actress)**
Collin
Corbin
**COOPER, STONEY
(Country Singer)**
Carol Lee
**COOPER, WILMA LEE
(Country Singer)**
Carol
**COPPOLA, CARMINE
(Composer)**
Francis Ford
**COPPOLA, FRANCIS
FORD (Director)**
Gian-Carlo
Roman
Sophia
**CORDERO, ANGEL
(Jockey)**
Angel Thomas
Merly Suzette
**COREA, CHICK
(Composer & Pianist)**
Liana
Thaddeus

**CORLEY, PAT (Actor)**
Christina
Jerry
Kevin
Michelle
Troy
Vickie
**CORMAN, ROGER
(Director & Actor)**
Brian William
Catherine Ann
Mary Tessa
Roger Martin
**CORRELL, CHARLIE
("Andy" on radio Amos 'n'
Andy)**
Richard [Correll]
**COSBY, BILL (Comedian
& Actor)**
Ennis William
Ensa Camille
Erika Ranee
Erinn Charlene
Evin Harrah
**COSELL, HOWARD
(Sportscaster)**
Hillary
Jill

---

### "FAMILY TIES"

Actor Nicholas Cage (*Moonstruck*) is the nephew of
director Francis Ford Coppola (*The Godfather,
Apocalypse Now,* and many others). (Cage was
born Nicholas Coppola.)

**COSTA-GAVRAS, CONSTANTIN (Director)**
Alexandre
Helene
Julie
**COSTAS, BOB (Sportscaster)**
Keith Michael Kirby
**COSTELLO, LOU (Comic)**
Chris
Paddy
**COSTELLO, MAURICE (Silent Film Star)**
Dolores [Costello]
**COSTER, NICOLAS (Actor)**
Candace
Dinean
Ian
**COSTNER, KEVIN (Actor & Director)**
Annie
Joe
Lily
**COULIER, DAVE (Actor)**
Luc
**COURIC, KATIE (TV's *The Today Show* co-host)**
Elinor Tully
**COUSINS, NORMAN (Writer)**
Amy
Andrea
Candis
Sara Kit

**COUSTEAU, JACQUES (Oceanographer & Writer)**
Jean-Michel
Philippe
**COWLEY, MALCOLM (Writer)**
Robert William
**CRADDOCK, BILLY "CRASH" (Country Singer)**
April
Billy
Steve
**CRANSTON, ALAN (U.S. Senator)**
Kim
Robin
**CRAWFORD, BRODERICK (Actor)**
Christopher
Kelley
**CRAWFORD, JOAN (Actress)**
Cathy
Chris [aka Phillip]
Christina [Crawford]
Cynthia
**CRAWFORD, MICHAEL (Singer)**
Emma
Lucy
**CRIST, JUDITH (Film and Drama Critic)**
Steven Gordon
**CROMWELL, OLIVER (British Lord Protector)**
Richard

**CRONKITE, WALTER**
**(Retired TV News**
**Journalist)**
Mary
Nancy
Walter Leland
**CRONYN, HUME (Actor)**
Christopher Hume
Susan
Tandy
**CROSBY, BING (Singer &**
**Actor)**
Dennis
Gary
Mary
Philip
**CROSS, CHRIS (Singer)**
Justin
**CROTHERS, SCATMAN**
**(Actor)**
Donna
**CRUISE, TOM (Actor)**
Isabella Jane
**CRYSTAL, BILLY (Actor)**
Jennifer [aka Jenny]
Lindsay
**CULKIN, KIT (Theatrical**
**Manager)**
Kiernan [Culkin]

Macaulay [Culkin]
**CUOMO, ANDREW**
**(Assistant Deputy**
**Secretary, HUD)**
Cara Ethel
Mariah Matilda
**CUOMO, KERRY**
**KENNEDY (Executive**
**Director, Robert F.**
**Kennedy Memorial)**
Cara Ethel
Mariah Matilda
**CUOMO, MARIO**
**(Former Governor of New**
**York)**
Andrew
Christopher [aka Chris]
Madeline
Margaret
Maria
**CURIE, MARIE (Scientist)**
Eve
Iréne
**CURTIS, JAMIE LEE**
**(Actress)**
Annie
**CURTIS, TONY (Actor)**
Alexandra
Allegra

---

### "FAMILY TIES"

Actress Denise Crosby (*Pet Sematary, Star Trek: The Next Generation*) is the granddaughter of Bing Crosby.

---

**SHAQ FACT**

Basketball legend Shaq O'Neal's complete name is Shaquille Rashan O'Neal. "Shaquille Rashan" means "Little Warrior" in Arabic.

---

Jamie Lee [Curtis]
Kelly
Nicholas Bernard
**CUSACK, SINEAD (Actress)**
Maximilian Paul
Samuel James
**CUSTER, GEORGE ARMSTRONG (Military Leader)**
Yellow Bird
**CYRUS, BILLY RAY (Country Singer)**
Braison Chance
Christopher Cody
Destiny Hope

# D

**D'AMATO, ALPHONSE (U.S. Senator)**
Christopher
Daniel
Lisa
Lorraine
**D'ARBANVILLE, PATTI (Actress)**
Jesse Wayne

**DAFOE, WILLEM (Actor)**
Jack
**DAHL, ARLENE (Actress)**
Carole Christine
Lorenzo [Lamas]
Sonny
**DAHL, RONALD (Writer)**
Lucy
Olivia Twenty
Ophelia Magdalene
Tessa Sophie
Theo Mathew Roald
**DALE, JIM (Actor)**
Adam
Belinda
Murray
Toby
**DALTON, ABBY (Actress)**
Kathleen [Kinmont]
**DALY, JAMES (Actor)**
Timothy [Daly] [aka Tim]
Tyne [Daly]
**DALY, TIMOTHY (Actress)**
Sam
**DALY, TYNE (Actress)**
Alyxandra
Elizabeth

Katherine [also reported as Kathryne]

**DANGERFIELD, RODNEY (Comedian & Actor)**
Brian
Melanie

**DANIELS, FAITH (TV Journalist)**
Alyx Rae
Andrew

**DANIELS, JEFF (Actor)**
Ben

**DANNER, BLYTHE (Actress)**
Gwyneth Kate
Jake
Laura

**DANO, LINDA (Actress, *Another World* & TV Host)**
Elisa

**DANSON, TED (Actor)**
Alexia
Katherine [aka Kate]

**DANZA, TONY (Actor)**
Emily
Gina
Katherine Anne [aka Katie]
Marc Anthony

**DAULTON, DARREN (Catcher, Philadelphia Phillies)**
Zack

**DAVID, HAL (Lyricist)**
Craig
Jim

**DAVIES, RAY (Singer/ Songwriter, the Kinks)**
Natalie

**DAVIS, BETTE (Actress)**
Barbara
Margot
Michael

**DAVIS, JIMMIE (Country Singer)**
Jimmie

**DAVIS, JOAN (Comic)**
Beverly [Wills]

**DAVIS, MAC (Country Singer)**
Joel Scott [aka Scotty]

**DAVIS, OSSIE (Actor)**
Guy
Laverne
Nora

**DAVIS, SAMMY JR. (Singer, Dancer, & Actor)**
Jeff

---

## HEY, SOMEBODY'S GOT TO DO GOD'S WORK, RIGHT?

Mormon leader Brigham Young ultimately fathered fifty-seven children by sixteen different wives.

Manny
Mark
Tracey
**DAWBER, PAM (Actress)**
Sean Thomas
Ty Christian
**DAWSON, RICHARD (TV Host)**
Shannon Nicole
**DAY, DORIS (Actress & Singer)**
Terry
**DE BAKEY, MICHAEL (Surgeon)**
Barry Edward
Denis Alton
Ernest
Michael Maurice
Olga Katerina
**DE CONCINI, DENNIS (U.S. Senator)**
Christina
Denise
Patrick Evo
**DE HAVILLAND, OLIVIA (Actress)**
Benjamin
Gisele
**DE LARROCHA, ALICIA (Concert Pianist)**
Alicia
Juan
**DE LAURENTIIS, DINO (Film Producer)**
Federico
Francesca
Rafaella

Veronica
**DE LUISE, DOM (Actor)**
David Dominick
Michael Robert
Peter John
**DE PAIVA, JAMES (Actor, *One Life to Live*)**
Dreama
**DE PALMA, BRIAN (Director)**
Lolita
**DEAN, JIMMY (Meat Processing Company Executive & Entertainer)**
Connie
Garry
Robert
**DEAVER, MICHAEL (Goverment Official)**
Amanda Judy
Blair Clayton
**DeBARTOLO, EDWARD J., JR. (Owner, San Francisco 49ers)**
Lisa Marie
Nicole Anne
Tiffanie Lynne
**DEBUSSY, CLAUDE (Composer)**
Claude-Emma [aka Claudette & Chou-Chou]
**DEE, RUBY (Actress)**
Guy
Laverne
Nora
**DEE, SANDRA (Actress)**
Dodd

**DEES, MORRIS (Lawyer & Activist)**
Ellie
John
Morris

**DELLA CORTE, ROSANNA (World's Oldest Woman [62] To Give Birth)**
Riccardo

**DELLUMS, RONALD (Legislator)**
Michael
Pamela

**DEMME, JONATHAN (Director)**
Brooklyn
Ramona

**DENEUVE, CATHERINE (Actress)**
Chiara
Christiaan [also reported as Christian]

**DeNIRO, ROBERT (Actor)**
Drina
Nina Nadjhea
Raphael Eugene

**DeNIRO, ROBERT, SR. (Abstract Expressionist Painter)**
Robert [DeNiro]

**DENTON, SANDY ("Pepa" of Salt-N-Pepa)**
Tyron

**DENVER, BOB (Actor— "Gilligan" on *Gilligan's***
*Island*)
Colin

**DENVER, JOHN (Singer/ Songwriter)**
Jesse Belle

**DEPARDIEU, GERARD (Actor)**
Guillaume
Julie

**DERN, BRUCE (Actor)**
Laura [Dern]

**DERRINGER, RICK (Songwriter/Rock Guitarist)**
Mallory Loving

**DERSHOWITZ, ALAN (Trial Lawyer)**
Ella
Elon Marc
Jamin Seth

**DEVANE, WILLIAM (Actor)**
Jake
Josh

**DeVITO, DANNY (Actor)**
Gracie Fan
Jake Daniel
Lucy Chet

**DeVITO, KARLA (Actress)**
Zephyr

**DEVRIES, WILLIAM (Surgeon)**
Adrie
Andrew
Diana
Janna

---

## THE DIANA DEPARTMENT

Princess Di's "close friend" James Gilbey provided Di with solace and a shoulder to lean on over the years, and he also christened her with a pet nickname: "Squidgy."

Princess Di's complete title reads, "Diana, Princess of Wales, Duchess of Cornwall, Duchess of Rothesay, Countess of Chester, Countess of Carrick, Baroness of Renfrew." No wonder everyone simply calls her Princess Di!

Princess Di's nickname for her son, William, is "Wills."

---

Jon
Kathryn
William
**DEWHURST, COLLEEN (Actress)**
Alexander
Campbell [Scott]
**DEXTER, AL (Country Singer)**
Helen Louise
Jimmie
Wayne
**DEY, SUSAN (Actress)**
Sarah
Susan
**DIAMOND, NEIL (Singer/Songwriter)**
Elyn
Jesse

Marjorie
**DIANA, PRINCESS (British Royalty)**
Henry Charles Albert David
William Arthur Philip Louis
**DICKENS, CHARLES (Writer)**
Alfred Tennyson
Charles Culliford Boz
Edward Bulwer Lytton [aka Plorn]
Francis Jeffrey
Henry Fielding
Kate
Sydney Smith Haldimand
Walter Landor
**DICKENS, LITTLE JIMMY (Country Singer)**

Pamela Jean
**DICKEY, JAMES (Writer)**
Bronwen Elaine
Christopher
Kevin Webster
**DICKINSON, ANGIE (Actress)**
Lea Nikki [aka Nikki]
**DICKINSON, JANICE (Model)**
Savannah
**DICOPOULOS, FRANK (Actor, *The Guiding Light*)**
Jaden Anderson
**DIDION, JOAN (Writer)**
Quintana Roo
**DIETRICH, MARLENE (Actress)**
Maria Riva
**DIGGS, CHARLES, JR. (Legislator)**
Alexis
Charles
Denise
**DILLER, PHYLLIS (Actress, Comedienne, & Writer)**
Perry
Peter
Sally
Stephanie
Suzanne
**DIMITROVA, GHENA (Opera Singer)**
Milena
**DINKINS, DAVID (Former Mayor, New York City)**
David
Donna
**DISNEY, ROY (Founder, Disney Company)**
Abigail Edna
Roy Patrick
Susan Margaret
Timothy John
**DITKA, MIKE (Football Coach)**
Mark
Matthew
Megan
Michael
**DIXON, ALAN (Former U.S. Senator)**
Elizabeth Jane
Jeffrey Alan
Stephanie Jo
**DIXON, DONNA (Actress)**
Belle Kingston
**DOCTOROW, E.L. (Writer)**
Caroline
Jenny
Richard
**DOLBY, RAY MILTON (Inventor, Dolby Sound System)**
David Earl
Thomas Eric
**DOLENZ, GEORGE (Actor)**
Mickey [Dolenz]
**DOLLAR, JOHNNY (Country Singer)**

John Washington
**DOLMAN, NANCY
(Actress)**
Katherine
**DOMENICI, PETE (U.S.
Senator)**
Clare
David
Helen
Lisa
Nanette
Nella
Paula
Peter
**DOMINGO, PLACIDO
(Operatic Tenor)**
Alvaro Maurizio
Jose
Placido
**DONAHUE, PHIL (TV
Talk Show Host)**
Daniel
Jim
Kevin
Maryrose
Michael
**DOSTOYEVSKY,
FYODOR (Writer)**
Fyodor
Lyubov
**DOUGLAS, BUSTER
(Professional Boxer)**
Lamar
**DOUGLAS, KIRK (Actor)**
Eric Anthony
Joel
Michael [Douglas]

Peter
**DOUGLAS, MICHAEL
(Actor)**
Cameron Morrell
**DOW, TONY (Actor—
"Wally" on *Leave It to
Beaver*)**
Christopher
**DOWNEY, MORTON
(Actor)**
Morton [Downey, Jr.]
**DOWNEY, MORTON, JR.
(TV Host)**
Kelli
Melissa
Tracey
**DOWNS, HUGH (TV
Journalist)**
Deirdre Lynn
Hugh Raymond
**DRAVECKY, DAVE
(Retired Professional
Baseball Player)**
Jonathan
Tiffany
**DREW, GEORGIANA
(Actress)**
Ethel [Barrymore]
John [Barrymore, Sr.]
Lionel [Barrymore]
**DREXLER, CLYDE
(Professional Basketball
Player)**
Austin
Elise
**DREYFUSS, RICHARD
(Actor)**

Benjamin [aka Ben]
Emily
Harry
**DRUCKER, PETER**
**(Writer)**
Cecily Anne
Joan Agatha
Kathleen Romola
**DRUSKY, ROY (Country**
**Singer)**
Roy Frank
Tracy
**DRYSDALE, DON**
**(Sportscaster)**
Kelly Eugenia
**DU PONT, PIERRE**
**(Former Governor of**
**Delaware)**
Benjamin
Eleuthere
Elise
Pierre
**DUFFY, JULIA (Actress)**
Daniel
**DUGUAY, RON**
**(Professional Hockey**
**Player)**
Noah
**DUKAKIS, MICHAEL**
**(Former Governor,**
**Massachusetts)**
Andrea
John
Kara
**DUCHESS OF KENT**
**(Royalty)**
Columbus George Donald

Taylor
Helen
**DUKAKIS, OLYMPIA**
**(Actress)**
Christina
Peter
Stefan
**DUKE OF KENT**
**(Royalty)**
Columbus George Donald
 Taylor
Helen
**DUKE, PATTY (Actress)**
Allen
David
Kevin
Mackenzie [Astin]
Sean [Astin]
Thomas
**DUKES, DAVID (Actor)**
Annie Cameron
**DUNAWAY, FAYE**
**(Actress)**
Liam
**DUNCAN, ISADORA**
**(Dancer)**
Deirdre
Patrick
**DUNCAN, JOHNNY**
**(Country Singer)**
Anje
Leslie
Lori
**DUNCAN, ROBERT**
**(Concert Singer & Actor)**
Charles
**DUNCAN, SANDY**

(Actress)
Jeffrey
Michael
**DUNHAM, KATHERINE**
**(Dancer & Choreographer)**
Marie-Christine
**DUNNE, DOMINICK**
**(Novelist)**
Griffin [Dunne]
**DURNING, CHARLES**
**(Actor)**
Douglas
Jeanine
Michele
**DYKSTRA, LENNY**
**(Professional Baseball**
**Player)**
Cutter
Gavin
**DZHANIBEKOV,**
**VLADIMIR (Soviet**
**Cosmonaut)**
Inna
Olya

# E

**E, ROB (Actress, *One Life***
***to Live*)**
Taylor
**EAGLETON, THOMAS**
**(Former U.S. Senator)**
Christin
Terence
**EASTWOOD, CLINT**
**(Actor & Director)**
Alison

Francesca Ruth
Kyle
**EBERSOL, DICK (TV**
**Producer)**
Charles [aka Charlie]
Edward
William
**EBSEN, BUDDY (Actor)**
Bonnie [Ebsen]
**EDDY, MARY BAKER**
**(Founder of Christian**
**Science)**
Foster
George
**EDELMAN, MARION**
**WRIGHT (Lawyer &**
**Activist)**
Ezra
Jonah
Joshua
**EDISON, THOMAS**
**(Inventor)**
Charles
Madeline
Marion
Theodore
Thomas
William
**EDWARD III (British**
**Royalty)**
Lionel
**EDWARDS, ANTHONY**
**(Actor)**
Bailey
**EDWARDS, BOB (Radio**
**Broadcaster)**
Brean

Nora
Susannah
**EDWARDS, HARRY**
**(Educator & Sports**
**Consultant)**
Changa Demany Imara
Fatima Malene Imara
Tazamisha Heshima Imara
**EINSTEIN, ALBERT**
**(Physicist)**
Eduard
Hans Albert
**EINSTEIN, HARRY**
**"PARKYAKARKUS"**
**(Comic)**
Albert [Brooks]
Dave [Osborne]
**EISNER, MICHAEL (Ex-**
**Disney Executive)**
Anders
Eric
Michael
**EKLAND, BRITT**
**(Actress)**
Victoria
**ELDERS, JOYCELYN**
**(Former U.S. Surgeon**
**General [Clinton**
**Administration])**
Kevin
**ELIKAN, LARRY (TV**
**Director)**
Jill
**ELIZABETH, QUEEN**
**(Royalty)**
Andrew Albert Christian
　Edward

Anne Elizabeth Alice Louise
Charles Philip Arthur
　George
Edward Antony Richard
　Louis
**ELKIN, STANLEY**
**(Writer & Educator)**
Bernard Edward
Molly Ann
Philip Aaron
**ELLERBEE, LINDA**
**(Journalist & Broadcaster)**
Joshua
Vanessa
**ELLINGTON, DUKE**
**(Bandleader, Composer, &**
**Pianist)**
Mercer
**ELLIOTT, BOB (Comic)**
Chris [Elliott]
**ELLIOTT, SAM (Actor)**
Cleo
**ELLIS, PERRY (Fashion**
**Designer)**
Tyler Alexandra
**ELWAY, JOHN**
**(Professional Football**
**Player)**
Jessica
John
Jordan
**EMBERG, KELLY**
**(Actress)**
Ruby
**ENG (Original Siamese**
**Twin)**
William

---

## "FAMILY TIES"

Actor and director Albert Brooks (*Defending Your Life*) is the son of Harry "Parkyakarkus" Einstein; brother of comic stuntman Super Dave Osborne (often seen on Showtime).

---

**ENGLUND, MORGAN (Actor, *The Guiding Light*)**
Anabel
Jackson Alexander

**EPHRON, NORA (Writer & Director)**
Jacob
Max

**EPSTEIN, JASON (Editor & Publishing Executive)**
Helen
Jacob

**ERDMAN, PAUL (Writer)**
Constance Anne
Jennifer Michele

**ESTEFAN, GLORIA (Singer)**
Nayib
Raphael

**ESTEVEZ, EMILIO (Actor)**
Paloma
Taylor Levi

**ESTRADA, ERIK (Actor)**
Anthony
Branden

**ESZTERHAS, ISTVAN (Hungarian Writer, Historical Novels)**
Joe [Eszterhas]

**ESZTERHAS, JOE (Screenwriter)**
Joseph Jeremiah [aka Joey]
Steven
Suzanne

**EUBANKS, BOB (TV Host)**
Corey [Michael Eubanks]

**EVANS, DALE (Country Singer)**
Cheryl
Deborah Lee
John
Linda Lou
Little Doe
Marion
Mary
Robin
Roy
Scottish Ward

**EVELYN, MILDRED (Actress)**
Faith [Brook]
Lyndon [Brook]

**EVERLY, DON (Singer)**
Eden
Erin
Stacey
**EVERS, MEDGAR (Civil Rights Leader)**
Darrell
James
Reena
**EVERT, CHRIS (Tennis Pro)**
Alexander James [aka Alex]
Nicholas

# F

**FAHD, KING (Saudi Royalty)**
Abdel
Faisel
Sultan
**FAIRBANKS, DOUGLAS, JR. (Actor)**
Daphne
Kay
Melissa
Victoria
**FAIRBANKS, DOUGLAS, SR. (Actor)**
Douglas [Fairbanks, Jr.]
**FALCO (Austrian Rock Musician)**
Katharina-Bianca
**FALK, PETER (Actor)**
Catherine
Jackie

**FALWELL, JERRY (Clergyman)**
Jeannie
Jerry
Jonathan
**FARENTINO, JAMES (Actor)**
David Michael
**FARR, JAMIE (Actor)**
Jonas Samuel
Yvonne Elizabeth
**FARRELL, MIKE (Actor)**
Erin
Josh
**FARROW, JOHN (Director)**
Mia [nee Maria]
Peter
Prudence
Stephanie
Tisa
**FARROW, MIA (Actress)**
Daisy
Dylan
Fletcher
Isaiah
Lark
Matthew
Moses
Sascha
Satchel
Soon-Yi
Tam
**FAULKNER, WILLIAM (Writer)**
Jill

**YOU MEAN, SHE WASN'T INSPIRED BY MOM'S PERFORMANCE IN *ROSEMARY'S BABY?***

Mia Farrow's adopted daughter Summer Song changed her name to Daisy after she saw her stepmom's performance as Daisy opposite Robert Redford in the 1974 film, *The Great Gatsby*.

**FAWCETT, FARRAH
(Actress)**
Redmond James
**FAYLEN, FRANK
(Actor—"Dobie Gillis" 's
Dad, Herbert)**
Kay [Faylen]
**FAZIO, GIUSEPPE
(Sicilian Director) [SEE
Caitlin Thomas]**
Francesco
**FEINSTEIN, DIANNE
(U.S. Senator & Former
Mayor of San Francisco)**
Katherine Anne [aka Kathy]
**FELD, KENNETH
(Owner, Ringling Brothers
and Barnum & Bailey
Circus)**
Alana
Juliette
Nicole
**FELICIANO, JOSÉ
(Singer/Songwriter)**
Jonathan
Melissa

**FELTS, NARVEL
(Country Singer)**
Narvel
Stacia
**FERGUSON, SARAH
(British Royalty—
"Princess Fergie")**
Beatrice [aka Bea]
Eugenie
**FERRARI, ENZO
(Executive, Ferrari
Motors)**
Alfredo [aka Dino]
Piero Lardi
**FERRARO, GERALDINE
(Former Vice Presidential
Candidate)**
Donna
John
Laura
**FERRER, JOSÉ (Actor)**
Gabriel
Lautitia
Maria
Miguel José
Monsita Teresa

Rafael
**FERRER, MEL (Actor)**
Sean
**FERRIGNO, LOU (Actor)**
Brent Adrian
Louis
Shanna Victoria
**FETCHIT, STEPIN
(Actor)**
Donald
Jemajo
**FIELD, SALLY (Actress)**
Eli
Peter
Samuel [aka Sam]
**FIELDER, CECIL
(Professional Baseball
Player)**
Cecilynn
Prince
**FIELDS, DEBBI
(Executive, Mrs. Fields
Cookies)**
Jennessa [also reported as
Janessa]
Jennifer
Jessica
**FIELDS, FREDDIE
(Theatrical Producer)**
Andrew
Kathy
Paris
Peter
Steven
**FIELDS, W.C. (Comedian
& Actor)**
Claude

**FINGERS, ROLLIE
(Professional Baseball
Player)**
Laurel Lynn
**FINKEL, FYVUSH (Actor,
*Picket Fences*)**
Elliot
Ian
**FINNBOGADÓTTIR,
VIGDÍS (President of
Iceland)**
Astridur
**FINNEY, ALBERT (Actor)**
Simon
**FISHER, CARRIE
(Actress & Writer)**
Billie Catherine
**FISHER, EDDIE (Actor)**
Carrie [Fisher]
Joely [Fisher]
Trishia
**FISHER, FRANCES
(Actress)**
Francesca Ruth
**FISK, CARLTON (Retired
Baseball Player)**
Carlyn
Casey
Courtney
**FISK, JACK (Film
Producer)**
Madison
Schuyler Elizabeth
Virginia
**FITZGERALD, ELLA
(Singer)**
Ray

**FITZGERALD, F. SCOTT**
(Writer)
Scottie
**FITZGERALD,**
**GERALDINE (Actress)**
Michael [Lindsay-Hogg,
British Director]
Susan
**FLATT, LESTER**
(Country Singer)
Brenda Carolyn
**FLEETWOOD, MICK**
(Singer, Fleetwood Mac)
Amy
**FLORIO, JAMES J.**
(Former Governor of New
Jersey)
Catherine
Christopher
Gregory
**FLOYD, RAY**
(Professional Golfer)
Raymond
Robert Loren
**FLYNN, ERROL (Actor)**
Arnella
Dierdre
Rory
Sean
**FLYNN, RAY (Former**
**Mayor of Boston)**
Catherine
Edward
Julie
Maureen
Nancy
Raymond

**FLYNT, LARRY**
(Publisher)
Larry
Lisa
Teresa
Tonya
**FOLEY, RED (Country**
**Singer)**
Betty
Jennie Lee
Julia Ann
Shirley Lee
**FOLLETT, KEN (Writer)**
Emanuele
Marie-Claire
**FOLLETT, WILSON**
(Writer & Editor)
Barbara
**FONDA, HENRY (Actor)**
Jane [Fonda]
Peter[Fonda]
**FONDA, JANE (Actress &**
**Exercise Instructor)**
Troy
Vanessa
**FONDA, PETER (Actor)**
Bridget [Fonda]
Justine
**FONTAINE, JOAN**
(Actress)
Deborah
Martita
**FOOTE, SHELBY (Writer**
**& Civil War Expert)**
Huger Lee
Margaret Shelby

**FORBES, MALCOLM
(Publisher & Writer)**
Christopher Charles [aka
Kip]
Malcolm [aka Steve]
Moira
Robert
Timothy Carter
**FORBES, MARY (Actress)**
Ralph [Forbes]
**FORD, BETTY (Former
First Lady)**
John
Michael Gerald
Steven
Susan Elizabeth
**FORD, GERALD (Former
U.S. President)**
John
Michael Gerald
Steven
Susan Elizabeth
**FORD, HARRISON
(Actor)**
Benjamin
Willard
**FORD, HENRY II
(Automobile Executive)**
Anne
Charlotte
Edsel Bryant
**FORD, JOHN (Director)**
Barbara
**FORD, TENNESSEE
ERNIE (Country Singer)**
Brian
Jeffrey

**FOREMAN, GEORGE
(Professional Boxer)**
George [several]
Michi
**FORSYTHE, JOHN
(Actor)**
Brooke
Dall
Page
**FOSSE, BOB
(Choreographer)**
Nicole
**FOSTER, DAVID
(Musician, Songwriter, &
Record Producer)**
Erin
Sara
**FOUTS, DAN
(Professional Football
Player)**
Dominic Daniel
Suzanne Marie
**FOX, MICHAEL J.
(Actor)**
Aquinnah Kathleen
Sam
Schuyler Frances
**FOXX, REDD (Comedian
& Actor)**
Debraca
**FOYT, A.J. (Race Car
Driver)**
Anthony Joseph
Jerry
Terry Lynn
**FRANCIOSA, TONY
(Actor)**

---

### NICKNAME DEPARTMENT

Sigmund Freud called his daughter Anna his Antigone—the daughter who cared for her blind father Oedipus. Anna took care of Sigmund when he lost his jaw to cancer.

---

Christopher
Marco
Nina
**FRANCIS, IVOR (Actor)**
Genie [Francis]
**FRANKLIN, ARETHA (Singer)**
Clarence
Edward
Kecalf
Teddy
**FRANKLIN, BENJAMIN (Writer, Inventor, & U.S. Founding Father)**
Sarah
William
**FRANZ, DENNIS (Actor, *NYPD Blue*)**
Krysta
Tricia
**FRAZIER, JOE (Retired Boxer)**
Jacquelyn
JoNetta
Marvis
Natasha
Weatta

**FREEMAN, MORGAN (Actor)**
Alphonse
Deena
Morgana
**FRENI, MIRELLA (Operatic Soprano)**
Micaela
**FREUD, SIGMUND (Founder of Psychoanalysis)**
Anna
**FRIEDAN, BETTY (Writer & Feminist Educator)**
Daniel
Emily
Jonathan
**FRIZELL, LEFTY (Country Singer)**
Lois Aleta
Marlan Jaray
Rick
**FULBRIGHT, JAMES (Former U.S. Senator)**
Elizabeth
Roberta

**FULTON, CHRISTINA (Model & Actress)**
Weston

**FUNT, ALLEN (TV Host)**
Juliet

# G

**GABLE, CLARK (Actor)**
John [Gable]
Judy

**GABOR, ZSA ZSA (Actress)**
Francesca

**GADDIS, RON (Country Musician)**
Morgan

**GALBRAITH, JOHN KENNETH (Economist)**
Alan
James
Peter

**GALILEI, GALILEO (Scientist)**
Livia [changed her name to Maria Celeste]
Vincenzio
Virginia

**GALLAGHER, BARBARA (Writer & Producer)**
Tyler Alexandra

**GALLO, ROBERT (AIDS Researcher & Scientist)**
Marcus
Robert Charles

**GALLUP, GEORGE III**

**(Research Organization Executive)**
Alison
George
Kingsley

**GALVIN, JOHN R. (NATO Commander)**
Elizabeth Ann
Eric
Kathleen Mary
Mary Jo

**GANDHI, MAHATMA (Indian Leader & Peace Activist)**
Devadas
Harilal

**GARAGIOLA, JOE (Radio & TV Personality)**
Gina
Joseph
Stephen

**GARCIA, ANDY (Actor)**
Alessandra
Dominik

**GARCIA, JERRY (Singer/ Songwriter & Founding Member, the Grateful Dead)**
Annabelle
Heather
Teresa
Trixie

**GARFUNKEL, ART (Singer & Actor)**
James Arthur

**GARIBALDI, GIUSEPPE (Italian Revolutionary)**

Manlio
**GARIBALDI, MARCO
(Italian Writer & Director)**
Lisa Marie
Navarone
**GARLAND, JUDY (Singer
& Actress)**
Liza
**GARNER, JAMES (Actor)**
Gretta
Kimberly
Scott
**GARVEY, CINDY
(Writer)**
Krisha Lee
Whitney Alyse
**GARVEY, STEVE
(Professional Baseball
Player)**
Krisha Lee
Whitney Alyse
**GATLIN, LARRY
(Country Singer)**
Joshua Cash
Kristin Kara
**GATTON, DANNY
(Guitarist)**
Holly
**GAUGUIN, PAUL
(Painter)**
Aline
Clovis
Emil
Emile
Jean
Pola
**GAULT, WILLIE**

**(Professional Football
Player)**
Shakari
**GAY, EUSTACE (Singer)**
Eustace
**GAYE, MARVIN (Singer)**
Nona
**GAYLE, CRYSTAL (Pop
Singer)**
Catherine Claire
**GELBART, LARRY (TV
Producer)**
Adam
Becky
Cathy
Gary
Paul
**GELDOFF, BOB (Rock
Musician)**
Fifi Trixiebelle
Peaches
Pixie
**GEORGE, PHYLLIS
(Sportscaster)**
Lincoln Tyler
Pamela
**GEPHARDT, RICHARD
(Politician)**
Christine
Katherine
Matthew
**GERARD, GIL (Actor)**
Gib
**GERALDO, NEIL
(Musician & Producer)**
Haley
**GERARDO (Actor)**

---

## "FAMILY TIES"

Emile Gauguin was Paul Gauguin's Tahitian son by a Tahitian native girl named Pau'ura. After an almost completely wasted life (which included jail time for vagrancy and public drunkenness), the 300-plus-pound Emile was found on the streets of Papeete, Tahiti, selling crayon drawings (signed "Gauguin," of course) to tourists for one dollar. Later, however, Emile's "artwork" became somewhat sought after and ended up selling in London for almost $1,500 each.

---

Bianca
**GERGEN, DAVID (Counselor to Bill Clinton)**
Christopher
Katherine
**GERONIMO (Apache Indian Leader)**
Eva
Robert
**GETTY, J.P., II (Financier & Businessman)**
Galaxy Gramaphone
Tara Gabriel
**GETZ, STAN (Saxophonist)**
Beverly
David
Nicholas
Pamela
Steven
**GIAMATTI, A.**

**BARTLETT (Former President, Yale University)**
Elena
Marcus Bartlett
Paul Edward
**GIBB, BARRY (Singer/ Songwriter, the Bee Gees)**
Ashley
Stephen
**GIBB, MAURICE (Singer/ Songwriter, the Bee Gees)**
Adam
Samantha
**GIBB, ROBIN (Singer/ Songwriter, the Bee Gees)**
Melissa
Spencer
**GIBBONS, LEEZA (TV Talk Show Host)**
Jenny Rose
Jordan Alexandra [aka Lexi]

Troy

**GIBSON, BOB (Professional Baseball Player)**
Annette
Renée

**GIBSON, DON (Country Singer)**
Autumn Scarlet

**GIBSON, MEL (Actor)**
Christopher
Edward
Hannah
Louis
Lucian
Will

**GIFFORD, FRANK (Sportscaster)**
Cassidy Erin
Cody Newton
Jeffery
Kyle
Victoria

**GIFFORD, KATHIE LEE (TV Talk Show Host)**
Cassidy Erin
Cody Newton

**GILBERT, MELISSA (Actress)**
Dakota Paul Mayi

**GILBERT, PAUL (Entertainer)**
Melissa [Gilbert]
Sara [Gilbert]

**GILFORD, JACK (Actor)**
Joseph Edward
Lisa

Sam

**GILL, VINCE (Singer/ Songwriter)**
Jennifer

**GILLEY, MICKEY (Country Singer)**
Gregory Brent

**GILLIAM, TERRY (Writer, Actor, & Director)**
Amy Rainbow
Holly

**GILLILAND, RICHARD (Actor)**
Connor

**GINGRICH, NEWT (Politician; Speaker of the House of Representatives)**
Jacqueline Sue
Linda Kathleen

**GINSBURG, RUTH BADER (U.S. Supreme Court Justice)**
James
Jane

**GIOVANNI, NIKKI (Poet)**
Thomas

**GIULIANI, RUDY (Mayor, New York City)**
Andrew
Caroline

**GLASGOW, RA'UF (Movie Producer)**
Maya

**GLASS, PHILIP (Composer & Musician)**
Juliet
Zachary

## "FAMILY TIES"

Actor Jason Patric (*The Lost Boys, Rush*) is the grandson of comic legend Jackie Gleason (and ex-squeeze of Julia Roberts).

**GLASSER, IRA (American Civil Liberties Union Executive)**
Andrew
David
Peter
Sally

**GLEASON, JACKIE (Actor)**
Genevieve
Geraldine
Linda

**GLEASON, LUCILLE (Actress)**
Russell [Gleason]

**GLENN, JOHN (U.S. Senator & Former Astronaut)**
Carolyn Ann
John David

**GOETHE, JOHANN VON (Writer)**
August

**GOLDBERG, GARY DAVID (TV Writer & Producer)**
Shana

**GOLDBERG, LEONARD (TV Executive)**
Amanda Erin

**GOLDBERG, WHOOPIE (Actress)**
Alexandrea

**GOLDIN, DANIEL (NASA Administrator)**
Ariel
Laura

**GOLDING, WILLIAM (Writer)**
David
Judith

**GOLDMAN, WILLIAM (Writer)**
Jenny
Susanna

**GOLDWATER, BARRY (Former U.S. Senator)**
Barry
Joanne
Margaret
Michael

**GOLDWYN, TONY (Actor)**
Anna

**GONZALES, PANCHO**

(Professional Tennis
Player)
Andrea
Christina
Danny
Jeanna Lynn
Michael
Richard
**GOODALL, JANE
(Ethologist & Writer)**
Hugo Eric Louis
**GOODMAN, BENNY
(Conductor & Clarinetist)**
Benjie
Rachel
**GOODMAN, ELLEN
(Journalist)**
Katherine Anne
**GOODMAN, JOHN
(Actor)**
Molly Evangeline
**GOODSON, MARK (TV
Producer)**
Jonathan
**GORDEEVA,
EKATERINA, (Olympic
Skater)**
Darya
**GORDON, DEXTER (Jazz**

Saxophonist)
Benjamin
Dee Dee
Robin
Woody
**GORDON, KIM (Singer,
Sonic Youth)**
Coco Chanel
**GORDY, BERRY (Record
Company Executive)**
Berry
Hazel Joy
Kennedy
Kerry
Rhonda [Ross]
Stefan
Terry James
**GORE, AL & TIPPER
GORE (U.S. Vice-
President and Spouse)**
Albert
Karenna
Kristin
Sarah
**GORMAN, LEON
(Executive, L.L. Bean)**
Ainslie
Jeffrey
Jennifer

---

## NAMESAKE DEPARTMENT

Sonic Youth's Kim Gordon and Thurston Moore
named their daughter Coco Chanel, in honor of the
legendary fashion designer.

**GORMÉ, EYDIE**
**(Entertainer)**
David [Lawrence]
Michael
**GOSSETT, LOUIS, JR.**
**(Actor)**
Satie
Sharron
**GOULD, ELLIOTT**
**(Actor)**
Jason
Jennifer
Sam Bazooka
**GOULD, JAY (Robber**
**Baron)**
Frank
George
**GOULD, STEPHEN JAY**
**(Paleontologist & Writer)**
Ethan
Jesse
**GOULET, ROBERT**
**(Actor & Singer)**
Christopher
Michael
Nicolette
**GOWDY, CURT**
**(Sportscaster)**
Cheryl Ann
Curtis
Trevor
**GRACE, PRINCESS**
**(Royalty)**
Stephanie [Princess
Stephanie]
**GRAHAM, BILL (Concert**
**Producer)**

Alex
David
Thomas
**GRAHAM, BILLY**
**(Evangelist)**
Anne
Nelson
Ruth
Virginia
William
**GRAHAM, KATHERINE**
**(Newspaper Executive)**
Donald Edward
Elizabeth
Stephen
William
**GRAHAM, NICHOLAS**
**(Fashion Designer)**
Christopher
**GRAMMER, BILLY**
**(Country Singer)**
Billy
Diane
Donna
**GRAMMER, KELSEY**
**(Actor)**
Kandace
**GRANGER, STEWART**
**(Actor)**
Tracy
**GRANT, AMY (Singer)**
Millie
**GRANT, CARY (Actor)**
Jennifer
**GRANT, LEE (Director &**
**Actress)**
Dinah [Manoff]

**GRANT, RODNEY (Actor)**
Walter

**GRAY, BARRY (Radio Personality)**
Dora
Melody

**GRAY, LINDA (Actress)**
Jeff
Kelly [also reported as Kehly]

**GRAY, OTTO (Country Singer)**
Owen

**GRAYSON, WILLIAM (Publisher)**
Geraldine
Gloria
William

**GREEN, RICHARD R. (Educator)**
Craig
Kelly
Kimberlee
Sherri

**GREENBERG, HANK (Baseball Hall of Famer)**
Alva
Glenn
Stephen

**GREENE, JACK (Country Singer)**
Barbara Lynn
Forest Anthony
Jackie Wayne
Jan Thomas
Mark Allen

**GREENFIELD, JERRY**
**(Jerry of "Ben & Jerry" Ice Cream)**
Tyrone

**GREGORY, CYNTHIA (Ballerina)**
Amanda
Lloyd

**GREGORY, DICK (Political Activist & Comedian)**
Ayanna
Christian
Gregory
Lynne
Michele
Missy [also reported as Miss]
Pamela
Paula
Stephanie
Yohance

**GRETZKY, WAYNE (Professional Hockey Player)**
Paulina
Trevor Douglas
Ty Robert

**GREY, JOEL (Actor)**
Jennifer [Grey]
Jimmy

**GREY, RAY (Silent Director)**
Virginia [Grey]

**GREYSON, BRUCE (Writer, Near-Death Experience Expert)**
Devon

Eric
**GRIEG, EDVARD**
**(Composer)**
Alexandra
**GRIFFEY, KEN**
**(Professional Baseball**
**Player)**
Ken [Griffey, Jr.]
**GRIFFIN, MERV (TV**
**Host & Singer)**
Anthony Patrick [aka Tony]
**GRIFFITH, ANDY (Actor)**
Andy Sam
Dixie Nan
**GRIFFITH, MELANIE**
**(Actress)**
Alexander
Dakota Mayi
**GRIMES, TAMMY**
**(Actress)**
Amanda [Plummer]
**GRINKOV, SERGEI**
**(Olympic skater)**
Darya
**GRISHAM, JOHN**
**(Writer)**
Shea
Ty
**GRODIN, CHARLES**
**(Actor & Writer)**
Marion
**GRODY, KATHRYN**
**(Actress)**
Gideon
Isaac
**GROENIG, MATT**

**(Cartoonist & Creator of**
*The Simpsons*)
Homer
**GROH, DAVID (Actor)**
Spencer Arthur
**GRUCCI, FELIX**
**(Executive, Grucci**
**Fireworks Co.)**
Donna
Felix
James
**GUCCIONE, BOB**
**(Publisher)**
Bob
**GUEST, CHRISTOPHER**
**(Actor)**
Annie
**GUIDRY, RON**
**(Professional Baseball**
**Player)**
Brandon
Jamie Rachael
**GUINNESS, ALEX**
**(Actor)**
Matthew
**GUMBEL, BRYANT (TV**
**Host)**
Bradley Christopher
Jillian Beth
**GUYER, DAVID**
**(Executive, Save the**
**Children)**
Alissa Carolyn
Cynthia Loraine
Grant
Leigh Jonathan

Marion Leslie
Shelly Diane

# H

**HACKMAN, GENE
(Actor)**
Christopher
Elizabeth
Leslie
**HAGEN, UTA (Actress)**
Lautitia
**HAGGARD, MERLE
(Singer/Songwriter)**
Dana
Kellie
Marty
Noel
**HAGLER, MARVELOUS
MARVIN (Professional
Boxer)**
Celeste
Charelle
Gentry
James
Marvin
**HAGMAN, LARRY
(Actor)**
Heidi
Preston
**HAIG, ALEXANDER
(Former U.S. Secretary of
State)**
Alexander
Barbara
Brian

**HAILEY, ARTHUR
(Writer)**
Diane
Jane
John
Mark
Roger
Steven
**HAIM, VICTOR (French
Playwright)**
Mathilda [May]
**HALBERSTAM, DAVID
(Writer)**
Julia
**HALE, ALAN (Actor—
"Skipper" on *Gilligan's
Island*)**
Alan [Hale, Jr.]
**HALE, BARBARA
(Actress—"Della Street"
on *Perry Mason*)**
William [Katt]
**HALEY, ALEX (Writer)**
Cynthia Gertrude [aka
Cindy]
Lydia Ann
William Alexander
**HALEY, JACK (Actor)**
Jack [Haley, Jr.]
**HALL, ANDREA (Actress)**
Emily
**HALL, BRAD (Writer)**
Henry
**HALL, DEIDRE (Actress)**
David Atticus
**HALL, GUS (Communist
Party Leader)**

Arvo
Barbara
**HALL, JERRY (Model)**
Elizabeth Scarlett
Georgia May Ayeesha
James Leroy Augustine
**HALLE, ANDRE (Deep-sea Diver)**
Raphaël
**HAMBLEN, STUART (Country Singer)**
Veeva Obee
**HAMEL, ALAN (Canadian TV Host)**
Leslie
Steve
**HAMILL, MARK (Actor)**
Nathan Elias
**HAMILTON, GEORGE (Actor)**
Ashley [Hamilton]
**HAMILTON, GEORGE IV (Country Singer)**
Edwin Peyton George
Mary
**HAMILTON, JANE (Writer)**
Ben
Hannah
**HAMILTON, LINDA (Actress)**
Dalton
Josephine
**HAMLIN, HARRY (Actor)**
Dmitri
**HAMMER, M.C. (Rap Singer)**

Akeiba Monique
**HAMMERSTEIN, OSCAR, II (Lyricist & Composer)**
James [aka Jimmy]
**HAMMOND, KAY (Actress)**
John [Standing]
**HANKS, TOM (Actor)**
Chester
Colin
**HANNA, BILL (Animated Cartoon Producer)**
Bonnie Janna
David William
**HANSEN, PATTI (Model)**
Alexandra
Theodora Dupree
**HARDISON, BETHANN (Model Mogul)**
Kadeem [Hardison]
**HARDISON, INGE (Painter & Sculptress)**
Yolande
**HARE, DAVID (Playwright)**
Darcy
Joe
Lewis
**HARGIS, BILLY JAMES (Clergyman)**
Becky Jean
Billy James
Bonnie Jane
Brenda Jo
**HARKIN, THOMAS (Congressman)**

Amy
Jenny
**HARMON, MARK (Actor)**
Sean Thomas
Ty Christian
**HARMON, TOM (Actor)**
Kelly [Harmon]
Mark [Harmon]
**HARPER, VALERIE
(Actress)**
Cristina
**HARRELSON, WOODY
(Actor)**
Denni Montana
**HARRIMAN, EDWARD
HENRY (Robber Baron)**
Mary
**HARRIMAN, WILLIAM
AVERELL (Former
Government Official)**
Kathleen
Mary
**HARRINGTON, PAT
(Vaudevillian)**
Pat [Harrington, Jr.]
**HARRIS, CASSANDRA
(Actress)**
Charlotte
Christopher
Sean William
**HARRIS, ED (Actor)**
Lily Delores
**HARRIS, EMMYLOU
(Singer/Songwriter)**
Hallie
Meghann Theresa [also
reported as Megan]

Shannon
**HARRIS, JULIE (Actress)**
Peter Allen
**HARRIS, LOU (Public
Opinion Analyst)**
Peter
Richard
Susan
**HARRIS, MEL (Actress)**
Byron
Madeline
**HARRIS, MOIRA
(Actress)**
Ella
McCanna
Sophie
**HARRIS, RICHARD
(Actor)**
Damien
Jamie
Jared
**HARRISON, GEORGE
(Singer/Songwriter,
Founding Member of the
Beatles)**
Dhani
**HARRYHAUSEN, RAY
(Special Effects Expert)**
Vanessa Ann
**HART, CECILIA (Actress)**
Flynn
**HART, GARY (Former
U.S. Senator)**
Andrea
John
**HART, MARY (TV Host)**
Alec

**HART, MICKEY**
**(Drummer, the Grateful**
**Dead)**
Taro
**HARTLEY, MARIETTE**
**(Actress)**
Justine
Sean
**HARTMAN, DAVID (TV**
**Host)**
Brian
Bridget
Conor
Sean
**HARVEY, PAUL (Radio**
**Commentator & Writer)**
Paul
**HASSELHOFF, DAVID**
**(Actor)**
Hayley
**HATCH, ORRIN (U.S.**
**Senator)**
Alysa
Brent
Jesse
Kimberly
Marcia
Scott
**HATFIELD, MARK (U.S.**
**Senator)**
Charles
Elizabeth
Mark
Theresa
**HATFIELD, WILLIAM**
**(Feuder, The Hatfields and**
**the McCoys)**

Johnse [short for Johnson]
**HATHAWAY, DONNY**
**(Singer)**
Leila
**HAWKING, STEPHEN**
**(Theoretical Physicist,**
**Mathematician, Educator,**
**& Writer)**
Lucy
Robert
Timothy
**HAWKINS, HAWKSHAW**
**(Country Singer)**
Don Robin
Harold Franklin
**HAWKINS, PAULA**
**(Former U.S. Senator)**
Genean
Kelley Ann
Kevin Brent
**HAWN, GOLDIE (Actress)**
Garry
Kate
Oliver
Wyatt
**HAWTHORNE,**
**NATHANIEL (Writer)**
Una
**HAYAKAWA, SAMUEL**
**(Writer & Former U.S.**
**Senator)**
Alan
Mark
Wynne
**HAYDEN, TOM**
**(Politician & Writer)**
Troy

**HAYES, HELEN (Actress)**
James [MacArthur]
Mary
**HAYES, ROLAND (Concert Singer)**
Afrika [Hayes Lambe]
**HAYWORTH, RITA (Actress)**
Rebecca
Yasmin [Aga Khan]
**HEALY, BERNADINE (Former Director, National Institute of Health)**
Bartlett Ann
Marie
**HEARST, PATTY (Actress)**
Gillian
Lydia
**HEARST, WILLIAM RANDOLPH (Editor & Publisher)**
David
George
John Augustine
Randolph
William Randolph
**HECKERLING, AMY (Director)**
Mollie Sara
**HECKERT, RICHARD (CEO, Du Pont)**
Alex
Andra
**HEDREN, TIPPI (Actress)**
Melanie [Griffith]

**HEFLIN, HOWELL (U.S. Senator)**
Howell Thomas
**HEFNER, HUGH (Publisher)**
Christie [Hefner]
Cooper Bradford
David
Marston
**HEIFETZ, JASCHA (Concert Violinist)**
Joseph
Josepha
Robert
**HEIMLICH, HENRY (Physician & Surgeon)**
Elizabeth
Janet
Peter
Philip
**HEINZ, HENRY (Former U.S. Senator)**
Andre
Christopher Drake
Henry John
**HELLER, JOSEPH (Writer)**
Erica Jill
Theodore Michael
**HELLER, WALTER (Kennedy Economic Advisor)**
Eric
Kaaren Louise
Walter
**HELMS, BOBBY (Country Singer)**

Bobby Bun
Debbie Kay
Randy Scott
**HELMS, JESSE (U.S. Senator)**
Charles
Jane
Nancy
**HELMSLEY, LEONA (Hotel Executive)**
Jay
**HEMINGWAY, ERNEST (Writer)**
Gregory
Jack
Pat
**HEMINGWAY, MARIEL (Actress)**
Dree Louise
Langley Fox
**HENDERSON, FLORENCE (Actress)**
Barbara
Elizabeth
Joey
Robert Norman
**HENDERSON, SKITCH (Musician & Bandleader)**
Heidi

**HENNER, MARILU (Actress)**
Nicholas
**HENNING, PAUL (TV Producer)**
Linda [Kaye Henning]
**HENRY VIII (King of England)**
Edward
Elizabeth
Henry
Mary
**HENRY, O. (Writer)**
Margaret
**HENSON, JIM (Puppeteer & TV Producer)**
Brian David [Henson]
Cheryl Lee
Heather Beth
John Paul
Lisa Marie
**HENTOFF, NAT (Writer)**
Jessica
Miranda
Nicholas
Thomas
**HEPBURN, AUDREY (Actress)**
Luca

---

### "FAMILY TIES"

Actress Mariel Hemingway (*Manhattan*) is the granddaughter of legendary writer Ernest Hemingway.

Sean
**HERMAN, WOODY**
**(Orchestra Leader)**
Ingrid
**HERRING, LYNN**
**(Actress, *General Hospital*)**
Grady
**HERSHEY, BARBARA**
**(Actress)**
Free (later changed to Tom]
**HERSHEY, JOHN**
**(Writer)**
Ann
Baird
Brook
John
Martin
**HERSHISER, OREL**
**(Professional Baseball**
**Player)**
Jordan Douglas
Orel Leonard
**HERVEY, IRENE**
**(Actress)**
Jack [Jones]
**HERZOG, WERNER**
**(Director)**
Rudolph Ames Achmed
**HESTON, CHARLTON**
**(Actor)**
Fraser Clark
Holly Ann
**HEXTALL, RON**
**(Professional Hockey**
**Player)**
Kristen

**HEYERDAHL, THOR**
**(Explorer & Writer)**
Anette
Bettina
Bjorn
Marian
Thor
**HILFIGER, TOMMY**
**(Fashion Designer)**
Alexandria
Richard
**HILL, GOLDIE (Country**
**Singer)**
Carl
Larry Dean
Lori Lynn
**HILLEGAS, CLIFTON**
**KEITH (Publisher, Cliff's**
**Notes)**
Diane
James
Kimberly
Linda
**HILLERMAN, TONY**
**(Writer)**
Anne
Anthony
Daniel
Janet
Monica
Steven
**HILLS, CARLA (U.S.**
**Trade Representative)**
Alison Macbeth
Laura
Megan Elizabeth
Roderick

**HILTON, CONRAD**
**(Hotelier)**
Francesca
**HINTON, S.E. (Writer)**
Nicholas David
**HINES, GREGORY**
**(Actor)**
Daria
Jessica
Zachary Evan
**HINES, MAURICE**
**(Dancer)**
Gregory [Hines]
**HIRSCHFELD, AL**
**(Artist)**
Nina
**HOBAN, RUSSELL**
**(Writer)**
Benjamin
Brom
Esmé
Jachin
Julia
Phoebe

Wieland
**HOFFA, JIMMY (Union**
**Leader)**
Charles
**HOFFMAN, ABBIE**
**(Political Activist)**
Andrew
**HOFFMAN, DUSTIN**
**(Actor)**
Alexandra
Jacob [aka Jake]
Jenna
Karina
Max
Rebecca
**HOFSTADTER, ROBERT**
**(Physicist & Writer)**
Douglas Richard
Laura
Mary
**HOGE, JAMES (Editor)**
Alicia
James Patrick
Robert

---

## WHERE'S NINA?

A cult following has developed around Al Hirschfeld and his drawings, thanks to his daughter, Nina. Since Nina's birth, Hirschfeld has been inserting hairline "NINA"s in his drawings, usually hidden in hair, the wrinkles of clothing, or in folds of skin. Hirschfeld also puts a number next to his distinctive signature that indicates the number of "NINA"s that can be found in the drawings.

## MA DADDY'S SO FUNNY—AIN'T HE, NOW?

For years it was rumored that Big Jim Hogg's daughter "Ima" (her real name) had two sisters named "Ura" and "Shesa," and a brother named "Hesa." Ima actually had three brothers named Will, Tom, and Mike. Big Jim didn't really do too much to discount the rumors. He seemed to actually enjoy the attention and uproar over his last name. It isn't known how Ima felt about it.

**HOGG, BIG JIM (1st Native Governor of Texas)**
Ima [Hogg]
Mike
Tom
Will
**HOLBROOK, HAL (Actor)**
David
Eve
Victoria
**HOLDEN, WILLIAM (Actor)**
Scott [Holden]
**HOLDER, GEOFFREY (Actor)**
Leo
**HOLLAND, VYVYAN (Writer & Oscar Wilde's Son)**
Merlin
**HOLLINGS, ERNEST (U.S. Senator)**
Ernest
Helen
Michael
Patricia
**HOLM, CELESTE (Actress)**
Daniel Schuyler
Theodor
**HOLMES, LARRY (Professional Boxer)**
Lisa
Listy
**HOLT, JACK (Actor)**
Tim [Holt]
**HOLTZ, LOU (College Football Coach, Notre Dame)**
Elizabeth
Kevin Richard
Luanne
Skip
**HOLYFIELD, EVANDER (Boxer)**

Ashley
Ebonné
Evander
Ewin

**HOOKS, REVEREND BENJAMIN (Former FCC Chairman)**
Patricia Louise

**HOOKS, ROBERT (Actor)**
Cecilia
Eric
Kevin

**HOPE, BOB (Actor)**
Anthony
Kelly
Linda
Nora

**HOPKINS, ANTHONY (Actor)**
Abigail

**HOPPER, DENNIS (Actor & Director)**
Henry

**HOPPER, DEWOLF (Silents Star)**
William [Hopper]

**HOPPER, HEDDA (Columnist)**
William [Hopper]

**HORNE, LENA (Singer)**
Gail
Teddy

**HORNSBY, BRUCE (Singer/Songwriter/Pianist)**
Keith Randall
Russell Ives

**HOROWITZ, VLADIMIR (Pianist)**
Sonia

**HOSKINS, BOB (Actor)**
Alex
Jack
Rosa
Sarah

**HOUSEMAN, JOHN (Actor & Director)**
Charles Sebastian
John Michael

**HOUSTON, CISSY (Singer)**
Whitney

**HOUSTON, WHITNEY (Singer & Actress)**
Bobbi Kristina

**HOWARD, LESLIE (Actor)**
Ronald [Howard]

**HOWARD, RANCE (Actor)**
Clint
Ron [aka Ronnie] [Howard]

**HOWARD, RON (Director)**
Bryce
Jocelyn
Paige
Reed

**HOWE, GORDIE (Former Professional Hockey Player)**
Cathleen Jill
Mark Steven
Marty Gordon

Murray Albert
**HOWSER, DICK (Professional Baseball Player)**
Jan
Jill
**HUBERT-WHITTEN, JANET (Actress, *The Fresh Prince of Bel Air*)**
Elijah Issac
**HUDSON, BILL (Singer/ Songwriter, the Hudson Brothers)**
Garry
Kate
Oliver
**HUFF, LEON (Songwriter & Music Producer)**
Debbie
Detira
**HUGHES, JOHN (Director)**
James
**HUGHES, TED (Poet)**
Frieda Rebecca
Nicholas
**HUGO, VICTOR (Writer, *Les Misérables*)**
Adèle
**HULL, BOBBY (Former Professional Hockey Player)**
Bart Alexander
Blake Anthony
Bobby Abbott
Brett Andrew

**HUMBARD, REX (TV Evangelist)**
Aimee Elizabeth
Charles Raymond
Don Raymond
Rex Emanuel
**HUMPERDINCK, ENGLEBERT (Singer)**
Jenna
**HUMPHRIES, BARRY (Actor—"Dame Edna Everage")**
Emily
Oscar
Rupert
Tessa
**HUNT, GORDON (Director)**
Helen [Hunt]
**HUNT, MARSHA (Actress)**
Karis
**HUNTER, EVAN (Writer)**
Amanda Eve
Mark
Richard
Ted
**HUNTER, MADELINE (Education Expert)**
Cheryl
Robin
**HUNTER, RACHEL (Model)**
Renée
Liam McAllister
**HURD, GALE ANNE (Producer)**

Lolita
**HURT, WILLIAM (Actor)**
Alexander Devon
Sam
**HUSSEIN, KING (King of Jordan)**
Hamzah
Hashim
Iman
**HUSSEY, OLIVIA (Actress)**
Alexander
India Joy
**HUSTON, JOHN (Director)**
Anjelica [Huston]
**HUSTON, WALTER (Vaudevillian)**
John [Huston]
**HUTTON, BARBARA (Woolworth Heiress)**
Lance
**HUTTON, JIM (Actor)**
Timothy [Hutton]
**HUTTON, TIMOTHY (Actor)**
Emanuel Noah [aka Noah]
**HYNDE, CHRISSIE (Singer/Songwriter, the Pretenders)**
Natalie

**I**

**IACOCCA, LEE (Former Automobile Company Executive)**

Kathryn Lisa
Lia Antoinette
**IDOL, BILLY (Rock Singer)**
Willem Wolf
**INMAN, BOBBY RAY (Electronics Executive)**
Thomas
William
**INNIS, ROY (Civil Rights Activist)**
Alexander
Cedric
Corinne
Kimathia
Niger
Patricia
**INOUYE, DANIEL (U.S. Senator)**
Daniel Ken
**IONESCO, EUGENE (Playwright)**
Anne-Marie-Therese
**IRELAND, JILL (Actress)**
Jason
**IRONS, JEREMY (Actor)**
Maximilian Paul
Samuel James
**IRVING, AMY (Actress)**
Gabriel
Max Samuel
**IRVING, JOHN (Writer)**
Brendan
Colin
**IRWIN, ELAINE (Model)**
Speck Wildhorse

ISOZAKI, ARATA
(Renowned Architect)
Horashi
Kan
IVAN THE TERRIBLE
(Russian Czar)
Feodor
Ivan
IVEY, JUDITH (Actress)
Maggie

# J

JACKSON, ALAN
(Country Singer)
Ali
Mattie
JACKSON, ANN (Actress)
Katherine
Roberta
JACKSON, BO (Athlete)
Garrett
JACKSON, CORDELL
(Guitarist)
Bexley Ryan
Dana Miller
JACKSON, GLENDA
(Actress)
Daniel
JACKSON, JESSE
(Clergyman & Civic
Leader)
Jacqueline Lavinia
Jesse Louis
Jonathan Luther
Santita
Yusef DuBois

JACKSON, JOE (Jackson
Family Patriarch)
Jackie
Janet
Jermaine
LaToya
Marlon
Michael
Randy
Tito
JACKSON, KATHERINE
(Jackson Family
Matriarch)
Jackie
Janet
Jermaine
LaToya
Marlon
Michael
Randy
Tito
JACKSON, KEITH (TV
Commentator)
Christopher Keith
Lindsey Keith
Melanie Ann
JACKSON, STONEWALL
(Country Singer)
Stonewall
JACKSON, WANDA
(Country Singer)
Gina Gail
Gregory
JACOBSON, MICHAEL
(Writer & Nutritional
Watchdog)
Sonya

**JACUZZI, CANDIDO
(Inventor, the Jacuzzi)**
Alba
Irene
John
Kenneth
**JAFFE, STAN (Film
Producer)**
Betsy
Bobby
**JAGGER, BIANCA
(Actress)**
Jade
**JAGGER, JADE (Mick's
Daughter)**
Assissi
**JAGGER, MICK (Rock
Musician, the Rolling
Stones)**
Elizabeth Scarlett
Georgia May Ayeesha
Jade
James Leroy Augustine
Karis
**JANEWAY, ELIOT
(Economist)**
Michael
William
**JANKLOW, MORT
(Attorney & Agent)**
Angela
Lucas
**JANKLOW, WILLIAM
(Former Governor of
South Dakota)**
Pam
Russell

Shonna
**JANSEN, DAN (Olympic
Speed Skater)**
Jane
**JARVIK, ROBERT
(Physician & Artificial
Organ Developer)**
Kate
Tyler
**JASMER, BRENT (Actor,
*The Bold and the Beautiful*)**
Alexa
**JAVITS, JACOB (Former
U.S. Senator)**
Carla
Joshua
Joy
**JENNER, BRUCE
(Professional Athlete)**
Brandon
Brendan
Brody
Burt
Cassandra
Robert
**JENNINGS, PETER (TV
News Anchor)**
Christopher
Elizabeth
**JENSEN, HOWARD
(Former New York Giant)**
Luke [Jensen]
Murphy [Jensen]
**JEWISON, NORMAN
(Director)**
Jennifer Ann
Kevin Jefferie

Michael Philip
**JILLIAN, ANN (Actress)**
Andrew Joseph
**JOEL, BILLY (Singer/ Songwriter)**
Alexa Ray
**JOHNSON, BETTY (Singer & Actress)**
Lydia
**JOHNSON, BEVERLY (Supermodel)**
Anansa
**JOHNSON, DON (Actor)**
Dakota Mayi
Jesse Wayne
**JOHNSON, EARVIN "MAGIC" (Retired Athlete)**
Earvin
**JOHNSON, JIMMY (Football Coach)**
Brent
Chad
**JOHNSON, LADY BIRD (Former U.S. First Lady)**
Luci
Lynda
**JOHNSON, LARRY (Professional Basketball Player)**
Gabrielle
**JOHNSON, LYNDA BIRD (Daughter, U.S. President)**
Catherine Lewis
Jennifer
Lucinda Desha

**JOHNSON, LYNDON (Former U.S. President)**
Luci
Lynda
**JOHNSON, VAN (Actor)**
Schuyler
**JOHNSON-MASTERS, VIRGINIA (Psychologist & Sex Researcher)**
Lisa
Scott
**JONES, ALLAN (Movie Singer)**
Jack [Jones]
**JONES, BOB (Minister)**
Bob
Jon Edward
Joy Estelle
**JONES, DAVEY (Singer, the Monkees)**
Annabelle
Jessica
Sarah
Talia
**JONES, GEORGE (Country Singer)**
Tamela
**JONES, GRANDPA (Country Singer)**
Elise June
Eloise
Mark Alan
**JONES, JAMES EARL (Actor)**
Flynn
**JONES, JANET (Actress)**
Paulina

Trevor Douglas
Ty Robert
**JONES, JENNIFER**
**(Actress)**
Robert [Walker, Jr.]
**JONES, MERVYN (Actor)**
Glynis [Johns]
**JONES, QUINCY (Music**
**Producer)**
Jolie
Kenya Julia Miambi Sarah
Kidada
Martina-Lisa [aka Martina]
Quincy
Rashida
**JONES, RICKY LEE**
**(Singer/Songwriter)**
Charlotte Rose
**JONES, SHIRLEY**
**(Actress)**
David [Cassidy]
**JONES, TERRY (Director**
**& Writer)**
Bill
Sally
**JONES, TOM (Singer)**
Mark
**JONES, TOMMY LEE**
**(Actor)**
Austin
Victoria
**JONG, ERICA (Writer)**
Molly
**JORDAN, CHARLES M.**
**(General Motors Car**
**Designer)**
Debra

Mark
Melissa
**JORDAN, MICHAEL**
**(Professional Basketball**
**Player)**
Jasmine Mickael
Jeffrey Michael
Marcus James
**JORDAN, VERNON**
**(Administrator)**
Vickee
**JOSEPHINE (Napoleon's**
**Empress)**
Eugène
Hortense
**JOVOVICH, GALINA**
**(Soviet Actress)**
Milla [Jovovich]
**JOYCE, JAMES (Writer)**
George
Lucia
**JUAN CARLOS I (King of**
**Spain)**
Christina
Elena
Felipe
**JUDD, NAOMI (Singer/**
**Songwriter)**
Ashley
Wynonna [nee Christina]

# K

**KAELIN, KATO (Actor)**
Tiffany
**KALLEN, JACKIE**

(Professional Boxing
Manager)
Brad
Bryan
**KANOKOGI, RUSTY
(Martial Arts Expert)**
Chris
Jean
Teddy
**KARAN, DONNA
(Fashion Designer)**
Gabrielle
**KARLOFF, BORIS
(Actor)**
Sara
**KASDAN, LAWRENCE
(Director)**
Jacob [aka Jake]
Jonathan
**KASEM, CASEY (TV &
Radio Personality)**
Julie
Kerri
Liberty Irene
Michael [aka Mike]
**KASSEBAUM, NANCY
(U.S. Senator)**
John Philip
Linda Josephine
Richard Landon
William Alfred
**KATZ, ALEX (Artist)**
Vincent
**KATZ, MICKEY
(Comedian)**
Joel [Grey]

**KAUFMAN, GEORGE S.
(Playwright)**
Anne
**KAUFMANN,
CHRISTINE (Actress)**
Allegra
**KAYE, DANNY (Actor &
Comedian)**
Dena
**KAZAN, ELIA (Director)**
Chris
Judy
Katharine
Leo
Nick
**KAZIN, ALFRED (Writer)**
Cathrael
Michael
**KEACH, STACY, SR.
(Actor)**
James
Stacy [Keach]
**KEAN, EDMUND (Actor)**
Charles
**KEAN, THOMAS (Former
Governor of New Jersey)**
Alexandra
Reed
Thomas
**KEATON, MICHAEL
(Actor)**
Sean Willie
**KEITEL, HARVEY
(Actor)**
Stella
**KEITH, BRIAN (Actor)**
Bobby

Daisy
Michael
Mimi
**KEITH, ROBERT (Actor)**
Brian [Keith]
**KELLEY, DAVID
(Producer & Writer, *Picket
Fences*)**
John Henry
**KELLY, GENE (Dancer &
Actor)**
Bridget
Kerry
Timothy
**KELLY, PRINCESS
GRACE (Royalty &
Former Actress)**
Stephanie
**KEMP, JACK (Politician)**
James [aka Jimmy]
Jeffrey [aka Jeff]
Jennifer
Judith
**KEMPER, MARGARET
TRUDEAU (Former Wife
of Canadian Prime
Minister)**
Alicia
Kyle
**KENNEDY, EDWARD
(U.S. Senator)**
Edward Moore
Kara Anne
Patrick Joseph
**KENNEDY, EDWARD,
JR. (Politician)**
Kiley Elizabeth
**KENNEDY, JEAN
(Ambassador to Ireland)**
Amanda
Kym
**KENNEDY, JOSEPH
(Kennedy Family
Patriarch)**
Edward
Eunice
Jean
John Fitzgerald
Joseph
Kathleen

---

## THIS IS MY BABY BOY, BABY

When Robert Kennedy, Jr., and his wife Mary had
their first child, a boy, they were undecided on
what to name him. RFK Jr. really wanted to dub the
lad Conor, but his wife wasn't so sure. Because of
their uncertainty, they called the boy "Baby" until
they made up their respective minds.

Patricia
Robert Francis
Rosemary
**KENNEDY, KATHLEEN
(Kennedy Family Member)**
Kerry Sophia
**KENNEDY, PAT (Kennedy
Daughter)**
Robin
Sydney
Victoria
**KENNEDY, ROBERT
(Assassinated Senator)**
Courtney
Joseph [aka Joe]
Kathleen
Kerry [Cuomo]
Rory
**KENNEDY, ROBERT, JR.
(Politician)**
Conor
Kathleen
Robert
**KENNEDY, ROSE
(Kennedy Family
Matriarch)**
Edward
Eunice
Jean
John Fitzgerald
Joseph
Kathleen
Patricia
Robert Francis
Rosemary
**KERCHEVAL, KEN**

(Actor—**"Cliff Barnes"** on
*Dallas*)
Aaron
Maddie
**KERN, JEROME
(Composer)**
Betty
**KERR, WALTER (Drama
Critic & Writer)**
Christopher
Colin
Gilbert
Gregory
John
Katharine
**KERREY, BOB
(Politician)**
Benjamin
Lindsey
**KERSHAW, DOUG
(Country Singer)**
Douglas James
Victor Conrad
**KESEY, KEN (Writer)**
Jed
Shannon
Sunshine
Zane
**KHAN, AGA (Royalty)**
Aly [Khan]
**KHAN, ALY (Royalty)**
Yasmin
**KHAN, GENGHIS
(Mongol Leader)**
Jöchi
Ögödei
Toluy

**KIDMAN, NICOLE**
(Actress)
Isabella Jane
**KIEFER, ANSELM**
(Artist)
Daniel
Julian
Sarah
**KIKO, PRINCESS**
(Royalty)
Princess Mako
**KILEY, RICHARD**
(Actor)
David
Dierdre
Dorothea
Erin
Kathleen
Michael
**KILGORE, MERLE**
(Country Singer)
Kimberly
Pamela Ann
Stephen
**KILMER, VAL (Actor)**
Jack
Mercedes

**KILPATRICK, JAMES**
(Newspaperman)
Christopher
Kevin
Michael Sean
**KING, ALAN (Comedian
& Actor)**
Andrew
Bobby
**KING, CAROLE (Singer/
Songwriter)**
Levi
Louise
Molly
Sherry
**KING, CLAUDE (Country
Singer)**
Bradley
Duane
Jerone
**KING, CORETTA
SCOTT (Lecturer &
Writer)**
Bernice Albertine
Dexter Scott
Martin Luther
Yolanda Denise

---

### "PAGING DR. FREUD"

Rainer Marie Rilke, the great German poet, was
brought up by his mother as a girl named Renée.
Rilke's mother had lost an infant daughter and
insanely wanted Rainer—a male—to replace her.

**KING, DON (Boxing Promoter)**
Carl
Carlie
Deborah
Eric
Gregory
Maximillian
**KING, MARTIN LUTHER, JR. (Civil Rights Leader & Writer)**
Bernice Albertine
Dexter Scott
Martin Luther
Yolanda Denise
**KING, MARTIN LUTHER, SR. (Clergyman)**
Alfred
Martin Luther
**KING, PEE WEE (Country Singer)**
Frank
Gene
Larry
Marietta Jo
**KING, PERRY (Actor)**
Hannah Perrin
**KING, STEPHEN & TABITHA KING (Writers)**
Joseph Hill
Naomi
Owen
**KING, LARRY (CNN Talk Show Host & Journalist)**
Chaia
**KINGSLEY, BEN (Actor)**

Edmund
**KINSKI, KLAUS (Actor)**
Nanhoi
Nastassja [Kinski]
Pola
**KINSKI, NASTASSJA (Actress)**
Aljosha
Kenya Julia Miambi Sarah
Sonia
**KIRKPATRICK, JEANE (Political Scientist & Former Government Official)**
Douglas
John
Stuart Alan
**KISSINGER, HENRY (Former U.S. Secretary of State)**
David
Elizabeth
**KLASS, PERRI (Pediatrician & Writer)**
Benjamin Orlando
Josephine Charlotte Paulina
**KLEIN, CALVIN (Designer)**
Marci
**KLEIN, ROBERT (Comedian)**
Alexander Stewart
**KLINE, KEVIN (Actor)**
Owen Joseph
**KLUGMAN, JACK (Actor)**
Adam

David
**KNIEVEL, EVEL**
**(Motorcycle Daredevil)**
Robbie [Knievel]
**KNIEVEL, ROBBIE**
**(Motorcycle Daredevil)**
Krysten
**KNIGHT, BOBBY**
**(Basketball Coach)**
Patrick Clair
Timothy Scott
**KNIGHT, GLADYS**
**(Singer/Songwriter)**
James
Kenya
Shanga
**KNIGHT, SHIRLEY**
**(Actress)**
Jennifer
**KNIGHT, TED (Actor)**
Elyse
Eric
Ted
**KNOTTS, DON (Actor)**
Karen Ann
Thomas Allen
**KOONS, JEFF (Artist)**
Ludwig Maximillian
**KOOP, C. EVERETT**
**(Former U.S. Surgeon**
**General)**
Allen
David Charles Everett
Elizabeth
Norman
**KOPPEL, TED (TV**
**Journalist)**

Andrea
Andrew
Deidre
Tara
**KOPPELL, OLIVER (New**
**York Attorney General)**
Carla
Jonathan
**KORDICH, JAY (Health**
**Food Entrepreneur—"The**
**Juiceman")**
Jayson
John
**KORMAN, HARVEY**
**(Actor)**
Christopher Peter
Maria Ellen
**KORN, SUSAN (TV Host)**
Jenna
**KRANTZ, JUDITH**
**(Writer)**
Anthony
Nicholas
**KRAVITZ, LENNY**
**(Musician)**
Zoe
**KREMENTZ, JILL**
**(Photographer & Writer)**
Lily
**KREUTZMAN, BILL**
**(Drummer, the Grateful**
**Dead)**
Justin
**KRIM, MATHILDE**
**(Virologist & Researcher)**
Daphna
**KRISTOFFERSON, KRIS**

(Singer/Songwriter &
Actor)
Casey
John Robert
Kris
Tracy
**KRZYZEWSKI, MIKE**
**(College Football**
**Coach)**
Debbie
Jamie
Lindy
**KÜBLER-ROSS,**
**ELISABETH (Physician)**
Barbara Lee
Kenneth Lawrence
**KUNTSLER, WILLIAM**
**(Lawyer)**
Emily
Jane
Karin
Sarah
**KUPCINET, IRV (Talk**
**Show Host)**
Karyn [Kupcinet]
**KURALT, CHARLES (TV**
**Host & Writer)**
Lisa Catherine
Susan
**KUROSAWA, AKIRA**
**(Japanese Director)**
Hisao
Kazuko
**KURTH, WALLY (Actor,**
*General Hospital*)
Meghan

**L**

**L'AMOUR, LOUIS**
**(Writer)**
Angelique Gabrielle
Beau
**L'ENGLE, MADELINE**
**(Writer)**
Bion
Josephine
Maria
**LADD, ALAN (Actor)**
David [Ladd]
**LADD, CHERYL (Actress)**
Jordan
Lindsay
**LADD, DIANE (Actress)**
Laura [Dern]
**LAEMMLE, CARL**
**(Founder of Universal**
**Studios)**
Carl
**LAHR, BERT (Actor)**
John [Lahr]
**LAHTI, CHRISTINE**
**(Actress)**
Emma
Joe
Wilson
**LAMAS, FERNANDO**
**(Actor)**
Lorenzo [Lamas]
**LAMAS, LORENZO**
**(Actor)**
Alvaro Joshua
Paton Lee

Shayne
**LAMBERT, CHRISTOPHER** (Actor)
Eleanor Jasmine
**LAMM, RICHARD** (Former Governor of Colorado)
Heather Susan
Scott Hunter
**LANCASTER, BURT** (Actor)
James Steven
Joanne Mari
John Martin
Susan Elizabeth
William Henry
**LANDER, DAVID** (Actor—"Squiggy" on *Laverne & Shirley*)
Natalie
**LANDERS, ANN** (Advice Columnist)
Margo
**LANDHAGE, GABY** (Swedish Model)
Erik
Sandrine
**LANDON, MICHAEL** (Actor)
Cheryl
Christopher Beau
Jennifer
Josh
Leslie Ann
Mark
Michael
Sean Mathew

Shawna Leigh
**LANDRY, TOM** (Professional Football Coach)
Kitty
Lisa
Thomas
**LANE, DIANE** (Actress)
Eleanor Jasmine
**LANGE, JESSICA** (Actress)
Alexandra
Hannah
Samuel
**LANSBURY, ANGELA** (Actress)
Anthony Peter
David
Deirdre Angela
**LARDNER, RING** (Writer)
David
James
John
Joseph
Katharine
Ring [aka Bill]
**LARROQUETTE, JOHN** (Actor)
Jonathan
Lisa
**LASORDA, TOMMY** (Retired Baseball Manager)
Laura
Tom Charles

**LATTANZI, MATT**
**(Actor)**
Chloe Rose
**LAUDER, ESTÉE**
**(Cosmetics Executive)**
Leonard Allen
Ronald
**LAUREN, RALPH**
**(Designer)**
Andrew
David
Dylan
**LAWFORD, PAT**
**KENNEDY (Kennedy**
**Family Member)**
Chris [Lawford]
**LAWRENCE, CAROL**
**(Actress & Singer)**
Christopher
Michael
**LAWRENCE, STEVE**
**(Entertainer)**
David [Lawrence]
Michael
**LAXALT, PAUL (Former**
**U.S. Senator)**
Gail
John
Kathleen
Kevin
Michelle
Sheila
**LeBROCK, KELLY**
**(Actress)**
Anneliese [also reported as
Anna Liza]
Arissa

Dominick [also reported as
Dominic]
**LE GUIN, URSULA K.**
**(Writer)**
Caroline
Elisabeth
Theodore
**LE MOND, GREG**
**(Professional Bicycle**
**Racer)**
Geoffrey James
**LEACH, PENELOPE**
**(Child Development**
**Expert)**
Matthew
Melissa
**LEAKEY, RICHARD**
**(Paleoanthropologist)**
Anna
Louise
Samira
**LEAR, FRANCES**
**(Publisher)**
Kate
Lear
Maggie
**LEAR, NORMAN (TV**
**Writer & Producer)**
Benjamin Davis
Ellen
Kate
Maggie
**LEARY, DENIS**
**(Comedian & Actor)**
Devin
Jack

**LEARY, TIMOTHY (Psychologist & Writer)**
John [aka Jack]
Susan
**LEDERMAN, LEON MAX (Winner, 1988 Nobel Prize for Physics)**
Heidi
Jesse
Rena
**LEE, BILL (Jazz Composer & Musician)**
Joie [Lee]
Spike [Lee]
**LEE, BRENDA (Country Singer)**
Jolie
Julie
**LEE, BRUCE (Actor)**
Brandon [Lee]
**LEE, GYPSY ROSE (Actress & Singer)**
Erik
**LEE, JOHNNY (Country Singer)**
Cherish
**LEE, MICHELE (Actress)**
David Michael
**LEE, ROSE (Country Singer)**
Dale
Jody
Lorrie
**LEE, STAN (Publisher & Writer, Marvel Comics)**
Jan
Joan [aka Joanie]

**LEHRER, JAMES (TV Commentator)**
Amanda
Jamie
Lucy
**LEIGH, JANET (Actress)**
Jamie Lee [Curtis]
Kelly
**LEITCH, DONOVAN (Singer/Songwriter)**
Donovan [Leitch]
Ione [Skye]
**LEMMON, JACK (Actor)**
Christopher [aka Chris]
Courtney
**LEMON, MEADOWLARK (Professional Basketball Player)**
Beverly
Donna
George
Jonathan
Robin
**LENDL, IVAN (Tennis Pro)**
Marika
**LENNON, ALFRED (John's Father)**
David Henry
Robin Francis
**LENNON, JOHN (Singer/Songwriter, Artist, Writer, & Founding Member of the Beatles)**
Julian
Sean Ono

## IMAGINE

Before John Lennon legally changed his name to John Ono Lennon, he was named John Winston Lennon, in honor of Winston Churchill.

**LENNON, JULIA (John's Mother)**
Jacqueline [aka Jacqui]
John
Julia
Victoria Elizabeth
**LENNOX, ANNIE (Rock Singer)**
Lola
Tali
**LEONARD, SUGAR RAY (Professional Boxer)**
Jarrel
Ray Charles
**LeROY, MERVYN (Director)**
Linda
**LESSING, DORIS (Writer)**
Jean
John
Peter
**LETTERMAN, DOROTHY (TV Correspondent)**
David [Letterman]
**LEVINE, JOSEPH (Conductor)**
David
Stephen
**LEVINSON, BARRY (Writer & Director)**
Jack
Sam
**LEWIS, HUEY (Singer/ Songwriter, Huey Lewis & the News)**
Austin
Kelly
**LEWIS, JERRY (Actor & Comedian)**
Anthony
Chris
Daniele Sarah
Gary [Lewis]
Joseph
Ronnie
Scotty
**LEWIS, JERRY LEE (Singer)**
Jerry Lee
Phoebe
**LEWIS, RAMSEY (Pianist & Composer)**
Dawn
Kendall

Marcus Kevin
Ramsey Emanuel
Vita Denise

**LEWIS, REGINALD
(Attorney & Financier)**
Christina
Leslie

**LEWIS, SHARI
(Puppeteer)**
Mallory

**LEWIS, SINCLAIR
(Writer)**
Michael

**LEWIS, TERRY (Music
Producer)**
Ashley Nicole
Brandon
Chloe
Tremayne

**LICHTENSTEIN, ROY
(Artist)**
David
Mitchell

**LIGHTFOOT, GORDON
(Singer/Songwriter)**
Fred
Ingrid

**LIMAN, ARTHUR (Chief
Counsel, Iran-Contra
Special Senate Committee)**
Douglas
Emily
Lewis

**LINDBERGH, CHARLES,
JR. (Aviator)**
Anne
Charles

Jon
Land
Reeve
Scott

**LINDEN, HAL (Actor)**
Amelia Christine
Ian Martin
Jennifer Dru
Nora Kathryn

**LINDFORS, VIVECA
(Actress)**
Kristoffer [Tabori]

**LINKLETTER, ART (TV
Host)**
Dawn
Diane
Jack [Linkletter]
Robert
Sharon

**LIPTON, PEGGY
(Actress)**
Kidada
Rashida

**LISZT, FRANZ
(Composer)**
Cosima

**LITHGOW, JOHN (Actor)**
Ian
Nathan George
Phoebe

**LITTLE, RICH
(Impressionist)**
Bria

**LOCKHART, GENE
(Actor)**
June [Lockhart]

**LOCKHART, JUNE**
**(Actress)**
Anne [Lockhart]
**LOCKHART,**
**KATHLEEN (Actress)**
June [Lockhart]
**LOCKLIN, HANK**
**(Country Singer)**
Beth
Margaret
Maurice
**LOCKWOOD, VICTORIA**
**(Royalty)**
Eliza
Katya
**LOEB, CHARLES**
**(Newspaper Executive)**
Jennie
Stella
**LOGGIA, ROBERT**
**(Actor)**
Cynthia
John
Kristina
Tracey
**LONDON, JACK (Writer)**
Joan
**LONG, RUSSELL**
**(Former U.S. Senator)**
Katherine
Pamela
**LONGFELLOW, HENRY**
**WADSWORTH (Poet)**
Alice
Allegra
Charles

Edith
Ernest
**LOPEZ, NANCY**
**(Professional Golfer)**
Ashley
Erinn
**LORD, BETTY BAO**
**(Chinese Pro-Democracy**
**Activist & Writer)**
Elizabeth
Winston
**LORD, BOBBY (Country**
**Singer)**
Robert Cabot Wesley
Sarah
**LORD, MARJORIE**
**(Actress)**
Anne [Archer]
Gregg
**LORD, WINSTON (U.S.**
**Diplomat)**
Elizabeth
Winston
**LOREN, SOPHIA**
**(Actress)**
Carlo [aka Cipi]
Edoardo [aka Eli]
**LORING, GLORIA**
**(Actress & Singer)**
Brennan
Robin
**LOUDERMILK, JOHN D.**
**(Country Singer)**
John
Michael Phillip
Ricky

**LOUIS, JOE (Professional Boxer)**
Jacqueline [aka Jackie]
Joe Louis
Joseph [aka Jo Jo]

**LOUIS-DREYFUSS, JULIA (Actress)**
Henry

**LOVE, COURTNEY (Singer/Songwriter)**
Frances Bean

**LOWE, ROB (Actor)**
Matthew Edward

**LUCCI, SUSAN (Actress)**
Susan

**LUCKINBILL, LAURENCE (Actor)**
Simon

**LUDLUM, ROBERT (Writer)**
Glynis
Jonathan
Michael

**LUGOSI, BELA (Actor)**
Bela

**LUMAN, BOB (Country Singer)**
Melissa

**LUMET, SIDNEY (Director)**
Amy
Jenny

**LUNDEN, JOAN (TV Host)**
Jamie

**LUPINO, STANLEY (British Comedian)**
Ida [Lupino]

**LuPONE, PATTI (Actress)**
Joshua

**LUTHER, MARTIN (The 1st Protestant)**
Hans
Paul
Peter

**LUTZ, ROBERT (Corporate Executive, Chrysler Corporation)**
Alexandra
Carolyn
Catherine
Jacqueline

**LYNCH, DAVID (Director & Writer)**
Jennifer [Lynch]

**LYNN, LORETTA (Singer/Songwriter)**
Betty Sue Lynn
Clara Marie
Ernest Ray
Jack Benny
Patsy Eileen
Peggy Jean

# M

**MAAZEL, LORIN (Conductor)**
Fiona
Ilann Sean

**MacCREADY, PAUL (Inventor)**
Marshall

Parker
Tyler
**MacDOWELL, ANDIE (Actress)**
Justin
Rainey
**MacGRAW, ALI (Actress)**
Joshua [aka Josh]
**MACK, JILLY (Actress)**
Hannah
**MACKIE, BOB (Fashion Designer)**
Robin Gordon
**MacLAINE, SHIRLEY (Actress & Writer)**
Sachi
Stephanie
**MacLEOD, GAVIN (Actor)**
David
Julie
Keith
Meghan
**MacNEIL, ROBERT (Broadcast Journalist)**
Alison
Catherine Anne
Ian
William
**MacRAE, GORDON (Actor & Singer)**
Amanda
Bruce
Heather
Meredith
**MADDEN, JOHN (TV Sports Commentator)**

Joe
Mike
**MADIGAN, AMY (Actress)**
Lily Delores
**MADSEN, VIRGINIA (Actress)**
Jack
**MAGLICH, BOGDAN (Physicist)**
Ivanko Taylor
Marko
Roberta
**MAILER, NORMAN (Writer)**
Danielle
Elizabeth
John Buffalo
Kate
Maggie
Michael
Steven
Susan
**MAINER, J.E. (Country Singer)**
Carolyn
Charles
Earl
Glen
Mary
**MAJOR, JOHN (Prime Minister of Great Britain)**
Elizabeth
James
**MAJORS, LEE (Actor)**
Dane Luke
Trey Kulley

**MAKEBA, MIRIAM
(Singer & Activist)**
Bongi
**MALAMUD, BERNARD
(Writer)**
Janna
Paul
**MALDEN, KARL (Actor)**
Carla
Mila
**MALLE, LOUIS
(Director) [SEE Candice
Bergen]**
Chloe
**MANCINI, HENRY
(Composer)**
Christopher
Felice
Monica
**MANDEL, HOWIE
(Comic)**
Jackelyn
Riley Paige
**MANDELA, NELSON
(President of South Africa)**
Maki
Zenani
Zinzi
**MANDRELL, BARBARA
(Singer)**
Jaime Nicole
Kenneth Matthew [aka Matt]
Nathaniel
**MANGIONE, CHUCK
(Musician & Composer)**
Diana

Nancy
**MANN, HERBIE (Flutist)**
Claudia
Laura
Paul
**MANN, THOMAS
(Writer)**
Erika
Klaus
Michael
**MANSFIELD, JAYNE
(Actress)**
Jayne Marie
Mariska [Hargitay]
Miklos
Tony
Zoltan
**MANTEGNA, JOE
(Actress)**
Gina Christine
Mia Marie
**MANTLE, MICKEY
(Former Professional
Baseball Player)**
Billy Giles
Danny Merle
David Harold
Mickey Elvin
**MANVILLE, LESLEY
(Actress)**
Alfie
**MAPHIS, JOE (Country
Singer)**
Dale
Jody
Lorrie

**MAPLES, MARLA**
(Actress)
Tiffany
**MARCEAU, MARCEL**
(Mime)
Sophie
**MARCONI,**
**GUGLIELMO (Scientist)**
Elettra
**MARGARET, PRINCESS**
(British Royalty)
Sarah
**MARLEY, BOB (Reggae**
**Singer/Songwriter)**
Rohan
Ziggy
**MARRINER, NEVILLE**
(Orchestral Conductor)
Andrew Stephen
Susan Frances
**MARSALIS, BRANFORD**
(Musician)
Reese Ellis
**MARSALIS, ELLIS (Jazz**
**Musician)**
Branford [Marsalis]
Delfeayo
Jason
Wynton [Marsalis]
**MARSHALL, BRENDA**
(Actress)
Scott [Holden]
**MARSHALL, E.G. (Actor)**
Degen
Jill
**MARSHALL, GARRY**
(Director)

Kathleen
Scott
**MARSHALL, JOHN (TV**
**Journalist)**
Vanessa
**MARSHALL, PENNY**
(Director & Actress)
Tracy Lee
**MARSHALL,**
**THURGOOD (Former**
**U.S. Supreme Court**
**Justice)**
John
Thurgood
**MARTIN, ALEXANDREA**
(Whoopi Goldberg's
Daughter)
Amarah Skye
**MARTIN, BILLY (Former**
**Baseball Manager)**
Billy Joe
Kelly Ann
**MARTIN, DEAN (Actor &**
**Singer)**
Claudia
Craig
Dean Paul [aka Dino]
Deanna
Gail
Gina
Ricci
**MARTIN, DEAN PAUL**
(Actor)
Alexander
**MARTIN, MARY**
(Actress)
Heller

---

### MAYBE SHE SHOULD HAVE NAMED HER "MOTRIN"

Mary Martin named her daughter "Heller" because "she kicked like mad" in utero.

---

Larry [Hagman]
**MARTIN, PAMELA SUE (Actress)**
Nickolas Garland
**MARTINS, PETER (Ballet Choreographer & Dancer)**
Nilas
**MARX, DICK (Composer & Conductor)**
Richard [Marx]
**MARX, KARL (Communist Writer)**
Fraziska
Freddy
Heinrich
Jenny
Laura
Leni [nee Eleanor]
**MARX, RICHARD (Singer/Songwriter)**
Brandon Caleb
**MARX, RUTH (Singer)**
Richard [Marx]
**MARY KAY (Cosmetics Executive)**
Ben
Marylyn
Richard

**MARY, QUEEN OF SCOTS (Royalty)**
James
**MASSEY, RAYMOND (Actor)**
Daniel [Massey]
**MASTROIANNI, MARCELLO (Actor)**
Barbara
**MATHESON, TIM (Actor)**
Cooper
**MATTHAU, WALTER (Actor)**
Charles [aka Charlie]
David
Jenny
**MATTINGLY, DON (Professional Baseball Player)**
Taylor Patrick
**MATTINGLY, THOMAS (Astronaut)**
Thomas
**MATISSE, HENRI (Painter)**
Jean
Marguerite
Pierre

MAUREEN (Actress—
"Marcia" on *The Brady
Bunch*)
Natalie
McCOY, CHARLIE
(Country Singer)
Charlie
Ginger
McCOY, RANDOLPH
(Feuder, the Hatfields and
the McCoys)
Rose Anne
McCULLOUGH,
GERALDINE (Painter &
Sculptress)
Lester
McDONALD, COUNTRY
JOE (Singer/Songwriter)
Seven

McDOWELL,
MALCOLM (Actor)
Charles [aka Charlie]
Lilly
McENROE, JOHN (Tennis
Pro)
Emily
Kevin Jack
Sean Timothy
McENTIRE, REBA
(Country Singer)
Shelby Stephen
McFADDEN, GATES
(Actress)
James Cleveland
McFADDEN, MARY
(Fashion Executive)
Justine
McFERRIN, BOBBY

## THE BEATLES OFF THE RECORD

In the sixties, the Beatles were so well-known
globally that they had to travel using code names.
For their 1964 vacation, the Fab Four and their
companions traveled under the following aliases:
**Paul:** Mr. Manning
**Jane Asher:** Miss Ashcroft
**Ringo:** Mr. Stone
**Maureen Starkey:** Miss Cockroft
[These four went to St. Thomas, the Virgin Islands.]
**John and Cynthia Lennon:** Mr. and Mrs. Leslie
**George:** Mr. Hargreaves
**Pattie Boyd:** Miss Bond
[These four went to Papeete, Tahiti.]

(Singer/Songwriter)
Jevon
Taylor
**McGILLIS, KELLY (Actress)**
Chelsea
Kelsey
Sondra
Sonora Ashley
**McGOVERN, GEORGE (Former U.S. Senator)**
Ann
Mary
Steven
Susan
Teresa
**McGUIRE, DOROTHY (Singer & Actress)**
Topo
**McKAY, JIM (TV Sports Commentator)**
Mary Edwina
Sean Joseph
**McKEAN, MICHAEL (Musician & Actor, Spinal Tap Founding Member)**
Colin
Fletcher
**McKENNA, TERRENCE (New Age Lecturer & Writer)**
Finn
**McKINNEY, STEWART (Politician)**
Jean
John
Libby

Lucie
Stewart
**McMAHON, ED (TV Personality)**
Claudia
Jeffrey
Katherine Mary
Linda
Michael
**McMURTRY, LARRY (Writer)**
James
**McQUEEN, STEVE (Actor)**
Chad
**McREYNOLDS, JESSE (Country Singer)**
Gwen
Keith
Michael
Randy
**MEADOWS, STEVE (Actor)**
Lexi
Troy
**MEARA, ANNE (Actress)**
Amy
Benjamin [aka Ben] [Stiller]
**MEHTA, ZUBIN (Conductor)**
Merwan
Zarina
**MELCHIOR, LAURITZ (Operatic Tenor)**
Ib [Melchior]
**MELLENCAMP, JOHN (Singer/Songwriter)**

Hud
Justice
Michelle
Speck Wildhorse
Teddi Jo
**MELVILLE, HERMAN
(Writer)**
Malcolm
Stanwix
**MENUHIN, YEHUDI
(Violinist)**
Gerard
Jeremy
Krov
Zamira
**MEREDITH, BURGESS
(Actor)**
Jonathan Sanford
Tala Beth
**MEREDITH, DON (Actor
& Sportscaster)**
Heather
Mary Donna
Michael
**MERRILL, CHARLES
(Founder, Merrill-Lynch)**
James [Merrill]
**MERRILL, DINA
(Actress)**
Heather
**MERRILL, ROBERT
(Baritone)**
David Robert
Lizanne
**MESSIER, MARK
(Professional Hockey
Player)**

Lyon
**METCALF, LAURIE
(Actress)**
Will
Zoe
**METZENBAUM,
HOWARD (U.S. Senator)**
Amy Beth
Barbara Jo
Shelley Hope
Susan Lynn
**MIDLER, BETTE (Actress
& Singer)**
Sophie Frederica Alohilano
**MILLAND, RAY (Actor)**
Daniel David
Victoria Francesca
**MILLER, ARTHUR
(Playwright)**
Jane Ellen
Robert
**MILLER, DENNIS
(Comic)**
Holden
**MILLER, GLENN
(Bandleader)**
Steve
**MILLER, JAMES
(Former Chairman,
Federal Trade
Commission)**
John Felix
Katrina Demaris
Sabrina Louise
**MILLER, JASON
(Playwright)**
Jason [Patric]

Jennifer
Jordan
**MILLER, ROGER**
**(Country Singer)**
Roger
**MILLS, SIR JOHN**
**(Actor)**
Hayley [Mills]
Juliet [Mills]
**MILNE, A.A. (Writer,**
*Winnie the Pooh*)
Christopher Robin
**MILNES, SHERRILL**
**(Baritone)**
Eric
Erin
Shawn
**MILSAP, RONNIE**
**(Singer/Songwriter)**
Ronald Todd [aka Todd]
**MILTON, JOHN (Poet)**
Anne
Deborah
Mary
**MINTZ, SHLOMO**
**(Concert Violinist)**
Eliau
**MITCHELL, GEORGE**
**(U.S. Senator)**
Andrea
**MITCHELL, NICOLE**
**(Model)**
Bria [aka Brea]
Miles Mitchell
Shayne [aka Shane]
**MITCHELSON, MARVIN**
**(Attorney)**

Morgan
**MITCHUM, ROBERT**
**(Actor)**
Christopher [aka Chris]
James [aka Jim] [Mitchum]
Petrine
**MIYAZAWA, KIICHI**
**(Former Prime Minister,**
**Japan)**
Hiro
Keiko
**MOBLEY, MARY ANN**
**(1958 Miss America)**
Mary Clancy
**MOLL, RICHARD (Actor)**
Cilo
**MONDALE, WALTER &**
**JOAN MONDALE**
**(Former U.S. Vice**
**President & Spouse)**
Eleanor Jane
Theodore
William Hall
**MONDAVI, ROBERT**
**(Wine Company**
**Executive)**
Marcia
Robert
Timothy
**MONK, ART (Professional**
**Football Player)**
Danielle
James Arthur
Monica
**MONROE, BILL (Country**
**Singer)**
James

Melissa
**MONTAGU, ASHLEY**
**(Anthropologist)**
Audrey
Barbara
Geoffrey
**MONTALBAN,**
**RICARDO (Actor)**
Anita
Laura
Mark
Victor
**MONTANA, JOE**
**(Professional Football**
**Player)**
Alexandra
Elizabeth
**MONTESSORI, MARIO**
**(Director, Montessori**
**International)**
Mario
Renilde
**MONTGOMERY,**
**ROBERT (Actor)**
Elizabeth [Montgomery]
**MOON, WARREN**
**(Professional Football**
**Player)**
Blair
Chelsea
Jeffrey
Joshua
**MOORE, ARCHIE**
**(Former Heavyweight**
**Champion)**
Anthony
Billy

D'Angelo
Hardy
Joanie
Rena
**MOORE, DEMI (Actress)**
Rumer Glenn
Scout Larue
Tallulah Belle
**MOORE, DUDLEY**
**(Actor)**
Patrick
**MOORE, HENRY**
**(Sculptor)**
Mary
**MOORE, JOANNA**
**(Actress)**
Tatum Beatrice [O'Neal]
**MOORE, MARY TYLER**
**(Actress)**
Richard [aka Ritchie]
**MOORE, MICHAEL**
**(Documentary Filmmaker)**
Natalie
**MOORE, ROGER (Actor)**
Christian
Deborah
Geoffrey
**MOORE, THURSTON**
**(Singer, Sonic Youth)**
Coco Chanel
**MOORER, MICHAEL**
**(Heavyweight Boxing**
**Champ)**
Michael
**MORENO, RITA (Actress)**
Fernanda

**MORGAN, GEORGE**
**(Country Singer)**
Bethany Bell
Candy Kay
Liana Lee
Lorrie [Morgan]
Matthew
**MORGAN, HARRY**
**(Actor, *M\*A\*S\*H*)**
Daniel
**MORGAN, HENRY**
**(Actor)**
Charles
Chris
Daniel
Paul
**MORGAN, LORRIE**
**(Country Singer)**
Jessie
Morgan
**MORGAN, ROBIN**
**(Writer)**
Blake Ariel
**MORIARTY, MICHAEL**
**(Actor)**
Matthew
**MORITA, PAT (Actor)**
Aly
Tia
**MORROW, VIC (Actor)**
Jennifer [Jason Leigh]
**MORSE, ROBERT (Actor)**
Allyn Elizabeth
Robin
**MOSTEL, ZERO (Actor)**
Josh [aka Joshua]

**MOYERS, BILL**
**(Journalist)**
Alice Suzanne [also reported as Suzanne]
John
William
**MOYNIHAN, DANIEL**
**(U.S. Senator)**
John
Maura
Timothy Patrick
**MOZART, WOLFGANG**
**AMADEUS (Composer)**
Franz Xavier Wolfgang [aka Wolfgang]
Karl
**MUBARAK, HOSNI**
**(President of the Arab Republic of Egypt)**
Alaa
Gamal
**MUDD, ROGER**
**(Broadcast Journalist)**
Daniel
Jonathan
Maria
Matthew
**MUHAMMAD, THE HONORABLE ELIJAH**
**(Leader, Nation of Islam)**
Akbar
Elijah
Emmanuel
Ethel
Herbert
Lottie
Nathaniel

Wallace

**MULRONEY, BRIAN
(Former Prime Minister,
Canada)**
Benedict Martin
Caroline Ann
Daniel Nicholas Dimitri
Robert Mark

**MURDOCH, RUPERT
(Publisher)**
Elisabeth
James
Lachlan
Prudence

**MURPHY, DALE
(Professional Baseball
Player)**
Chad
Shawn
Travis

**MURPHY, EDDIE (Actor
& Comedian)**
Brea
Miles Mitchell
Shayne Audra [also reported
as Shane]

**MURRAY, ANNE (Singer)**
Dawn Joanne
William Stewart

**MURRAY, BILL (Actor)**
Homer Banks
Luke

**MUSBURGER, BRENT
(Sportscaster)**
Blake
Scott

**MUSGRAVE, F. STORY
(Astronaut)**
Bradley Scott
Christopher Todd
Holly Kay
Jeffrey Paul
Lorelei Lisa

**MUSIAL, STAN (Baseball
Executive)**
Dickie
Geraldine

**MUSTAINE, DAVE
(Singer/Songwriter,
Whitesnake)**
Justis David

# N

**NAMATH, JOE (Retired
Professional Football
Player)**
Jessica Grace

**NAMUTH, HANS
(Photographer &
Filmmaker)**
Peter
Tessa

**NASH, OGDEN (Poet)**
Linell

**NATION, CARRY
(Fanatical Prohibitionist)**
Charlien

**NEAL, PATRICIA
(Actress)**
Lucy
Olivia Twenty
Ophelia Magdalene

Tessa Sophie
Theo Mathew Roald
**NEAL, VINCE (Rock Musician, Motley Crüe)**
Skylar Lynnae
**NEHRU, JAWAHARLAL (1st Prime Minister of Independent India)**
Indira
**NEIL, ELEANOR (Artist & Filmmaker)**
Gian Carlo
Sophia
**NELSON, CRAIG, T. (Actor)**
Chris
**NELSON, HORATIO (British Admiral)**
Horatio
**NELSON, RICKY (Singer)**
Gunnar Eric [Nelson]
Matthew Gray [Nelson]
Sam Hilliard
Tracy Kristine [Nelson]
**NELSON, TRACY (Actress)**
Remington Elizabeth
**NELSON, WILLIE (Singer/Songwriter)**
Amy
Billy
Jacob
Lana
Lucas Autry [also reported as Lukas]
Paula Carlene
Susie

**NERO, FRANCO (Actor)**
Carlo Gabriel
**NERO, PETER (Pianist & Composer)**
Beverly
Jedd
**NESMITH, MICHAEL (Singer/Songwriter & Former "Monkee")**
Jason
**NESPRAL, JACKIE (TV Host)**
Frances
**NEUHARTH, ALLEN (Publisher, *USA Today*)**
Daniel
Janet Ann
**NEWELL, HOPE (Actress)**
Timothy [Daly] [aka Tim]
Tyne [Daly]
**NEWLEY, ANTHONY (Songwriter)**
Sasha [also spelled Sacha]
**NEWMAN, ARNOLD (Photographer)**
David
Eric
**NEWMAN, EDWIN (Retired News Commentator)**
Nancy
**NEWMAN, JIMMY "C" (Country Singer)**
Gary Wayne
**NEWMAN, JOSEPH**

(Inventor, Plastic-Coated
Barbells)
Gyromas
**NEWMAN, PAUL (Actor)**
Clea Olivia
Elinor Terese
Melissa
Scott
Stephanie
Susan
**NEWTON-JOHN,
OLIVIA (Singer)**
Chloe Rose
**NICHOLAS II, CZAR
(Last Russian Czar)**
Alexis
Anastasia
**NICHOLSON, JACK
(Actor)**
Caleb
Jennifer
Lorraine
Raymond Nicholas
**NICKLAUS, JACK
(Professional Golfer)**
Gary Thomas
Jack William
Michael Scott
Nancy Jean
Steven Charles
**NICKLES, DON (U.S.
Senator)**
Donald Lee
Jennifer Lynn
Kim Elizabeth
Robyn Lee

**NIMOY, LEONARD
(Actor & Director)**
Adam
Julie
**NIPON, ALBERT
(Executive, Albert Nipon
Fashions)**
Andrew
Barbara Joy
Lawrence
Leon
**NIXON, PAT (Former
First Lady)**
Julie
Patricia
**NIXON, RICHARD
(Former U.S. President)**
Julie
Patricia
**NOLTE, NICK (Actor)**
Brawley King
**NOONAN, PEGGY
(Writer)**
Will
**NORMAN, GREG
(Professional Golfer)**
Gregory
Morgan-Leigh
**NORRIS, CHUCK (Actor)**
Eric
Mike
**NORTH, ALEX
(Composer)**
Dylan
Eilssa
Steven

Mia [nee Maria]
Peter
Prudence
Stephanie
Tisa
**O'TOOLE, PETER
(Actor)**
Kate
Pat
**OCASEK, RIC (Singer/
Songwriter, the Cars)**
Jonathan Raven
**OLDMAN, GARY (Actor)**
Alfie
**OLIN, KEN (Actor)**
Clifford
Roxanne [aka Roxie]
**OLIN, LENA (Actress)**
August
**OLIVIER, LAURENCE
(Actor)**
Julie Kate
Richard
Simon
Tamsin Agnes Margaret
**OLMOS, EDWARD
JAMES (Actor)**
Brodie
Mico
**OLSEN, KENNETH H.
(Founder, Digital
Equipment Corporation)**
Ava-Lisa
Glenn Charles
James Jonathan
**OLSEN, MERLIN (Sports
Analyst)**

Jill Catherine
Kelly Lynn
Nathan Merlin
**ONASSIS, ARISTOTLE
(Shipping & Airline
Mogul)**
Alexander
Christina
**ONASSIS, CHRISTINA
(Heiress)**
Athina
**ONASSIS, JACQUELINE
KENNEDY (Former U.S.
First Lady)**
Caroline [Kennedy,
Schlossberg]
John [Kennedy, Jr.]
Patrick
**ONO, YOKO (Singer/
Songwriter, Artist, Writer,
& John Lennon's Widow)**
Kyoko
Sean Ono [Lennon]
**ONTKEAN, MICHAEL
(Actor)**
Sadie
**OPHULS, MARCEL
(Director)**
Catherine Julie
Danielle
Jeanne Dorothee
**ORBACH, JERRY (Actor
& Singer)**
Anthony Nicholas
Christopher Ben
**OSBORNE, BOB (Country
Singer)**

---

### AND THEY NEVER ORDERED PICKLES FROM ROOM SERVICE

During the seventies, John Lennon and Yoko Ono frequently traveled under the names of Reverend Fred and Ada Gerkin.

---

Robby
Tina Renea
Wynn
**OSBORNE, SONNY
(Country Singer)**
Karen Deanna
Steve Russell
**OSBOURNE, OZZIE
(Rock Singer)**
Jack
**OSMOND, DONNY
(Singer)**
Donald Clark
**OSMOND, GEORGE
(Father of the Osmonds)**
Alan
Donny
Jay
Jimmy
Marie
Merrill
Wayne
**OSMOND, MARIE
(Singer)**
Rachel
Stephen James
**OSMOND, OLIVE**

**(Mother of the Osmonds)**
Alan
Donny
Jay
Jimmy
Marie
Merrill
Wayne
**OVERMYER, ROBERT
(Astronaut)**
Carolyn Marie
Patricia Ann
Robert
**OVERSTREET, TOMMY
(Country Singer)**
Elizabeth Nan
Thomas Cary
**OWENS, BUCK (Country Singer)**
Buddy
Mike
**OWENS, JESSE (Former Olympic Champion)**
Beverly
Gloria
Marlene
**OXENBERG,**

**CATHERINE (Actress)**
India Raven
**OZAWA, SEIJI**
**(Conductor)**
Seira
Yukiyoshi
**OZICK, CYNTHIA**
**(Writer)**
Rachel Sarah

## P

**PACINO, AL (Actor)**
Julie
**PAGE, GERALDINE**
**(Actress)**
Angelica
Anthony
Jonathan
**PALLENBERG, ANITA**
**(Actress)**
Dandelion [later Angela]
Marlon
**PALMER, JIM (Former**
**Professional Baseball**
**Player)**
Jamie
Kelly
**PALTROW, BRUCE (TV**
**Producer)**
Gwyneth Kate [Paltrow]
Jake
Laura
**PAPP, JOE (Theater**
**Producer)**
Anthony
Barbara

Michael
Miranda
Susan
**PARSONS, ESTELLE**
**(Actress)**
Abbie
Abraham
Martha
**PASTEUR, LOUIS**
**(Scientist)**
Camille
Cécile
Jeanne
**PATINKIN, MANDY**
**(Actor & Singer)**
Gideon
Isaac
**PATTEN, CHRISTOPHER**
**(Governor of Hong Kong)**
Alice
Kate
Laura
**PATTERSON, FLOYD**
**(Former Heavyweight**
**Boxer)**
Janene
Jennifer
**PATTON, GEORGE S.**
**(Army General)**
Beatrice
George
Ruth Ellen
**PAUL, LES (Musician &**
**Guitar Designer)**
Colleen
Gene
Lester

Mary
Robert
**PAULEY, JANE (TV Host)**
Garry
Rachel
Richard
**PAULING, LINUS (Writer
& Chemistry Researcher)**
Edward
Linda Helen
Linus Carl
Peter Jeffress
**PAVAROTTI, LUCIANO
(Lyric Tenor)**
Cristina
Giuliana
Lorenza
**PAYNE, LEON (Country
Singer)**
Leon Roger
Myrtie Lee
Patricia Lee
Rene
**PAYS, AMANDA (Actress)**
Angus Moore
Henry
Oliver
**PAYTON, WALTER
(Former Professional
Football Player)**
Brittney
Jarrett
**PEALE, NORMAN
VINCENT (Clergyman)**
Elizabeth
John
Margaret

**PEARY, ADMIRAL
ROBERT (Explorer)**
Anaukap
Kali
Marie
Robert
**PECK, GREGORY
(Actor)**
Anthony [aka Tony] [Peck]
Carey
Cecilia
Jonathan [aka Jon]
Steve
**PECK, J. EDDIE (Actor,
*The Young and the
Restless*)**
Austin
Dalton
**PECK, TONY (Actor)**
Zachary Anthony
**PECKINPAH, SAM
(Director)**
Kristen
Matthew
Melissa
Sharon
**PEELE, BEVERLY
(Actress & Model)**
Cairo
**PEI, I.M. (Architect)**
Chien
Li
Liane
T'ing
**PELÉ (Professional Soccer
Player)**
Edson

Genima
Jennifer
Kely Cristina
**PELL, CLAIBORNE (Former U.S. Senator)**
Christopher
Herbert Claiborne
Julia
Nuala Dallas
**PENDERECKI, KRZYSZTOF (Composer)**
Dominique
Lukasz
**PENDERGRASS, TEDDY (Singer/Songwriter)**
Ladonna
Tamon
Teddy
Tisha
**PENN, ARTHUR (Movie & Theater Director)**
Matthew
Molly
**PENN, IRVING (Photographer)**
Tom
**PENN, LEO (Director)**
Christopher [aka Chris] [Penn]
Sean [Penn]
**PENN, SEAN (Actor & Director)**
Dylan Frances [also reported as Frances]
Hooper Jack
**PEPPARD, GEORGE (Actor)**

Bradford
Christian
Julie
**PERELMAN, RON (Revlon Executive)**
Samantha
**PERKINS, ANTHONY (Actor & Director)**
Elvis
Osgood
**PERKINS, CARL (Country Singer)**
Debra
Greg
Stan
Steve
**PERKINS, OSGOOD (Actor)**
Anthony [Perkins]
**PERLMAN, RHEA (Actor)**
Gracie Fan
Jake Daniel
Lucy Chet
**PERLMAN, RON (Actor)**
Blake Amanda
**PEROT, H. ROSS (Business Executive & Former Presidential Candidate)**
Carolyn
Katherine
Nancy
Ross
Suzanne
**PERRIN, NOEL (Writer & Educator)**

Amy
Elisabeth
**PERRY, CARRIE SAXON (Mayor, Hartford, CT)**
James
**PERPICH, RUDY (Former Governor of Minnesota)**
Mary Susan
Ruby George
**PERSICHETTI, VINCENT (Composer)**
Garth
Lauren
**PESCI, JOE (Actor)**
Tiffany
**PESCOW, DONNA (Actress)**
Jack
**PETER, KING (Yugoslavian Royalty)**
Alexander
**PETERS, JON (Producer)**
Caleigh
Chris
**PETERS, ROBERTA (Soprano)**
Bruce

Paul
**PETERSON, ROGER TORY (Ornithologist & Artist)**
Lee
Tory
**PETTY, RICHARD (Auto Racer)**
Kyle [Petty]
Lisa
Rebecca
Sharon
**PFEIFFER, MICHELLE (Actress)**
Claudia Rose
John Henry
**PHILBIN, REGIS (TV Host)**
Amy
Danny
Jennifer
Joanna
**PHILLIPS, BILL (Country Singer)**
William George
**PHILLIPS, JOHN (Singer/ Songwriter)**

---

### THIS IS MY MOM, THE DIVA

Barbra Streisand has publicly referred to Jon Peters's daughter Caleigh as "my daughter." It is generally assumed to be a term of endearment rather than a description of their actual biological relationship.

Chynna [Phillips]
Mackenzie [Phillips]
**PHILLIPS, JULIA (Writer & Producer)**
Kate
**PHILLIPS, MICHELLE (Actress)**
Chynna [Phillips]
**PICASSO, PABLO (Artist)**
Paloma [Picasso]
**PICKETT, WILSON (Singer)**
Brandy
**PIERCE, WEBB (Country Singer)**
Debbie
Webb
**PILLOW, RAY (Country Singer)**
Dale
Daryl Ray
Selena
**PINCAY, LAFFIT, JR. (Jockey)**
Laffit
Lisa
**PINTER, HAROLD (Playwright)**
Daniel
**PISCOPO, JOE (Actor)**
Joseph [aka Joey]
**PIZZARELLI, BUCKY (Jazz Musician)**
John [Pizzarelli]
**PLANCK, MAX (Scientist)**
Erwin

Karl
**PLATO, DANA (Actress)**
Tyler
**PLATH, SYLVIA (Poet)**
Frieda Rebecca
Nicholas
**PLIMPTON, GEORGE (Writer)**
Medora
Taylor
**PLOWRIGHT, JOAN (Actress)**
Julie Kate
Richard
Tamsin Agnes Margaret
**PLUMMER, CHRISTOPHER (Actor)**
Amanda [Plummer]
**POCAHONTAS (Native American Princess)**
Thomas
**PODHORETZ, NORMAN (Editor & Writer)**
John
Naomi
Rachel
Ruth
**POINTER, PRISCILLA (Actress)**
Amy [Irving]
**POINTER, RUTH (Pop Singer)**
Ali
Connor
**POITIER, SIDNEY (Actor & Director)**
Anika

Beverly
Gina
Messenger
Pamela
Sherri
Sydney
**POLANSKI, ROMAN
(Director)**
Morgane
**POLLACK, SYDNEY
(Director)**
Rachel
Rebecca
Steven
**POLLAN, TRACY
(Actress)**
Aquinnah Kathleen
Sam
Schuyler Frances
**POMPADOUR, MADAME
DE (Louis XV's Mistress)**
Alexandrine
**PONTI, CARLO
(Director)**
Carlo [aka Cipi]
Edoardo [aka Eli]
**POPE, GENEROSO
(Publisher, *The National
Enquirer*)**
Generoso
Gina
Lorraine
Maria
Michele
Paul
**PORIZKOVA, PAULINA
(Model & Actress)**

Jonathan Raven
**PORTER, SYLVIA
(Writer)**
Cris Sarah
Sumner Campbell
**POST, MARKIE (Actress)**
Daisy
Kate Armstrong
**POTOK, CHAIM (Writer)**
Akiva
Naama
Rena
**POTTS, ANNIE (Actress)**
Clay
James Powell
**POVICH, MAURY (TV
Host)**
Amy
Susan
**POWELL, COLIN
(Former Chairman of the
Joint Chiefs of Staff)**
Annemarie
Linda
Michael
**POWELL, LEWIS (U.S.
Supreme Court Justice)**
Ann
Josephine
Lewis
Mary
**POWER, TYRONE
(Actor)**
Romina
Taryn [Power]
Tony
Tyrone

**POWER, TYRONE, SR.**
**(Actor)**
Tyrone [Power]
**POWHATAN (Native**
**American Chief)**
Pocahontas [aka Rebecca]
**PREDOCK, ANTOINE**
**(Architect)**
Hadrian
Jason
**PREMINGER, OTTO**
**(Director)**
Erik
Mark William
Victoria Elizabeth
**PRENTISS, PAULA**
**(Actress)**
Russ Thomas
**PRESLEY, ELVIS (King)**
Lisa Marie [Presley]
**PRESLEY, LISA MARIE**
**(Elvis's Daughter)**
Benjamin Storm
Danielle Riley
**PRESLEY, PRISCILLA**
**(Actress)**
Lisa Marie [Presley]
Navarone Anthony
**PRESTON, KELLY**
**(Actress)**
Jett
**PREVIN, ANDRÉ**
**(Conductor)**
Daisy
Fletcher
Lark
Matthew

Sascha
Soon-Yi
**PRICE, RAY (Country**
**Singer)**
Clifton Ray
**PRICE, VINCENT (Actor)**
Mary Victoria
Vincent
**PRIDDY, NANCY**
**(Actress, *Days of our Lives*)**
Christina [Applegate]
**PRIDE, CHARLEY**
**(Singer/Songwriter)**
Angela
Dion
Kraig
**PRINCE, HAROLD**
**(Theatrical Producer)**
Charles
Daisy
**PRITIKIN, NATHAN**
**(Nutritionist)**
Jack
Janet
Kenneth
Ralph
Robert
**PROPHET, ELIZABETH**
**CLARE (Religious Leader)**
Erin
Moira
Sean
Tatiana
**PROST, ALAIN (Grand**
**Prix Driver)**
Nicolas

**PROWSE, JULIET**
**(Dancer)**
Seth
**PRUETT, JEANNE**
**(Country Singer)**
Jack
Jael
**PRYOR, RICHARD**
**(Actor & Comedian)**
Elizabeth Ann
Rain [Pryor]
Renée
Richard
**PUCCINI, GIACOMO**
**(Composer)**
Fosca
Tonio
**PULITZER, JOSEPH**
**(Publisher)**
Herbert
Joseph
Ralph
**PULITZER, ROXANNE**
**(Writer)**
Mac
Zach
**PUZO, MARIO (Writer)**
Anthony
Dorothy
Eugene
Joey
Virginia

## Q

**QUAID, DENNIS (Actor)**
Jack Henry

**QUAYLE, DAN &**
**MARILYN QUAYLE**
**(Former U.S. Vice**
**President & Attorney)**
Benjamin Eugene
Mary Corinne
Tucker Danforth
**QUINDLEN, ANNA**
**(Writer)**
Christopher
Maria
Quindlen [aka Quin]
**QUINN, ANTHONY**
**(Actor)**
Christina
Daniele
Danny
Duncan
Francesco
Kathleen
Lorenzo
Patricia
Valentina
**QUINN, JANE BRYANT**
**(Financial Columnist &**
**Writer)**
Martha [Quinn]

## R

**RABE, DAVID**
**(Playwright)**
Lily
**RABIN, YITZHAK (Prime**
**Minister, Israel)**
Dalia
Yuval

**RADZIWILL, LEE**
**(Jacqueline Kennedy**
**Onassis's Sister)**
Anna
Anthony
**RAITT, JOHN (Broadway**
**Musical Star)**
Bonnie [Raitt]
**RALEIGH, SIR WALTER**
**(Writer & Explorer)**
Carew
**RAMIS, HAROLD (Actor,**
**Writer, & Director)**
Violet Isadora
**RAMPAL, JEAN-PIERRE**
**(Flutist)**
Isabelle
Jean-Jacques
**RANDALLS, ANTHONY**
**(Country Dancer, the**
**Nashville Network)**
Arielle
**RANDALLS, CHRISTINA**
**(Country Dancer, the**
**Nashville Network)**
Arielle
**RANDOLPH, BOOTS**
**(Country Singer)**

Linda
Randy
**RANDOLPH, JENNINGS**
**(Former U.S. Senator)**
Frank
Jennings
**RANGEL, CHARLES**
**(Legislator)**
Alicia
Steven
**RANKIN, KENNY**
**(Musician)**
Chris
**RAPHAËL, SALLY**
**JESSY (TV Talk Show**
**Host)**
Allison
Andrea
Robby
**RASHAD, PHYLICIA**
**(Actress)**
Condola Phylea
William Lancelot
**RASPBERRY, WILLIAM**
**(Journalist & Newspaper**
**Columnist)**
Angela
Patricia

---

### "FAMILY TIES"

Musician Kenny Rankin's son Chris was a roadie for
the literary (Stephen King, Dave Barry, Amy Tan)
rock band, the Rock Bottom Remainders. His road
nickname was "Hooper."

**RASPUTIN (Advisor to Russian Tsar Nicholas II)**
Maria
Varvara

**RATHER, DAN (Broadcast Journalist)**
Daniel Martin
Dawn Robin

**RATTLE, SIMON (Conductor)**
Sasha

**RATZENBERGER, JOHN (Actor)**
Nina

**RAUSCHENBERG, ROBERT (Artist)**
Christopher

**REAGAN, NANCY (Former U.S. First Lady)**
Loyal
Patricia Ann [aka Patti]
Ronald Prescott

**REAGAN, RONALD (Former U.S. President)**
Maureen
Michael
Patricia Ann [aka Patti]
Ronald Prescott

**REASONER, HARRY (TV Journalist)**
Ann
Elizabeth
Ellen
Jane
Jonathan
Mary Ray
Stuart

**REDFORD, ROBERT (Actor & Director)**
Amy
David James
Jamie
Scott
Shauna

**REDGRAVE, LYNN (Actress)**
Annabel
Benjamin
Kelly

**REDGRAVE, MICHAEL (Actor)**
Corin
Lynn
Vanessa [Redgrave]

**REDGRAVE, VANESSA (Actress)**
Carlo Gabriel
Joely Kim
Natasha Jane [Richardson]

**REDSTONE, SUMNER (Entertainment Corporate Executive)**
Brent Dale
Shari Ellin

**REED, BEN (Actor)**
Beau Grayson
Presley Tanita

**REED, DONNA (Actress)**
Anthony
Mary Anne
Penny Jane
Timothy

**REED, JERRY (Country Singer)**

Lottie
Sedina
**REED, SHANNA (Actress)**
Jonathan Joseph
**REEVE, CHRISTOPHER
(Actor)**
Alexandra
Matthew
Ninna Priscilla
Owen
Will
**REEVES, DEL (Country
Singer & Grand Ole Opry
Star)**
Ann
Bethany
Kari [Reeves]
**REHNQUIST, WILLIAM
(U.S. Supreme Court
Justice)**
James
Janet
Nancy
**REID, TIM (Actor)**
Christopher
Tim
Tori
**REINER, CARL (Director
& Actor)**
Lucas
Rob [Reiner]
Sylvia Ann
**REINER, ROB (Director
& Actor)**
Tracy Lee [Reiner]
**REMBRANDT (Painter)**
Titus

**REMICK, LEE (Actress)**
Kate
Matthew
**RENOIR, PIERRE-
AUGUSTE (Painter)**
Claude
Jean [Renoir]
Pierre
**REUBEN, DAVID
Psychiatrist & Writer)**
Amy
Catherine
David Robert
Giselle
**REUSSEL, THIERRY
(French Pharmaceutical
Heir)**
Athina
Erik
Sandrine
**REVERE, PAUL
(Revolutionary)**
Deborah
Frances
John
Joseph
Paul
**REYNOLDS, BURT
(Actor)**
Quinton Anderson
**REYNOLDS, DEBBIE
(Actress)**
Carrie [Fisher]
Todd
**RHODES, CYNTHIA
(Actress)**
Brandon Caleb

**RICE, BOBBY G.**
**(Country Singer)**
Connie
Tamara
**RICE, GRANTLAND**
**(Sportswriter)**
Florence [Rice]
**RICE, JERRY**
**(Professional Football**
**Player)**
Jacqui
**RICH, BUDDY**
**(Drummer)**
Kathy
**RICH, CHARLIE (Singer/**
**Songwriter)**
Charles Allan
Jack Michael
Laurie Lynn
Renée Annette
Rich Lee
**RICHARDS, ANN**
**(Governor of Texas)**
Cecile
Clark
Dan
Ellen
**RICHARDS, KEITH**
**(Guitarist, the Rolling**
**Stones)**
Alexandra
Dandelion [later Angela]
Marlon
Theodora Dupree
**RICHARDS, MICHAEL**
**(Actor—"Kramer" on**
*Seinfeld*)

Sophia
**RICHARDSON, TONY**
**(Director)**
Joely Kim
Natasha Jane
**RICHIE, LIONEL (Singer/**
**Songwriter)**
Miles
Nicole
**RICKLES, DON**
**(Comedian & Actor)**
Lawrence Corey
Mindy Beth
**RICKOVER, ADMIRAL**
**HYMAN (Retired Naval**
**Officer)**
Robert
**RIDDLE, NELSON**
**(Composer & Conductor)**
Bettina Marie
Cecily Jean
Christopher Robert
Maureen Alicia
Nelson
Rosemary Ann
**RIGBY, PAUL (Editorial**
**Cartoonist)**
Bay
**RIGG, DIANA (Actress)**
Rachel
**RILEY, JEANNIE C.**
**(Country Singer)**
Kim
**RILKE, RAINER MARIE**
**(Poet)**
Ruth
**RIPKIN, CAL, JR.**

(Professional Baseball Player)
Rachel
Ryan
**RITTER, TEX (Country Actor & Singer)**
Jonathan Southworth [aka John] [Ritter]
Thomas Matthews
**RIVERA, CRAIG (Geraldo's Brother & TV Journalist)**
Austin Cruz
**RIVERA, GERALDO (TV Talk Show Host)**
Gabriel Miguel
Isabella Holmes
Simone
**RIVERS, JOAN (Entertainer)**
Melissa
**ROBARDS, JASON, JR. (Actor)**
David
Jake
Jason
Sam
Sarah Louise
Shannon
**ROBARDS, JASON, SR. (Actor)**
Jason [Robards, Jr.]
**ROBB, CHARLES (Former Governor of Virginia)**
Catherine
Jennifer

Lucinda Desha
**ROBBINS, HAROLD (Writer)**
Adreana
Caryn
**ROBBINS, MARTY (Country Singer)**
Ronnie
**ROBBINS, TIM (Actor)**
Jack Henry
Miles Guthrie
**ROBBINS, TOM (Writer)**
Fleetwood Starr
**ROBERTS, COKIE (TV Journalist)**
Lee Harriss
Tebecca
**ROBERTS, ERIC (Actor)**
Emma
**ROBERTSON, CLIFF (Actor)**
Heather
Stephanie
**ROBERTSON, PAT (Televangelist & Politician)**
Ann
Elizabeth
Gordon
Timothy
**ROBERTSON, ROBBIE (Singer/Songwriter, the Band)**
Delphine
**ROBINSON, DAVID (San Antonio Spur)**
David

**ROBINSON, DOLORES**
**(Celebrity Manager)**
Holly [Robinson]
**ROBINSON, EDWARD G.**
**(Actor)**
Edward
**ROBINSON, FRANK**
**(Professional Baseball**
**Manager)**
Frank Kevin
Nichelle
**ROBINSON, MARY**
**(President, Ireland)**
Aubrey
Tessa
William
**ROBINSON, SMOKEY**
**(Singer/Songwriter)**
Berry William
Tamla Claudette
**ROCKEFELLER, DAVID**
**(Banker)**
Abby
David
Eileen
Margaret
Neva
Richard
**ROCKEFELLER, JOHN**
**D. (Financial Mogul)**
Alta
Edith
John
**ROCKEFELLER, JOHN**
**D., JR. (Former Governor**
**of West Virginia)**
Charles
Jamie
Justin
Valerie
**RODDENBERRY, GENE**
**(Writer & Producer)**
Darlene
Dawn Alison
Eugene Wesley
**RODDICK, ANITA**
**(Cosmetics Executive)**
Justine
Samantha
**RODGERS, JIMMIE**
**(Country Singer)**
Anita
**ROEBLING, JOHN**
**(Engineer, the Brooklyn**
**Bridge)**
Washington
**ROEBLING, PAUL**
**(Actor)**
Kristian
**ROGERS, DAVID**

---

## NICKNAME DEPARTMENT

Rush Limbaugh's high school nickname was
"Rusty."

(Country Singer)
Anthony Kyle
Tonya Lynn
**ROGERS, KENNY**
**(Singer/Songwriter)**
Carol
Kenneth
**ROGERS, KENNY (Texas**
**Rangers Pitcher)**
Jessie
**ROGERS, PAUL (Novelist)**
Chris
**ROGERS, ROY (Country**
**Singer**
Cheryl
Deborah Lee
John
Linda Lou
Little Doe
Marion
Mary
Robin
Roy
Scottish Ward
**ROGERS, WAYNE (Actor)**
Billy
Laura
**ROGERS, WILL**
**(Humorist)**
Will [Rogers, Jr.]
**ROONEY, ANDY (Writer**
**& TV Commentator, *60***
***Minutes*)**
Brian
Ellen
Emily

Martha
**ROONEY, MICKEY**
**(Actor)**
Chris
Joe
Kelly Ann
Kerry
Kimmy Sue
Kyle
Mark
Mickey
Timothy
**ROSE, PETE (Baseball**
**Player)**
Cara
Fawn
Peter [aka Petey]
Tyler
**ROSEANNE (Actress &**
**Comedienne)**
Brandi [also reported as
Brandy]
Jacob [aka Jake]
Jennifer
Jessica
**ROSENBERG, ETHEL**
**(Executed Spy)**
Michael
Robert
**ROSENBERG, EVELYN**
**(Artist)**
Mica
Oren
**ROSENBERG, JULIUS**
**(Executed Spy)**
Michael

Robert
**ROSENBERG, STEPHEN**
**(Cancer Researcher)**
Beth
Naomi
Rachel
**ROSS, DIANA (Singer)**
Chudney
Evan
Rhonda Suzanne [Ross]
Ross Arne
Tracee Joy
**ROSS, KATHARINE**
**(Actress)**
Cleo
**ROSSELLINI, ISABELLA**
**(Actress)**
Elettra Ingrid
Roberto
**ROSSELLINI, ROBERTO**
**(Director)**
Isabella [Rossellini]
**ROSSNER, JUDITH**
**(Writer)**
Daniel
Jean
**ROSTENKOWSKI, DAN**
**(U.S. Congressman)**
Gail
**ROSTROPOVICH,**
**MSTISLAV (Cellist)**
Olga
Yelena
**ROUNDTREE, RICHARD**
**(Actor)**
Kelly

Nicole
**ROWAN, CARL**
**(Journalist & Newspaper**
**Columnist)**
Barbara
Carl
Geoffrey
**ROWLANDS, GENA**
**(Actress)**
Alexandra
Nicholas
Zoe
**ROYKO, MIKE (Writer)**
David
Robert
**ROZELLE, PETE**
**(Football Executive)**
Ann Marie
**RUCKLESHAUS,**
**WILLIAM (Lawyer)**
Catherine Kiley
Jennifer Lea
Mary Hughes
Robin Elizabeth
William Justice
**RUDMAN, WARREN**
**(Former U.S. Senator)**
Alan
Debra
Laura
**RUNDGREN, TODD**
**(Rock Musician)**
Rebop
**RUPPE, LORET MILLER**
**(Former Director, the**
**Peace Corps)**

Adele
Antoinette
Katherine
Loret
Mary
**RUSHDIE, SALMAN
(Writer)**
Zafar
**RUSK, DEAN (Former
U.S. Secretary of State)**
David Patrick
Margaret Elizabeth
Richard
**RUSSELL, BERTRAND
(Mathematician &
Philosopher)**
Conrad
John
Katharine [aka Kate]
**RUSSELL, KEN (Director)**
Alexander
James
Molly
Toby
Victoria
Xavier
**RUSSELL, KURT (Actor)**
Boston
Wyatt
**RUSSERT, TIM
(Broadcaster)**
Luke
**RUSSO, RENÉE (Actress)**
Rose
**RUTH, BABE (Baseball
Legend)**

Dorothy
George
Helen
Margaret
**RUTHERFORD,
JOHNNY (Professional
Race Car Driver)**
Angela Ann
John
**RYAN, LEO
(Congressman Slain by
Jim Jones's Followers)**
Chris
Erin
Kevin
Patricia
Shannon Jo
**RYAN, MEG (Actress)**
Jack Henry
**RYAN, NOLAN
(Professional Baseball
Player)**
Reese
Reid
Wendy

# S

**SABERHAGEN, BRETT
(Professional Baseball
Player)**
Drew William
**SAGAL, KATY (Actress &
Singer)**
Sarah Grace
**SAGAN, CARL (Writer,
Educator, & Astronomer)**

Alexandra
Dorion Solomon
Jeremy Ethan
Nicholas
**SAGANSKY, JEFF
(CBS-TV Executive)**
Gillian
**SAGER, CAROLE
BAYER (Songwriter)**
Christopher Elton
**SAGET, BOB (Actor)**
Lara
**SAINT, EVA MARIE
(Actress)**
Darrell
Laurette
**SALAZAR, ALBERTO
(Runner)**
Antonio Roberto
**SALES, SOUPY (Comic)**
Tony
**SALINAS, CARLOS
(Former President of
Mexico)**
Cecilia
Emiliano
Juan Cristobal
**SALK, JONAS (Physician
& Scientist)**
Darrell John
Jonathan Daniel
Peter
**SANDERS, DEION
(Professional Basketball
Player)**
Deion

Deiondra
**SANDRICH, MARK (TV
Director)**
Jay [Sandrich]
**SARANDON, SUSAN
(Actress)**
Eva Maria Livia
Jack Henry
Miles Guthrie
**SASSOON, BEVERLY
(Writer & Cosmetics
Executive)**
Catya [Sassoon]
**SASSOON, VIDAL (Hair
Stylist & Cosmetics
Executive)**
Catya [Sassoon]
David
Eden
Elan
**SAVALAS, TELLY (Actor)**
Ariana
Candace
Christian
Christina
Nicholas
Penelope
**SAYERS, GALE (Writer
& Former Professional
Football Player)**
Gale
Scott
Timothy
**SCACCHI, GRETA
(Actress)**
Leila

---

### IT DOESN'T MEAN "TRUST FUND"?

King Hussein of Jordan's wife, Queen Noor, was actually born in Washington, D.C., as Lisa Halaby. When she wed the king, she took an Arabic name, "Noor," which means "light."

---

**SCAGGS, BOZ (Singer/ Songwriter)**
Austin
Oscar
**SCALIA, ANTONIN (U.S. Supreme Court Justice)**
Ann
Catherine Elizabeth
Christopher James
Eugene
John Francis
Margaret Jane
Mary Clare
Matthew
Paul David
**SCHANK, ROGER (Educator)**
Hana
Joshua
**SCHEIDER, ROY (Actor)**
Maximillia
**SCHEMBECHLER, BO (CEO, the Detroit Tigers)**
Glenn Edward
**SCHENKEL, CHRIS (Sportscaster)**
Christiana
Johnny
Ted
**SCHIEFFER, BOB (Broadcast Journalist)**
Sharon
Susan
**SCHILDKRAUT, RUDOLPH (Actor)**
Joseph [Schildkraut]
**SCHISGAL, MURRAY (Screenwriter, *Tootsie*)**
Jane
Zachary
**SCHLAFLY, PHYLLIS (Writer, Lawyer, & Conservative Spokesperson)**
Andrew
Anne
Bruce
John
Phyllis Liza
Roger
**SCHLESINGER, ARTHUR (Writer & Historian)**
Andrew

Christina
Katharine
Robert
Stephen
**SCHLESINGER, JAMES**
**(Economist)**
Ann
Charles
Clara
Cora
Emily
James Rodney
Thomas
William
**SCHLOSSBERG,**
**CAROLINE KENNEDY**
**(Philanthropist)**
John [aka Jack]
Rose
Tatiana Celia
**SCHMIDT, MIKE**
**(Professional Baseball**
**Player)**
Jessica Rae
Jonathan Michael
**SCHORR, DANIEL**
**(Journalist & Writer)**
Jonathan
Lisa
**SCHRAGER, IAN**
**(Hotelier)**
Sophia
**SCHULBERG, BUDD**
**(Writer & Screenwriter,**
*On the Waterfront*)
Ben Stuart
David

Jessica
Stephen
Victoria
**SCHULLER, ROBERT**
**(Writer & Clergyman)**
Carol
Gretchen
Jeanne
Robert
Sheila
**SCHULZ, CHARLES**
**(Cartoonist, *Peanuts*)**
Amy
Charles
Craig
Jill
Meredith
**SCHWARZENEGGER,**
**ARNOLD (Actor)**
Christina Maria
Katherine Eunice
Patrick Arnold
**SCHWARZKOPF,**
**NORMAN (Retired U.S.**
**Army General)**
Christian
Cynthia
Jessica
**SCHWINDEN, TED**
**(Former Governor of**
**Montana)**
Chrys
Dore
Mike
**SCIALFA, PATTI (Rock**
**Musician)**

## BUT THEN HE WOULDN'T HAVE BEEN ABLE TO TELL DAVID LETTERMAN HOW HIS NAME MEANS "BLACK PLOWMAN" IN AUSTRIAN

In the seventies, veteran actress Shelley Winters gave newcomer Arnold Schwarzenegger some advice: Change your name, she told him. No one will ever be able to remember "Schwarzenegger" and you'll never be a success. When asked what he should change it to, Winters told him to use his first name, "Arnold," as his last name. When prodded for an appropriate first name, she suggested "Tom." If "Ahnold" had acted on this suggestion, he would have become "Tom Arnold," which means that there would have been *two* "Tom Arnold"s in Schwarzenegger's 1994 box-office hit, *True Lies*. (The other one being, of course, the ex-Mr. Roseanne.) This brings to mind something Henry David Thoreau said in *Walden*: "I have lived some thirty years on this planet, and I have yet to hear the first syllable of valuable or even earnest advice from my seniors."

Evan James
Jessica
Sam Ryan
**SCORSESE, MARTIN (Director)**
Catherine Terese
Domenica Elizabeth
Glinora Sophia
**SCOTT, GEORGE C. (Actor)**
Campbell [Scott]
**SCOTT, WILLARD (TV Weatherman)**
Anne
David
Robert
**SCOTTO, ROSANNA (News Anchor)**
Louis
**SCRIBNER, CHARLES, JR. (Publisher)**
Blair
Charles
John

**SCRUGGS, EARL (Singer/ Songwriter)**
Gary Eugene
Randy Lynn
Steven Earl [aka Steve]

**SCULLY, VINCE (Sportscaster)**
Catherine Anne
Erin
Kelly
Kevin
Michael
Todd

**SEAGAL, STEVEN (Actor)**
Anneliese [also reported as Anna Liza]
Arissa
Dominick [also reported as Dominic]

**SEALE, BOBBY (Political Activist)**
Malik Nkrumah Stagolee

**SEAVER, TOM (Professional Baseball Player)**
Anne Elizabeth
Sarah

**SEDAKA, NEIL (Singer/ Songwriter)**
Dara Felice
Marc Charles

**SEDGWICK, KYRA (Actress)**
Sosie Ruth
Travis Sedg

**SEEGER, PETE (Singer/ Songwriter)**
Daniel Adams
Mika
Tinya

**SEGAL, GEORGE (Actor)**
Elizabeth
Polly

**SEGAL, GEORGE (Sculptor)**
Jeffrey
Rena

**SEGAL, JERRY (Playwright)**
Robby [Benson]

**SEGOVIA, ANDRÉS (Classical Guitarist)**
Andrés
Beatrice
Carlos Andrés
Leonardo

**SELES, XAROLJ (Documentary Filmmaker & Cartoonist)**
Monica [Seles]

**SELLECCA, CONNIE (Actress)**
Gib
Prima Sellicchia

**SELLECK, TOM (Actor)**
Hannah Margaret
Kevin

**SELLERS, PETER (Actor)**
Victoria

**SERKIN, RUDLOPH (Pianist)**
Elisabeth

John
Judith
Marguerite
Peter
Ursula
**SEVERINSEN, DOC**
**(Musician & Conductor)**
Allen
Cindy
Judy
Nancy
Robin
**SEYMOUR, JANE**
**(Actress)**
Katie
Sean
**SEYMOUR, STEPHANIE**
**(Model)**
Dylan
Peter
**SHABAZZ, BETTY**
**(Widow of Malcolm X &**
**Activist)**
Attallah
Gamilah
Ilyasah
Malaak
Malikah
Qubilah
**SHAFFER, PAUL**
**(Musician & Bandleader,**
*Late Show with David*
*Letterman*)
Victoria Lily
**SHAKESPEARE,**
**WILLIAM (Playwright)**
Hamnet

Judith
Susanna
**SHANKER, ALBERT**
**(Labor Union Official)**
Adam
Jennie
Michael
**SHANNON, DEL (Singer)**
Craig
Jody
Kym
Shannon
**SHAPIRO, ROBERT**
**(Attorney)**
Brent
**SHATNER, WILLIAM**
**(Actor)**
Leslie
Lisabeth
Melanie [Shatner]
**SHAW, ARTIE (Composer**
**& Musician)**
Jonathan
Steven
**SHAWN, DICK (Actor)**
Adam
Amy
Jennifer
Wendy
**SHEEDY, CHARLOTTE**
**(Literary Agent)**
Ally [Sheedy]
**SHEEHY, GAIL (Writer)**
Maura
Mohm
**SHEEN, MARTIN (Actor)**
Carlos [Charlie Sheen]

Emilio [Estevez]
Ramon
Renée
**SHELDON, SIDNEY**
**(Writer)**
Mary
**SHELLEY, PERCY**
**BYSSHE (Poet)**
Charles Bysshe
Eliza Lanthe
Percy Florence
William
**SHEPARD, ALAN**
**(Astronaut)**
Juliana
Laura
**SHEPARD, SAM**
**(Playwright)**
Hannah
Jesse Mojo
Samuel
**SHEPHERD, CYBILL**
**(Actress)**
Ariel
Clementine
Zachariah
**SHERMAN, BOBBY**
**(Former Teen Idol)**
Chris

Tyler
**SHIELDS, TERI**
**(Theatrical Manager)**
Brooke [Shields]
**SHIRE, TALIA (Actress)**
Jason Francesco
Matthew Orlando
Robert
**SHOEMAKER, WILLIE**
**(Jockey)**
Amanda Elisabeth
**SHORE, DINAH (Singer)**
John David
Melissa Ann
**SHORE, MITZI (Actress)**
Paul [aka Pauly]
**SHORE, SAMMY (Comic)**
Paul [aka Pauly]
**SHORT, MARTIN (Actor)**
Henry
Katherine
Oliver
**SHRINER, HERB**
**(Humorist)**
Kin [Shriner]
Will [Shriner]
**SHRIVER, EUNICE**
**(Philanthropist)**
Maria [Shriver]

---

### THE CEEDS OF CYBILL

According to Cybill Shepherd, her unusual first
name comes from her grandfather's name, Cyrus
and her father's name, Bill.

Robert [Shriver]
**SHRIVER, MARIA (TV Journalist)**
Christina Maria
Katherine Eunice
Patrick Arnold
**SHRIVER, SARGENT (Businessman)**
Robert [Shriver]
**SHULA, DON (Football Coach)**
Anne
David [Shula]
Donna
Michael
Sharon
**SHULTZ, GEORGE (Former U.S. Secretary of State)**
Alexander George
Barbara
Kathleen
Margaret Ann
Peter Milton
**SIEGEL, BERNIE (Healing Researcher, Physician, & Writer)**
Carolyn
Jeffrey
Jonathan
Keith
Stephen
**SILLS, BEVERLY (Soprano & Opera Company Director)**
Diana
Lindley

Meredith [aka Muffy]
Nancy
Peter [aka Bucky]
**SILVERMAN, FRED (Broadcasting Executive)**
Melissa Anne
William Lawrence
**SIMMONS, ADELE SMITH (Educator)**
Eric
Ian
Kevin
**SIMMONS, GENE (Singer, Kiss)**
Sophie
**SIMMONS, JEAN (Actress)**
Kate
Tracy
**SIMON, CARLY (Singer/ Songwriter)**
Benjamin Simon
Sarah Maria
**SIMON, PAUL (Congressman & Writer)**
Martin
Sheila
**SIMON, PAUL (Singer/ Songwriter)**
Adrian Edward
Harper
**SIMPSON, ALAN K. (U.S. Senator)**
Colin
Susan Lorna
William Lloyd

**SIMPSON, CAROLE (TV Journalist)**
Mallika

**SIMPSON, O.J. (Former Professional Football Player)**
Aaren
Arnelle
Jason
Justin Ryan
Sydney Brook

**SINATRA, BARBARA (Frank's Wife)**
Robert

**SINATRA, FRANK (Singer & Actor)**
Christine [aka Tina]
Frank Wayne
Nancy

**SINGER, ISAAC BASHEVIS (Writer)**
Israel

**SINGLETARY, MIKE (Professional Football Player)**
Jill
Kristen
Mathew

**SINISE, GARY (Actor)**
Ella
McCanna
Sophie

**SISKEL, GENE (Film Critic)**
Callie Gray
Kate Adi

**SKINNER, B.F. (Psychologist & Educator)**
Deborah
Julie

**SKINNER, SAM (Former White House Chief of Staff)**
Jane
Steven
Thomas

**SLEZAK, LEO (Operatic Tenor)**
Walter [Slezak]

**SLEZAK, WALTER (Actor)**
Erika [Slezak]

**SLICK, GRACE (Singer/ Songwriter, Jefferson Airplane)**
China

**SLIM, MONTANA (Country Singer)**
Carol Joyce
Sheila Rose

**SLOTNICK, BARRY (Criminal Lawyer)**
Deborah Anne
Melissa Lynn
Michelle Elisa
Stuart Philip

**SMART, JEAN (Actress)**
Connor

**SMEAL, ELEANOR (National Organization of Women Executive)**
Lori
Tod

**SMIRNOFF, YAKOV (Comedian)**
Alexander
Natasha
**SMITH, ANNA NICOLE (Model & Actress)**
Daniel
**SMITH, CARL (Country Singer)**
Carl
Larry Dean
Lori Lynn
Rebecca Carlene
**SMITH, HARRY (TV's *CBS This Morning* co-host)**
Grady Thomas
**SMITH, JACLYN (Actress)**
Gaston
Spencer Margaret
**SMITH, JEFF (Celebrity Chef—"The Frugal Gourmet")**
Channing
Jason
**SMITH, PATTI (Singer/ Songwriter)**
Jackson Frederick
**SMITH, ROGER (Automobile Manufacturing Executive)**
Drew Johnston
Jennifer Anne
Roger
Victoria Belle
**SMITH, WILLIAM**

**(Former U.S. Attorney General)**
Gregory Hale
Scott Cameron
Stephanie
William French
**SMITHERS, JAN (Actress)**
Molly Elizabeth
**SMITS, JIMMY (Actor)**
Joaquin
Taina
**SMOTHERS, DICKIE (Comic)**
Andrew
Remick
**SMOTHERS, TOMMY (Comic)**
Beau
**SNEAD, SAM (Professional Golfer)**
Samuel Jackson
Terrance
**SNIDER, DEE (Singer/ Songwriter, Twisted Sister)**
Jesse
**SNIPES, WESLEY (Actor)**
Jelani
**SNODGRASS, CARRIE (Actress)**
Zeke
**SNOW, HANK (Country Singer)**
Jimmie [Rodgers]
**SNOWDEN, LORD (Royalty)**
Linley

**SOLTI, SIR GEORGE (Conductor)**
Claudia [Solti]

**SOLZHENITSYN, ALEKSANDR (Writer)**
Ignat
Stepan

**SOMERS, SUZANNE (Actress & Writer)**
Bruce
Leslie
Steve

**SORVINO, PAUL (Actor)**
Mira [Sorvino]

**SOVINE, RED (Country Singer)**
Bill
Janet Carol
Mike
Roger

**SPAAK, CHARLES (Belgian Screenwriter)**
Catherine [Spaak]

**SPACEK, SISSY (Actress)**
Madison
Schuyler Elizabeth
Virginia

**SPADER, JAMES (Actor)**
Sebastian

**SPEAKES, LARRY (Former Reagan Administration Official)**
Barry Scott
Jeremy Stephen
Sondra LaNell

**SPECTER, ARLEN (U.S. Senator)**
Shannin
Stephen

**SPECTOR, PHIL (Record Producer & Songwriter)**
Donte
Gary
Louis
Nicole
Phillip

**SPELLING, AARON (Producer & Writer)**
Randall Gene
Victoria [aka Tori]

**SPHEERIS, PENELOPE (Director)**
Anna

**SPIELBERG, STEVEN (Director)**
Max Samuel
Sasha
Sawyer
Theo

**SPILLANE, MICKEY (Writer)**
Carolyn
Kathy
Mike
Ward

**SPINDERELLA [Dee Dee Roper] (Singer, Salt-n-Pepa)**
Christy

**SPOCK, BENJAMIN (Physician & Writer)**
John
Michael

**SPRINGSTEEN, BRUCE (Singer/Songwriter)**
Evan James
Jessica
Sam Ryan

**ST. JACQUES, RAYMOND (Actor)**
Raymond
Sterling

**ST. JAMES, SUSAN (Actress)**
Charles [aka Charlie]
Edward Bright
Harmony
Sunshine
William

**STACK, ROBERT (Actor)**
Charles Robert
Elizabeth

**STALIN, SVETLANA (Writer & Joseph's Daughter)**
Olga

**STALLONE, JACKIE (Astrologer & Writer)**
Frank [Stallone]
Sylvester [aka Sly] Stallone

**STALLONE, SYLVESTER (Actor, Director, & Writer)**
Sage Moonblood
Sergio
Seth

**STANDING, SIR GUY (English Actor)**
Kay [Hammond]

**STANLEY, PAUL (Singer, Kiss)**
Evan Shane

**STAPLETON, MAUREEN (Actress)**
Daniel
Katharine

**STARKEY, ZAK (Rock Musician)**
Tatia Jayne

**STARR, RINGO (Singer/Songwriter, Member of the Beatles & Actor)**
Jason
Lee
Zak [Starkey]

**STEEL, DAWN (Motion Picture Executive)**
Rebecca

**STEENBURGEN, MARY (Actress)**
Charles [aka Charlie]
Lilly

**STEIGER, ROD (Actor)**
Anna

**STEINBERG, DAVID (Director)**
Rebecca
Sasha

**STEINBRENNER, GEORGE (Baseball Executive)**
Harold
Henry
Jennifer Lynn
Jessica Joan

**STEPHANIE, PRINCESS (Royalty)**
Louis

---

## THE RISEN RINGO

Beatle Ringo Starr was a sickly child. In fact, he was ill so often that his grandfather Starkey gave him an appropriate nickname: Lazarus.

---

Pauline
**STERN, DANIEL (Actor)**
Henry
**STERN, DAVID (Commissioner, NBA)**
Andrew
Eric
**STERN, HOWARD (Radio Personality)**
Ashley Jade
Debra
Emily
**STERN, ISAAC (Violinist)**
David
Michael
Shira
**STEVENS, CONNIE (Actress)**
Joely [Fisher]
Trishia
**STEVENS, JAMES (Philanthropist & Founder of Home for Leper Children)**
Ashu
**STEVENS, STELLA (Actress)**
Andrew [Stevens]
**STEVENS, TED (U.S. Senator)**
Ben
Elizabeth
Lily Irene
Susan
Theodore
Walter
**STEVENSON, ADLAI (Former U.S. Senator)**
Adlai [Stevenson]
Katherine
Lucy
Warwick
**STEVENSON, PARKER (Actor)**
William True Parker
**STEVENSON, ROBERT LOUIS (Writer)**
Belle
Lloyd
**STEWART, JIMMY (Actor)**
Judy
Kelly
Michael
Ronald
**STEWART, MARTHA**

(Style Consultant &
Writer)
Alexis
**STEWART, POTTER
(Retired U.S. Supreme
Court Justice)**
David
Harriet Potter
Potter
**STEWART, ROD (Rock
Singer)**
Alana
Kimberly
Liam McAllister
Renée
Ruby
Sean
**STILLER, JERRY (Actor)**
Amy
Benjamin [aka Ben] [Stiller]
**STING (Singer/
Songwriter)**
Coco
Eliot Pauline
Joseph [aka Joe]
Katherine [aka Kate]
**STOKES, CARL (TV
Journalist)**
Carl
Cordell
Cordi
**STOKES, LOUIS
(Legislator)**
Angela
Lorene
Louis
Shelley

**STONE, IRVING (Writer)**
Kenneth
Paula
**STONE, OPAL (Fashion
Designer)**
Blake Amanda
**STRAM, HANK (Former
Football Coach & TV
Commentator)**
Dale Alan
Gary Baxter
Henry Raymond
Julia Anne
Mary Nell
Stuart Madison
**STRANGE, CURTIS
(Professional Golfer)**
David Clark
Thomas
**STRASBERG, ANNA
(Acting Teacher)**
Adam
**STRASBERG, LEE
(Acting Teacher)**
Susan [Strasberg]
**STRAVINSKY, IGOR
(Composer)**
Milene
Sviatoslav [aka Soulima]
Theodore
**STREEP, MERYL
(Actress)**
Grace Jane
Henry
Louisa Jacobson
Mary Willa
**STREISAND, BARBRA**

(Singer, Actress, & Director)
Jason

**STRONG, MAURICE (Environmentalist)**
Frederick Maurice
Kenneth Martin
Mary Anne
Maureen Louise

**STYRON, WILLIAM (Writer)**
Claire Alexandra
Paola Clark
Susanna Margaret
Thomas

**SUGARMAN, BERT (TV Producer)**
Alec

**SULZBERGER, ARTHUR (Newspaper Executive)**
Arthur
Cathy
Cynthia
Karen

**SUMMER, DONNA (Singer/Songwriter & Actress)**
Brook Lyn
Mimi

**SUNG, KIM IL (Ruler, North Korea)**
Kim [Il Sung]

**SUNUNU, JOHN (TV Journalist & Former White House Chief of Staff)**
Catherine
Christina
Christopher
Elizabeth
James
John
Michael
Peter

**SUSSKIND, DAVID (TV, Movie, & Theatrical Producer)**
Andrew
Diana
Pamela
Samantha

**SUTHERLAND, DONALD (Actor)**
Angus
Kiefer [Sutherland]
Rachel
Roeg
Rossif

**SUTHERLAND, KIEFER (Actor)**
Michelle Kath
Sarah

**SUU KYI, AUNG SAN (Activist & Nobel Laureate)**
Alexander
Kim

**SUZY (Newspaper Columnist)**
Roger

**SWAGGART, JIMMY (Televangelist)**
Donnie

# T

**TAGLIABUE, PAUL
(Commissioner of the
National Football League)**
Drew
Emily
**TAKEI, KEI
(Choreographer & Dancer)**
Raishun
**TALLCHIEF, MARIA
(Ballerina)**
Elise
**TAMBO, OLIVER
(President-General of the
African National Congress)**
Dalindlela
Dudalani
Tambi
**TANDY, JESSICA
(Actress)**
Christopher Hume
Susan
Tandy
**TARBOX-WEILL, EDYE
(TV Newscaster)**
Bubba
**TARCHER, JEREMY
(Publisher)**
Mallory
**TARKANIAN, JERRY
(Basketball Coach,
University of Nevada at
Las Vegas)**
Danny
George

Jodie
Pamela
**TAYLOR, ELIZABETH
(Actress)**
Christopher
Elizabeth Frances
Liza
Maria
Michael
**TAYLOR, JAMES (Singer/
Songwriter)**
Benjamin Simon
Sarah Maria
**TAYLOR, LAWRENCE
(Professional Football
Player)**
Lawrence
Paula
Tanisha
**TAYLOR-YOUNG,
LEIGH (Actress)**
Patrick [O'Neal]
**TE KANAWA, KIRI
(Operatic Soprano)**
Antonia Aroha
Thomas Desmond
**TENNYSON, ALFRED
LORD (Writer)**
Hallam
**TERKEL, STUDS (Writer)**
Paul
**TESH, JOHN (TV Host)**
Prima Sellecchia
**THACKERAY, WILLIAM
MAKEPEACE (Novelist)**
Anne

**THARP, TWYLA (Dancer & Choreographer)**
Jesse

**THATCHER, MARGARET (Former Prime Minister of Great Britain)**
Carol
Mark

**THEISMANN, JOE (Professional Football Player)**
Amy Lynn
Joseph Winton
Patrick James

**THICKE, ALAN (Actor)**
Brennan
Robin

**THIEBAUD, WAYNE (Artist)**
Mallary Ann
Matthew Bult
Paul
Twinka

**THOMAS, CAITLIN (Dylan's Widow)**
Aeronwyn
Francesco
Colm
Llewelyn

**THOMAS, CLARENCE (U.S. Supreme Court Justice)**
Jamal

**THOMAS, DANNY (Entertainer)**
Charles Anthony

Margaret Julia [aka Marlo] [Thomas]
Theresa Cecilia

**THOMAS, DAVE (Founder of Wendy's)**
Kenneth
Lori
Molly Jo
Pamela
Wendy [originally Melinda Lou]

**THOMAS, DYLAN (Poet)**
Aeronwyn
Colm
Llewelyn

**THOMAS, ISIAH (Professional Basketball Player)**
Joshua Isiah

**THOMAS, RICHARD (Actor)**
Barbara
Gwyneth
Pilar
Richard Francisco

**THOMAS, THURMAN (Professional Football Player)**
Angelica
Olivia

**THOMPSON, HUNTER S. (Writer)**
Juan

**THOMPSON, JAMES (Former Governor of Illinois)**
Samantha Jayne

**THOMPSON, JOHN**
**(College Basketball Coach,**
**Georgetown University)**
John
Ronald
Tiffany
**THOMPSON, LEA**
**(Actress)**
Madeline
**THORNBURGH, DICK**
**(Former Governor of**
**Pennsylvania)**
David
John
Peter
William
**THRELKELD, RICHARD**
**(Broadcast Journalist)**
Julia Lynn
Susan Anne
**THURMOND, STROM**
**(U.S. Senator)**
Juliana Gertrude
Nancy
Paul
**TICOTIN, RACHEL**
**(Actress)**
Greta
**TIEGS, CHERYL (Model)**
Zachary Anthony
**TIFFANY (Pop Singer)**
Elijah
**TILLIS, MEL (Singer/**
**Songwriter)**
Carrie
Cindy
Connie

Melvin
Pam [Tillis]
**TILTON, CHARLENE**
**(Actress)**
Cherish
**TINY TIM (Singer)**
Tulip
**TISCH, LAURENCE**
**(Executive, CBS)**
Andrew
Daniel
James
Thomas
**TOFFLER, ALVIN**
**(Writer)**
Karen
**TOLSTOY, LEO (Writer)**
Alexandra
Andrei
Leo
Sasha
Timothy
**TORN, RIP (Actor &**
**Director)**
Angelica
Anthony
Danae
Jonathan
**TOSCANINI, ARTURO**
**(Conductor)**
Walter
**TOWER, JOHN (Former**
**U.S. Senator)**
Jeanne
Marian
Penelope

**TRACY, SPENCER**
**(Actor)**
John
Susie
**TRAIN, RUSSELL**
**(Environmentalist, World**
**Wildlife Fund)**
Emily
Errol
Nancy
**TRAUB, MARVIN (Ex-**
**Executive, Bloomingdale's)**
Andrew
James
Peggy Ann
**TRAVIS, MERLE**
**(Country Singer)**
Cindy
Dennis
Merlene
Mildred
Pat
**TRAVOLTA, JOHN**
**(Actor)**
Jett
**TREBECK, ALEX (Host**
**of TV Game Show**
*Jeopardy*)
Emily Grace
Matthew Alexander
**TRENT, LES (TV**
**Journalist,** *American*
*Journal*)
Victoria Iris
**TREVINO, LEE**
**(Professional Golfer)**
Lesley Ann

Richard Lee
Tony Lee
Troy Liana
**TRILLIN, CALVIN**
**(Writer)**
Abigail
Sarah
**TROTTIER, BRYAN**
**(Professional Hockey**
**Player)**
Bryan
**TRUDEAU, GARY**
**(Cartoonist)**
Garry
Rachel
Richard
Ross
Tommy
**TRUITT, ANNE (Artist)**
Alexandra
Mary
Samuel
**TRUMP, DONALD**
**(Businessman)**
Donald [aka Donny]
Eric
Ivanka
Tiffany
**TRUMP, IVANA (Writer)**
Donald
Eric
Ivanka
**TSONGAS, PAUL**
**(Former U.S. Senator)**
Ashley
Katina
Molly

---

**I WONDER HOW THE UMPIRES FELT ABOUT THIS, DON'T YOU?**

Babe Ruth supposedly got his name because that's what he called a person he had just met, rather than going to the trouble of remembering their name.

---

**TSUPEI, CORINNA (Miss Universe, 1968) [SEE Freddie Fields]**
Andrew
Paris
Steven
**TUBBS, ERNIE (Country Singer)**
Justin [Tubbs]
**TUBBS, JUSTIN (Country Singer)**
Leah
Lisa
**TUCHMAN, BARBARA (Writer & Historian)**
Alma
Jessica
Lucy
**TUCKER, FORREST (Actor)**
Cynthia Brooke
Forrest Sean
Pamela Brooke
**TUCKER, TANYA (Country Singer)**
Beau Grayson

Ben
Presley Tanita
**TURNER, KATHLEEN (Actress)**
Rachel Ann
**TURNER, LANA (Actress)**
Cheryl [Crane]
**TURNER, TED (Media Mogul)**
Beauregard
Laura Lee
Rhett
Robert Edward
Sarah Jean
**TURNER, TINA (Singer)**
Craig
Ike
Michael
Ronald
**TURTURRO, JOHN (Actor)**
Amadeo
**TURTURRO, NICK (Actor)**
Erica
**TWAIN, MARK (Writer)**

### NOW HE & JANE ARE WORKING ON A "SCARLETT," RIGHT?

Ted Turner *really* likes the movie *Gone With the Wind*. In fact, he likes it so much that he bought the MGM movie library so he could own the flick, and he named his son Rhett, after *GWTW*'s Rhett Butler.

Clara
Jean
Susie [aka Susy]
**TWEED, SHANNON (Actress)**
Sophie
**TWITTY, CONWAY (Singer/Songwriter)**
Cathy
Conway
Jimmy
Joni
Mike
**TYLER, STEVEN (Singer, Aerosmith)**
Liv [Tyler]
Chelsea
Taj
**TYLER, TEXAS T. (Country Singer)**
David Luke
Rodger
**TYSON, LAURA D'ANDREA (Economist & Clinton Cabinet Member)**

Elliott
**TYSON, MIKE (Boxer)**
D'Amato

# U

**UGGAMS, LESLIE (Entertainer)**
Danielle Nicole
Jason Harolde John
**ULLMAN, LIV (Actress)**
Linn
**ULLMAN, TRACY (Actress)**
John Albert Victor [aka Johnny]
Mabel Ellen
**UMBERTO, KING (Italian Royalty)**
Vittorio Emanuele
**UNITAS, JOHNNY (Former Professional Football Player)**
Alicia Ann
Chad Elliott
Christopher

Francis Joseph
Janice
John Constantine
Kenneth
Robert
**UNSER, AL (Auto Racer)**
Alfred Richard [Unser, Jr.]
Debra Ann
Mary Linda
**UNSER, BOBBY (Auto Racer)**
Bobby
Cyndi
Jeri
Robby
**UPDIKE, JOHN (Writer)**
David
Elizabeth
Michael
Miranda
**URICH, ROBERT (Actor)**
Emily
Ryan
**URIS, LEON (Writer)**
Karen Lynn
Mark Jay
Michael Cady
**USTINOV, PETER (Actor, Director, & Writer)**
Andrea
Igor
Pavla
Tamara

# V

**VADIM, ROGER (Director)**
Christiaan
Vanessa
**VALENZUELA, FERNANDO (Professional Baseball Player)**
Fernando
**VALVANO, JIM (Basketball Coach)**
Jamie
Lee Ann
Nicole
**VAN ARK, JOAN (Actress)**
Vanessa
**VAN BUREN, ABIGAIL (Columnist, *Dear Abby*)**
Edward Jay
Jeanne
**VAN DYKE, DICK (Actor)**
Barry [Van Dyke]
Carrie Beth
Christian
Stacey
**VAN DYKE, LEROY (Country Singer)**
Adam
Carla
Lee
**VAN HALEN, EDDIE (Rock Musician, Van Halen)**
Wolfgang

**VAN NOSTRAND, AMY (Actress)**
Sam

**VAN PATTEN, DICK (Actor)**
Vincent [Van Patten]

**VAN PEEBLES, MARIO (Writer & Actor)**
Mario
Megan

**VAN SLYKE, ANDY (Professional Baseball Player)**
Jared
Scott

**VANDERBILT, CORNELIUS (Shipping & Railroad Mogul)**
Cornelius
George
William

**VANDERBILT, GLORIA (Fashion Designer)**
Anderson
Carter
Christopher
Stanislaus

**VANOCUR, SANDER (Broadcaster)**
Christopher
Nicholas

**VAUGHN, MARK (Actor)**
Margaux

**VAUGHN, ROBERT (Actor)**
Caitlin
Cassidy

**VAUGHN, SARAH (Singer)**
Paris

**VERDI, GIUSEPPE (Italian Operatic Composer)**
Icilio Romano
Virginia

**VERDON, GWEN (Actress & Dancer)**
James
Nicole

**VEREEN, BEN (Actor)**
Benjamin
Kabara
Karon
Malaika
Naja

**VERNON, JOHN (Actor)**
Kate [Vernon]

**VICKERS, JON (Operatic Tenor)**
Allison
Jonathan
Kenneth
Wendy
William

**VICTORIA, QUEEN (British Royalty)**
Alice
Arthur
Beatrice
Bertie
Leopold
Victoria

**VIDALE, THEA (Actress)**
Magdalen

Medea

**VIDOV, OLEG (Soviet Actor & Director)**
Slava

**VIERA, MEREDITH (TV Journalist)**
Lily Max

**VILA, BOB (TV Host)**
Christopher
Monica
Susannah

**VINCENT, FAY (Commissioner of Major League Baseball)**
Anne
Edward
William

**VINCENT, MARJORIE (1991 Miss America)**
Cameron

**VITALE, DICK (Sportscaster)**
Sherri
Terri

**VOIGHT, JON (Actor)**
Angelina Jolie
James Haven

**VOLCKER, PAUL (Former Chairman, Federal Reserve Board)**
James
Janice

**VON ARX, MARC (Writer & Director)**
Aimee Madeline

**VON FURSTENBERG, DIANE (Fashion Designer)**
Alexandre
Tatiana

**VON KARAJAN, HERBERT (Conductor)**
Arabel
Isabel

**VON SYDOW, MAX (Actor)**
Clas Wilhelm
Per Henrik

**VON TRAPP, MARIA (Matriarch, the Trapp Family Singers)**
Agathe
Eleonore
Hedwig
Johanna
Johannas
Maria
Martina
Rosemarie
Rupert
Werner

**VONNEGUT, KURT, JR. (Writer)**
Edith
James
Kurt
Mark
Nanette
Steven

**VUITTON, HENRY-LOUIS (Designer)**
Colette
Daniele
Philippe-Louis

# W

**WAGNER, JACK (Actor,**
***General Hospital*)**
Petey
**WAGNER, KRISTINA**
**(Actress, *General Hospital*)**
Petey
**WAGNER, LINDSAY**
**(Actress)**
Alex
Dorian
**WAGNER, RICHARD**
**(Composer)**
Eva
Isolde
Siegfried
**WAGNER, ROBERT**
**(Actor)**
Courtney
Katherine [aka Kate]
Natasha
**WAGONER, PORTER**
**(Singer/Songwriter)**
Debra
Denise
Richard
**WAKELY, JIMMY**
**(Country Singer)**
Carol
Deanna
Johnny
Linda
**WALDRON, HICKS**
**(Executive, Avon)**
Ben

Janet
**WALESA, LECH (Polish**
**Solidarity Leader)**
Anna
Bogdan
Brygida
Jaroslaw
Magdalena
Maria
Przemyslaw
Slawomir
**WALGREEN, CHARLES,**
**III (Executive, Walgreen)**
Charles Richard
Christ Patrick
Kevin Patrick
Leslie Ray
Tad Alexander
**WALKER, BILLY**
**(Country Singer)**
Deana
Judy
Julie
Lina
**WALKER, CHARLIE**
**(Country Singer)**
Art
Carrie Lucinda
Ronnie
**WALKER, ROBERT**
**(Actor)**
Robert [Walker, Jr.]
**WALLACE, GEORGE**
**(Former Governor of**
**Alabama)**
Bobbie Jo
George

Janie Lee
Peggy Sue
**WALLACE, IRVING (Writer)**
Amy
David
**WALLACE, JANE (TV Journalist)**
Zachariah Max
**WALLACE, MIKE (TV Journalist, *60 Minutes*)**
Christopher
Peter
**WALLACH, ELI (Actor)**
Katherine Beatrice
Peter Douglas
Roberta Lee
**WALLIS, HAL (Movie Producer)**
Hal Brent
**WALSH, BILL (Professional Football Coach)**
Craig
Elizabeth
Steve
**WALTERS, BARBARA (TV Journalist)**
Jacqueline Dena
**WALTERS, JULIE (Actress)**
Maizie
**WALTON, BILL (Professional Basketball Player)**
Adam
Luke

Nathan
**WAPNER, JOSEPH (TV Jurist—"Judge Wapner" on *The People's Court*)**
David
Frederick
Sarah
**WARD, SELA (Actress)**
Austin Ward
**WARNER, JOHN (U.S. Senator)**
John William
Mary
Virginia
**WARREN, LESLEY ANNE (Actress)**
Chris
**WARWICK, DIONNE (Singer)**
Damion
David
**WASHINGTON, DENZEL (Actor)**
John David
Katia
Malcolm
Olivia
**WASHINGTON, GROVER, JR. (Musician & Composer)**
Grover
Shana
**WATSON, DOC (Country Singer)**
Merle
**WATSON, JAMES**

(Educator & Molecular
Biologist)
Duncan James
Rufus Robert
**WATSON, TOM
(Professional Golfer)**
Margaret Elizabeth
Michael
**WATTLETON, FAYE
(Planned Parenthood
Executive)**
Felicia Megan
**WAYANS, DAMAN
(Actor)**
Fuddy
Trixie
**WAYNE, JOHN (Actor)**
Patrick [Wayne]
**WEAVER, CHARLIE
(Actor)**
Lewis [Arquette]
**WEAVER, DENNIS
(Actor)**
Rick
Robby
Rusty
**WEAVER, EARL
(Baseball Manager)**
Michael Earl

Rhonda Lee
Theresa Ann
**WEAVER, PAT (TV
Producer)**
Sigourney [Weaver]
**WEAVER, SIGOURNEY
(Actress)**
Charlotte
**WEBBER, ANDREW
LLOYD (Composer)**
Imogen
Nicholas
**WEDGEWORTH, ANN
(Actress)**
Danae
**WEBER, PETE
(Professional Bowler)**
Nicole
**WEICKER, LOWELL
(Former Governor of
Connecticut)**
Brian
Gray Godfrey
Lowell Palmer
Palmer
Scot
Sonny
**WEINBERGER, CASPAR
(Former U.S. Secretary of**

---

## NAMESAKE DEPARTMENT

The actor Stepin Fetchit (*Miracle in Harlem*) took
his stage name from a winning racehorse who was
very lucky for him.

Defense)
Arlin Cerise
Caspar Willard
**WEINTRAUB, JERRY (Theatrical Manager & Promoter)**
Jamie Lee
Jody Christine
Julie Caroline
Michael
**WEISS, ROBERT (Composer)**
Bobby
**WELCH, BOB (Professional Baseball Player)**
Dylan
Riley
**WELCH, JACK (CEO, General Electric)**
Anne
John
Katherine
Mark
**WELCH, RAQUEL (Actress)**
Damon
Tahnee [Welch]
**WELD, TUESDAY**

(Actress)
Natasha
Patrick
**WELLES, ORSON (Actor & Writer)**
Beatrice
Christopher
Rebecca
**WELLS, H.G. (Writer)**
Anthony Panther
**WELLS, KITTY (Country Singer)**
Bobby
Carol Sue
Ruby
**WEST, DOTTIE (Singer/ Songwriter)**
Dale
Kerry
Morris
Shelly
**WEST, MORRIS (Writer)**
Christopher
Melanie
Michael
Paul
**WEST, REBECCA (Writer)**
Anthony Panther

---

### "FAMILY TIES"

H.G. Wells's son with writer Rebecca West was named "Anthony Panther." "Panther" was Wells's affectionate nickname for West.

**WESTHEIMER, DR. RUTH (Sex Authority & Writer)**
Joel
Miriam
**WETTIG, PATRICIA (Actress)**
Clifford
Roxanne [aka Roxie]
**WEXNER, LESLIE (Owner, Victoria's Secret)**
Harrison
**WHALLEY-KILMER, JOANNE (Actress)**
Jack
Mercedes
**WHEELER, BILLY ED (Country Singer)**
Lucy
**WHITE, BYRON (U.S. Supreme Court Justice)**
Charles
Nancy
**WHITE, JACK (Country Singer)**
Sarah Grace
**WHITE, KARYN (Singer/ Songwriter)**
Ashley Nicole
Brandon
Chloe
Tremayne
**WHITE, REGGIE (Professional Football Player)**
Jecolia
Jeremy

**WHITE, THEODORE (Writer)**
Ariana
David
**WHITE, VANNA (TV Hostess, *Wheel of Fortune*)**
Nicholas
**WHITLEY, KEITH (Country Singer)**
Jessie
**WHITMAN, SLIM (Country Singer)**
Charlene
**WHITTY, MAY (Actress)**
Margaret [Webster]
**WIDMARK, RICHARD (Actor)**
Anne
**WIESEL, ELIE (Writer)**
Shlomo Elisha
**WIEST, DIANNE**
Emily
Lily
**WILCOX, LARRY (Actor, *CHiPs*)**
Wendy
**WILDE, OSCAR (Writer)**
Cyril
Vyvyan [Holland]
**WILDER, DOUGLAS L. (Governor of Virginia)**
Douglas
Lawrence
Loren
Lynn
**WILDER, GENE (Actor)**
Katharine Anastasia

**WILDMON, DONALD**
**(Minister)**
Angela
Donna Lou
Mark Ellis
**WILHELM, FRIEDRICH**
**(Royalty)**
Louis
**WILHELM, KAISER II**
**(Royalty)**
Friedrich [Wilhelm]
**WILL, GEORGE**
**(Columnist)**
Geoffrey
Jonathan
Victoria
**WILLIAMS, ANDY**
**(Entertainer)**
Christian
Noelle
Robert
**WILLIAMS, BILL**
**(Actor—"Kit Carson")**
William [Katt]
**WILLIAMS, BILLY DEE**
**(Actor)**
Corey Dee
Hanako
Miyako
**WILLIAMS, DOUG**
**(Professional Football**
**Player)**
Ashley
**WILLIAMS, HANK JR.**
**(Country Singer)**
Katherine Diana

**WILLIAMS, MARSHA**
**(Producer)**
Cody Alan
**WILLIAMS, MITCH**
**(Houston Astros Pitcher)**
Damon
**WILLIAMS, MONTEL**
**(TV Host)**
Montel
**WILLIAMS, ROBIN**
**(Actor)**
Cody Alan
Zachary
Zelda
**WILLIAMS, VANESSA**
**(Singer & Actress)**
Devin Christian
Jillian
Melanie
**WILLIAMS, WILLIE C.**
**(Chief of Police, Los**
**Angeles)**
Eric
Lisa
Willie
**WILLIAMSON,**
**MARIANNE (Writer)**
India Emmaline
**WILLIS, BRUCE (Actor)**
Rumer Glenn
Scout Larue
Tallulah Belle
**WILLS, GARY (Writer)**
Garry
John
Lydia

WILLSON, S. BRIAN
(Anti-War Activist)
Gabriel
WILSON, BRIAN (Singer/
Songwriter, The Beach
Boys)
Carnie
Wendy
WILSON, EARL (Writer
& Radio Commentator)
Earl
WILSON, GAHAN
(Cartoonist & Writer)
Paul
Randy
WILSON, MARY (Singer,
the Supremes)
Willie
WILSON, RITA (Actress)
Chester
Colin
WINGER, DEBRA
(Actress)
Emanuel Noah [aka Noah]
WINKLER, HENRY
(Actor & Director)
Jed
Max
Zoe Emily
WINTERS, JONATHAN
(Actor & Artist)
Jonathan
Lucinda Kelley
WINTERS, SHELLEY
(Actress & Writer)
Vittoria
WOLFE, TOM (Writer)

Alexandra
WONDER, STEVIE
(Singer/Songwriter)
Aisha
Keita
Mumtaz
WOOD, NATALIE
(Actress)
Courtney
Natasha
WOODRUFF, JUDY
(Broadcast Journalist)
Benjamin
Jeffrey
Lauren Ann
WOODWARD, BOB
(Journalist)
Tali
WOODWARD, EDWARD
(Actor)
Emily Beth
Peter
Sarah
Timothy
WOODWARD, JOANNE
(Actress)
Clea Olivia
Elinor Terese
Melissa
WORDSWORTH,
WILLIAM (Poet)
Ann Caroline
WORTH, MARION
(Country Singer)
Joyce Lea
WORTHY, JAMES
(Professional Athlete)

Sable Alexandria
Sierra Alexis
**WOUK, HERMAN (Writer)**
Abraham Isaac
Joseph
Nathaniel
**WRIGHT, FRANK LLOYD (Architect)**
Catherine
David
Frances
John
Lloyd
Robert Llewellyn
**WRIGHT, JOHNNY (Country Singer)**
Bobby
Carol Sue
Rudy
**WRIGHT, JULANN (Comedienne)**
Anthony Patrick
**WRIGHT, ROBIN (Actress)**
Dylan Frances
Frances
Hopper Jack
**WYMAN, BILL (Musician, the Rolling Stones)**
Katharine Noelle
**WYMAN, JANE (Actress)**
Maureen
Michael
**WYNETTE, TAMMY (Country Singer)**

Georgette
**WYNN, ED (Actor)**
Keenan [Wynn]
**WYNN, KEENAN (Actor)**
Edmond Keenan [Wynn]
Edwina Keenan
Hilda Keenan
Tracy Keenan

# Y

**YABLANS, FRANK (Movie Producer)**
Edward
Robert
Sharon
**YARD, MOLLY (Former President, NOW)**
James
Joan
John
**YORK, JOHN J. (Actor, *General Hospital*)**
Schuyler
**YOUNG, ANDREW (Civil Rights Leader & Former Mayor)**
Andrea
Andrew
Lisa
Paula Jean
**YOUNG, BRIGHAM (Mormon Leader)**
Brigham
Clarissa
John
Mabel

Willard
**YOUNG, FARON**
**(Country Singer)**
Alana
Damion Ray
Kevin Robert
Robin Farrell
**YOUNG, JOHN**
**(Astronaut)**
John
Sandra
**YOUNG, LORETTA**
**(Actress)**
Judy
**YOUNG, NEIL (Singer/**
**Songwriter)**
Amber
Ben
Zeke
**YOUNG, ROBERT**
**(Actor)**
Barbara Queen
Carol Ann
Elizabeth Louise
Kathleen Joy
**YOUNGBLOOD,**
**JOHNNY RAY (Church**
**Leader)**
Jason
Joel
Johnny Jernell
**YOUNGMAN, HENNY**
**(Comedian)**
Gary
Marilyn
**YOUNT, ROBIN**

**(Professional Baseball**
**Player)**
Amy
Jenna
Melisa

# Z

**ZAHN, PAULA (Co-Host,**
**TV's *CBS This Morning*)**
Haley
Jared Brandon
**ZALM, WILLIAM**
**ZANDER (Premier, British**
**Columbia)**
Jeffrey
Juanita
Lucia
Wim
**ZANUCK, DARRYL**
**(Movie Mogul)**
Richard
**ZAPATO, ANTONIO**
**(Actor)**
Jack
**ZAPPA, FRANK (Rock**
**Composer)**
Ahmet Emuukha Rodan
Diva
Dweezil
Moon Unit
**ZELAZNY, ROGER**
**(Science Fiction Writer)**
Devin
Shannon
Trent

**ZEMAN, JACKIE**
**(Actress, *General Hospital*)**
Cassidy Zee
Lacey Rose
**ZEMECKIS, ROBERT**
**(Director)**
Mary Ellen
**ZIGLER, EDWARD**
**(Founder, Project Head**
**Start)**
Perrin
**ZIMBALIST, EFREM, JR.**
**(Actor)**

Stephanie [Zimbalist]
**ZIMBALIST, EFREM, SR.**
**(Concert Violinist)**
Efrem [Zimbalist, Jr.]
**ZIMMER, KIM (Actress,**
***The Guiding Light*)**
Jake
Max
Rachel
**ZUKERMAN, PINCHAS**
**(Concert Violinist)**
Arianna
Natalia

# About the Author

**STEPHEN J. SPIGNESI** is a writer who specializes in popular culture subjects, including television, film, and contemporary fiction. His other books include:

*Mayberry, My Hometown: The Ultimate Guidebook to America's Favorite TV Small Town* (Popular Culture, Ink.)

*The Complete Stephen King Encyclopedia* (Popular Culture, Ink; Contemporary Books)

*The Stephen King Quiz Book* (Signet)

*The Second Stephen King Quiz Book* (Signet)

*The Woody Allen Companion* (Andrews and McMeel; Plexus Ltd.; Popular Culture, Ink)

*The Official "Gone With the Wind" Companion* (Plume)

*The V.C. Andrews Trivia and Quiz Book* (Signet)

*The Odd Index: The Ultimate Compendium of Bizarre and Unusual Facts* (Plume)

*What's Your "Mad About You" IQ?* (Citadel Press)

*The Gore Galore Video Quiz Book* (Signet)

*What's Your "Friends" IQ?* (Citadel Press)

*The "ER" Companion* (Citadel Press)

*The Italian 100: A Ranking of the Most Influential Italians, Past and Present* (forthcoming, Citadel Press)

*Stephen King A to Z* (forthcoming, Popular Culture, Ink)

In addition to writing, Spignesi also lectures widely on a variety of popular culture subjects and is the founder and Editor-in-Chief of the small press publishing company, The Stephen John Press. He lives in New Haven, CT, with his wife, Pam.